BEACHHEAD NORMANDY

Related Potomac Titles

Shattered Sword: The Untold Story of the Battle of Midway
—Jonathan Parshall and Anthony Tully

War in the Boats: My WWII Submarine Battles
—William J. Ruhe

TOM CARTER

BEACHHEAD NORMANDY

AN LCT'S ODYSSEY

Potomac Books
Washington, D.C.

Copyright © 2012 by Potomac Books, Inc.

Published in the United States by Potomac Books, Inc. All rights reserved. No part of this book may be reproduced in any manner whatsoever without written permission from the publisher, except in the case of brief quotations embodied in critical articles and reviews.

Library of Congress Cataloging-in-Publication Data
Carter, Tom, 1955–
 Beachhead Normandy : an LCT's odyssey / Tom Carter. — 1st ed.
   p. cm.
 Includes bibliographical references and index.
 ISBN 978-1-59797-710-4 (hardcover : alk. paper)
 ISBN 978-1-59797-797-5 (electronic)
 1. World War, 1939–1945—Campaigns—France—Normandy. 2. World War, 1939–1945—Amphibious operations. 3. World War, 1939–1945—Tank warfare. 4. World War, 1939–1945—Naval operations, American. 5. Landing craft—United States—History—20th century. I. Title.
 D756.5.N6C378 2012
 940.54'21422—dc23
                                                                2012018882

Printed in the United States of America on acid-free paper that meets the American National Standards Institute Z39-48 Standard.

Potomac Books
22841 Quicksilver Drive
Dulles, Virginia 20166

First Edition

Since I intended this book to honor
my dad and his World War II shipmates,
it seems fitting that it should be dedicated
to the memory of my mom,

Alta Mae Brantley Carter
1926–2009

Tennessee farm girl,
Manhattan Project security clerk, Oak Ridge, 1945–1946,
bookkeeper,
mentor,
pal

CONTENTS

	Preface	xi
	Acknowledgments	xxi
1	Pearl Harbor to Boot Camp	1
2	LCTs Enter the War	11
3	Solomons Island	26
4	Long, Slow Trip to War	39
5	The Near Shore	57
6	Omaha Beach	74
7	Frenzy and Storm	96
8	Calm and Oblivion	119
9	Return to Near Shore	144
10	Slogging Across the Pacific	158
11	The Far East	174
12	Odysseus in Tennessee	187
	Bibliography	197
	Index	201
	About the Author	209

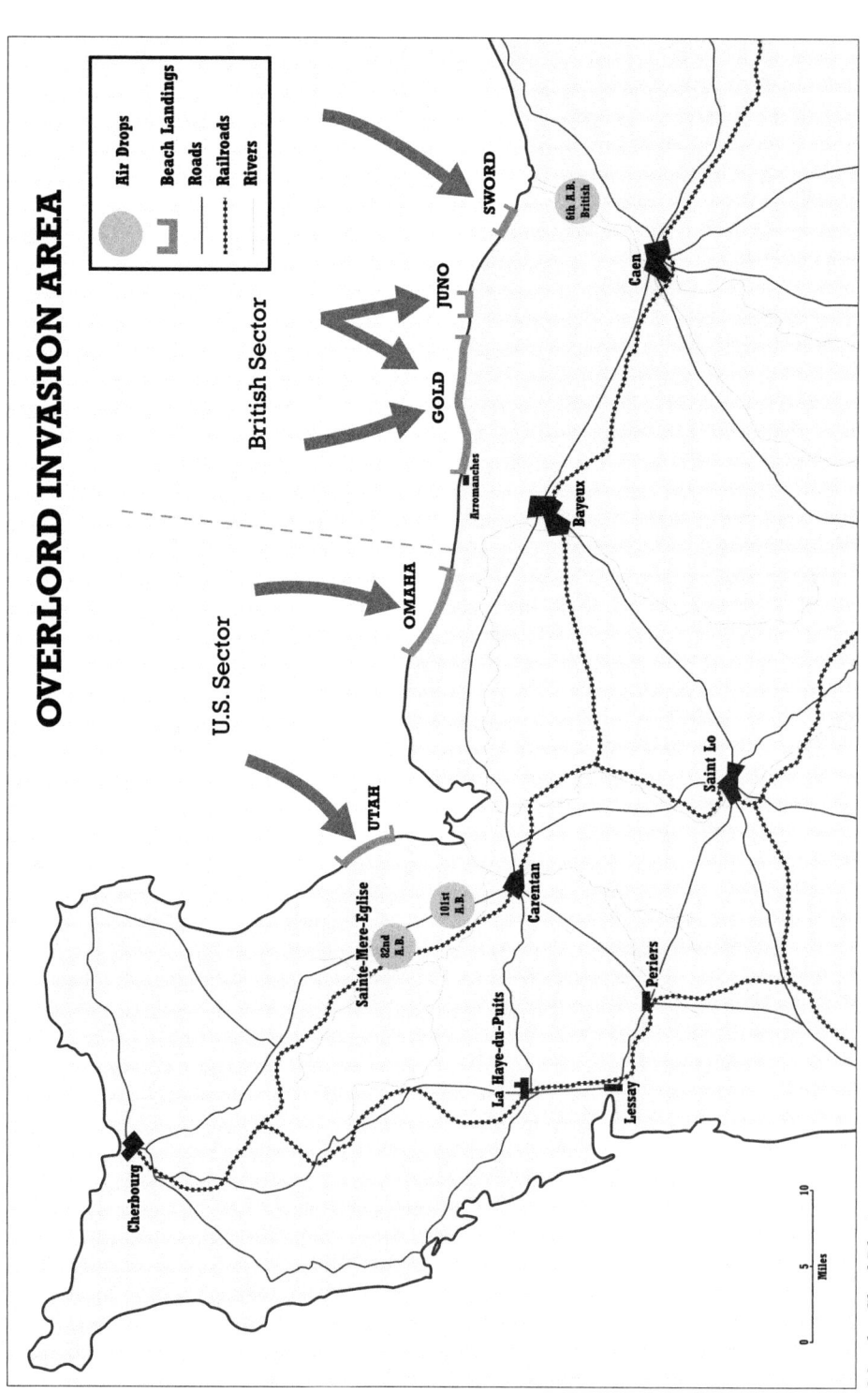

Map by Chad Blevins

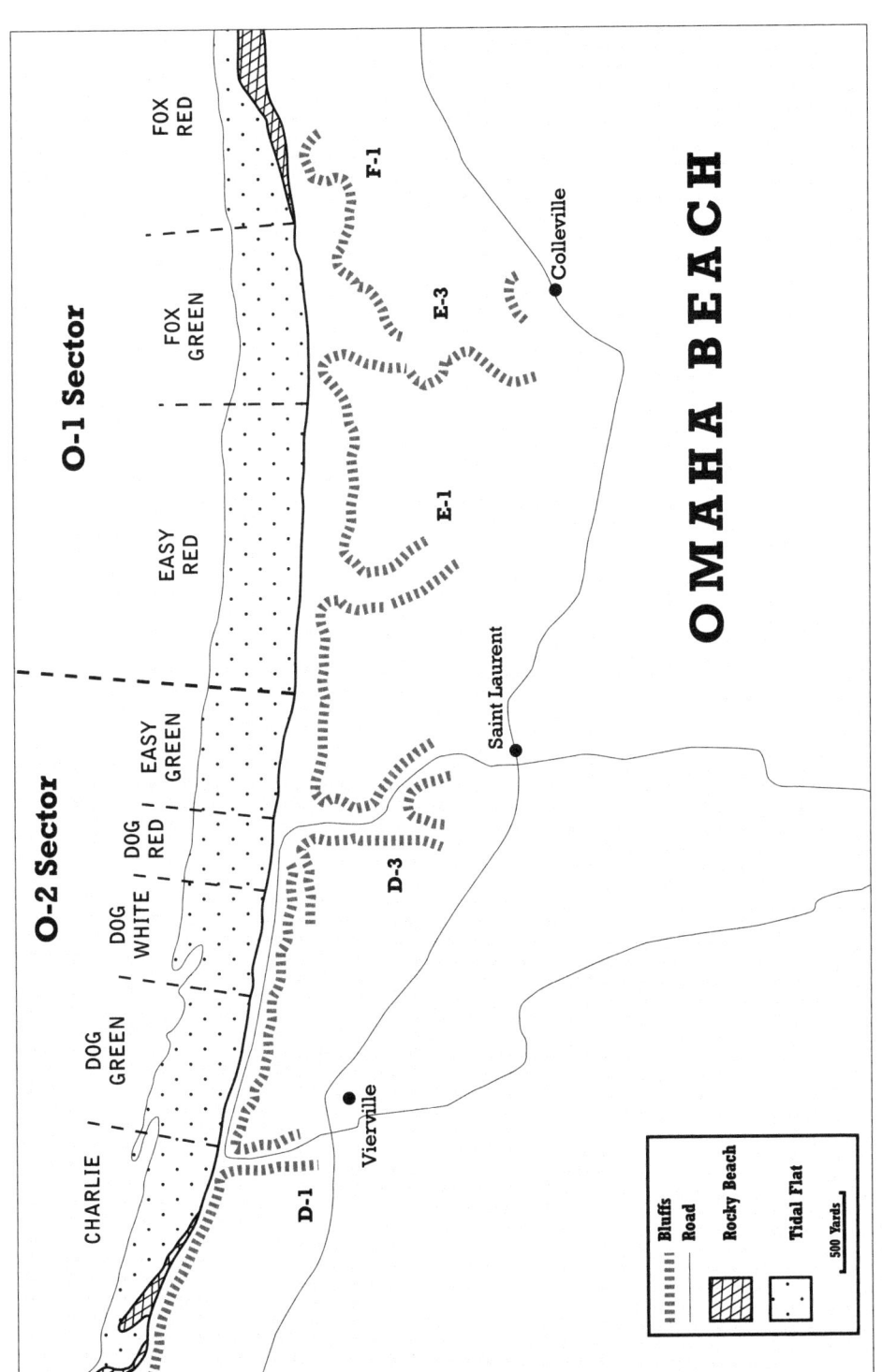

Map by Chad Blevins

PREFACE

The three brown and brittle pages of my father's "D-Day Diary" and the story behind it have always been a major part of my family's history. To my two older brothers, my younger sister, and I, his service as a gunner's mate aboard a landing craft at Normandy was somehow clearer than his job as an accountant. At an early age, we learned the significance of terms like "LCT" and "Omaha Beach." We grew up knowing the difference between a 20mm and a quad 40 the way other kids grew up knowing the difference between a tricycle and a bicycle. At first, Dad's story stayed in a box at our grandparents' house, and on many Sunday afternoons while the adults chatted over the remains of dinner we would dig it out of the closet and read it once more.

Another box at home contained his small, out-of-focus photographs of men named Pequigney and Carlson and Johnson, Cromer and Kelly and Kleen, and we studied them until we thought we knew these men. Dad's hobby was painting, and of course our favorite was his painting of the little ship LCT 614 hitting the beach, guns blazing, surrounded by dead and wounded soldiers in the water. And he had lots of funny stories about his shipmates, of how he lied about his age to join the navy when he was fifteen, of getting wounded while souvenir hunting, and of how he ended his navy service as a quad 40 mount captain on the pre-commissioning crew of the destroyer USS *Joseph P. Kennedy, Jr.* (DD 850).

But as childhood interests turned into careers, we read his story and looked at the photographs less and less. We didn't even notice when Dad gave the painting away to a veteran's organization. The stories ended in September 1984 when Dad died of cancer. That last June, Dad closely followed the television coverage of the fortieth anniversary of the invasion, and he mentioned how he wished he had had the chance to return to Normandy. At that point, my brother Steve was determined to be on Omaha Beach on June 6, 1994.

In 1992, my brother Robert decided to accompany Steve, and in 1993 a generous gift from my mother-in-law allowed me to go along. As we began preparing for the trip in earnest, we all realized how little specific detail we knew about the 614. Where in England did it deploy? Where on Omaha Beach did it land? When? What army units did it carry? What happened after that morning?

Although we had grown up reading stories of D-Day, we began rereading the classic works of the invasion to get some idea of what Dad experienced. However, we were surprised to learn that landing craft, tanks (LCTs), were disappointingly absent from popular history. Books written from the army's perspective mention LCTs only as the men go ashore from them. Cornelius Ryan's *The Longest Day*, for instance, or Joseph Balkoski's *Beyond the Beachhead* give LCTs one-sentence passing references.

Even books chronicling the navy's role in the invasion, like Samuel Eliot Morison's *History of the U.S. Naval Operations in World War II*, give only the briefest comments about these craft. The only LCT exploits to get much attention at all were Lt. Dean Rockwell's decision not to launch the amphibious (Duplex Drive [DD]) tanks into the rough sea but to land them directly onto the beach and LCT 30's fatal charge through the obstacles to land her cargo. Edward Ellsberg's *The Far Shore* chronicled Operation Mulberry, the construction and use of the artificial harbors through which the invading armies were kept supplied, but he never mentions any individual LCT or describes their work in any detail.

Oddly, despite such skimpy coverage in the books, LCTs are an inescapable presence in the photographs of the invasion. Flipping through several books about the invasion, I counted fully a third of the pictures of the invasion fleet that either featured an LCT prominently or caught one lurking in the background. The photographs attest clearly to the important, busy, ubiquitous role of LCTs both during and after the invasion, but the writers for some reason do not give the little craft commensurate coverage in their stories. Going by the written word alone, a reader could get the impression that LCTs pop up out of nowhere, deposit men and vehicles on the beach, and then promptly return to limbo.

At the height of all this catch-up learning, I was finishing work toward a PhD in journalism at the University of Tennessee. Having been in the navy (like Dad, I left the service as a third-class gunner's mate aboard a destroyer) and a newspaper reporter, and now as a newly trained academic researcher, I decided to put my experience and skills to work to fill in these gaps. Since the secondary sources (published histories) had painted only broad strokes, I knew we would have to turn to primary sources—navy records and first-person accounts.

The first place to look was in the "primary" sources we already had at hand. Dad's diary seemed to give us the most direct detail about his experience during the invasion itself. It has several obvious historical errors, such as mentioning the battleships *Oklahoma* (sunk at Pearl Harbor and never repaired) and *Nevada* (which supported the landing at Utah Beach, not Omaha). These errors indicated we couldn't take his account as complete truth, but it was the fullest description we had of an LCT in action on D-Day.

Even if it were short on fact, it was perhaps long on leads, although they were quite subtle. For instance, it did not tell us which army unit the 614 carried ashore or where, but it did say the craft carried bulldozers rather than tanks, indicating an engineering unit. Dad wrote that Pequigney relieved him at the wheel right at H-Hour, the time the first wave of assault troops began reaching shore, so we knew that the 614 went ashore after the first wave but still relatively early in the day—probably around 7 a.m. Also, the mention of LCT 590 seemed to be an interesting lead. Since Dad mentioned that ship landed alongside the 614, the report of its loss might provide circumstantial information about what was happening at that particular place and time. One of Dad's photographs pictured the men of an LCT crew and had a full paragraph on the back:

> LCT 590 received 8 direct hits D-Day. This picture was taken in May, '44. All the boys in this picture except three were killed D-Day. The living ones are marked with arrows. They are:
> Hugh Alsworth, Minn.
> James Holland, Penn.
> the Skipper.

I thought this note would lead to good information. Certainly navy records would include reports on casualties and the loss of a ship.

We also had some information from Dad's separation papers, outlining his stints at boot camp and gunner's mate school in Bainbridge, Maryland; amphibious training at Solomons Island, Maryland, and Camp Bradford, Virginia; duty aboard USS LST 291 and USS LCT (6) Flotilla Twelve and then stateside service until his discharge in December 1945. With the names of these units and the dates of his service with them, I was fairly sure getting logbooks and other official navy records would be a simple matter of making a few phone calls and writing a few letters. Having been in the navy myself, I knew something about the extent and detail of military record keeping, and I thought I knew where to look and whom to ask to get official navy records.

As it turned out, the navy and National Archives that I thought would provide specific details, ended up yielding helpful but circumstantial information. Apparently, the navy thought so little of the tiny, ubiquitous LCTs that very few records concerning them still exist, if they were kept at all. The most important and informative early acquisition from the archives was the logbook of the LST 291, the ship that carried the LCT 614 and its crew to England. The logbook provided a list of the crew and an outline of their adventures from New Orleans to Plymouth, including a quarantine in Halifax that almost made them miss the invasion. Much of the information that makes up chapter 4 comes directly from it.

The navy archives yielded two action reports that concerned craft from Flotilla Twelve. The first report I received was written by William Leide, who was commander of Flotilla Twelve and in charge of all LCTs in Assault Group O-2 (the western half of Omaha Beach). The action report does not mention LCT 614 directly, but it does describe events going on around Dad's craft, especially the confusion that ensued after the first few waves. It also deepened a mystery. It placed LCT 590 among Lieutenant Rockwell's craft carrying the DD tanks. The 590 was indeed hit but suffered three dead rather than all but three dead, as Dad's diary and photo caption said. This mystery continues with the other action report—Dean Rockwell's account of LCT Group Thirty-five, which carried the DD tanks to the O-2 sector of Omaha Beach. It includes a handwritten report by the skipper of LCT 590, but none of the names of casualties mentioned in it are names on the back of Dad's photograph of the supposed LCT 590 crew. We now had no idea which craft Dad had misidentified as the 590.

Other documents supplied by the navy help sketch in the big picture, but they did not provide the specific details I had wanted. The operation order for the invasion describes how Lieutenant Commander Leide was supposed to take charge of the craft in Flotillas Twelve and Twenty-six while they operated in the British sector. Most important for us, it told us that LCT 614 was scheduled to land in the Dog Red sector of Omaha Beach in the H+60 wave (one hour into the landings) and that it carried sixty-five men and fourteen vehicles from three army units: the 149th Combat Engineer Battalion, the Third Battalion of the 116th Infantry Regiment of the Twenty-ninth Division, and the 3565th Ordnance Company (we later learned it was an automotive salvage unit). The navy registry card for the 614 told its ultimate fate. But despite the apparent prominent role Flotilla Twelve played in Operation Neptune (the assault) and the subsequent Operation Mulberry (the supply effort), the navy had no further records of its activities—no logbook, no war diary, no casualty reports, nothing else.

We began to realize why LCTs figured so little in the histories of D-Day—they left no records. Well, not exactly "no" records, but not the wealth of information left by bigger ships. Reasons for this are that LCTs were not commissioned warships, and they did not have commanding officers. Instead, LCTs were simply placed "in service" with an officer in charge. Dad's service record hinted at this when it listed him as a crew member not of LCT 614 but of LCT Flotilla Twelve. But even as the "commissioned" unit, the flotilla did not always keep full records. When the commanding officer of Flotilla Twelve, Lieutenant Commander Leide, filed his action report, he did not do as commander of Flotilla Twelve but as commander of LCTs, Assault Group O-2.

I later learned that I was not the first researcher to encounter this lack of archival evidence for LCTs. In his *The Amphibians Came to Conquer*, Vice Adm. George C. Dyer writes:

> They had insufficient personnel to keep a ship's log, much less a war diary, and by and large they passed in and out of their service in the Navy leaving no individual record, except in the memories of those who served in them or had some service performed by them. Presumably, the LCT Flotilla and LCT Group Commanders kept a log and a war diary, but if they did so, by and large they have not survived to reach the normal repositories of such documents.[1]

My only consolation in this passage was that my inability to find the documents I wanted was not a commentary on my skill as a researcher or reporter.

Ultimately, Dad's photographs proved to be the most fruitful lead to information. Dad's short notes on the back of some of them were usually just a last name or

---

1. Dyer, *The Amphibians Came to Conquer*, 464.

worse ("Tex, from Texas"), but others were a bit more helpful: "Frank Pequigney, The Bronx," or "Francis Kelly, Chicago." I started working with the notes that provided names and cities. These, coupled with the library's phone fiche and some good luck, soon yielded contacts with several of Dad's shipmates. I started with Frank Pequigney, since he had the most unusual name. The Manhattan phone book listed only one Pequigney, who happened to be his distant relative and had the address of Frank Pequigney's son. I was soon in contact with him, and he sent other photographs, names and addresses of crew members, and plenty of other information. Robert and I were also able to visit him, the first of Dad's shipmates we met.

Each instance of finding another of Dad's shipmates was unique. A very helpful telephone operator provided the contact with the skipper of the 614, Don Irwin. I had his 1944 hometown, but the current phone book did not list him. I called information for that area code and was asking for Don Irwins in several of the large cities around, and finally the operator said, "I have only one Don Irwin listed in this area code. I can give you that number." It was the right Don Irwin. He provided us very early with a twelve-page version of his "D-Day Diary," which he had written up after he provided an oral history for Stephen Ambrose's Eisenhower Center.

Other contacts came through the men themselves. I tracked down Roy Carlson, the anchor winch operator who spent much of the time during the invasion in Dad's gun tub, simply by finding his name listed in the phone book. He lived in the same Oregon town that he did fifty years ago. He knew that Dad's loader, Walter Stefanowicz, had died and that John Jarvis, the one member of the crew to be wounded during the invasion, was living in Minnesota. It also turned out that Carlson's son was marrying a woman who had graduated from the college in Georgia where I was teaching, and when he came to Georgia for the wedding he made a special effort to drop by my mother's house to chat with me. Mr. Pequigney provided information that led to contacts with Richard Gudger and William Cromer. Mr. Irwin knew something of the background of the ship's second officer, George Pillmore, and soon I was in touch with him.

Within a few months, we had accounted for almost half of the 614's crew. These men have provided plenty of stories that picked up where Dad's had left off. Indeed, their stories quickly corrected many of the embellishments Dad had put into his written account; we learned the diary had more than offhand historical errors. Case in point: Dad's diary describes shooting up a machine gun nest. All his shipmates agree, however, that he never fired on D-Day. In fact, the ship was under strict orders not to shoot except under specific guidelines.

More important, some of the men were able to get back in touch with one another. On his way to Georgia, Mr. Carlson visited Mr. Irwin in Iowa and taped some of their conversations for me. Although John Jarvis's health prevented him from participating in the reconstruction of this story, finding him meant that Mr. Irwin could complete some unfinished business and get Mr. Jarvis the Purple Heart he had been due since 1944. That alone was worth the time and the effort that I had put into the research.

About the time that we began finding Dad's shipmates, two new books about the Normandy invasion appeared, based largely on first-person accounts, that gave LCTs slightly more attention than previous books had. Paul Stillwell's *Assault on Normandy: First-Person Accounts from the Sea Services* provides an account from Rockwell and a few other isolated anecdotes about crewmen aboard LCTs. Stephen Ambrose's *D-Day, June 6, 1944: The Climactic Battle of World War II*, probably the most thorough account of the invasion, treats LCTs as a mostly background presence in the book. However, he mentions more of them individually than any previous book about the invasion. Our biggest and most pleasant surprise came when we learned that Ambrose gave LCT 614 almost two full pages of attention, drawn from Irwin's oral history.

So we had a fairly good idea of what happened to LCT 614 during the Normandy invasion and afterward when we went to England and France in May and June 1994. We spent a few days in southern England, including a day at Weymouth and Portland, and we were able to stand on the "hard" where LCT 614 likely took on its load. We traveled to France by ferry to simulate Dad's seaborne crossing. Our "second longest day" on June 6 started with a predawn trip to be on Dog Green at H-Hour (we couldn't be at Dog Red because it was sealed off for the international ceremony that included heads of state), a lunch of military meals ready to eat (MREs) at the church wall in Vierville (we wondered how many GIs sat under that same wall on D-Day to wolf down their C or K rations), and an afternoon at the U.S. cemetery in Colleville. One highlight of the trip occurred the next day, when we happened to meet Dean Rockwell on the beach. The trip resulted in a profound reconnection with our Dad, then some ten years dead.

Upon our return, we visited with several of Dad's shipmates who had provided information. We showed them our pictures of the trip (Robert became infamous for clicking his shutter every fifteen seconds) and thanked them for the invaluable help they had given us. Without them, the trip would not have been nearly as successful. It was then that I realized an LCT book needed to be written.

Ultimately, the heart of this book is the memory of these men. As I've mentioned, my background is in journalism, not history. As a result, I have been more interested in the story than trying to nail down specific factual details. I have especially not bothered (too much) to chase the impossible wild goose of chronology. That doesn't mean, of course, that I have been cavalier with the facts. Several members of the crew have read these chapters and corrected the more egregious errors. But after fifty years, memories are not accurate, and remembering picky factual details or exactly when something happened is simply not possible. When two or more of the men had similar memories, I tried to conflate them into a single event. Where memories have conflicted, I have tried to fit in as much of both versions as I could. That means that perhaps the same event appears in this book more than once in slightly different guise or, conversely, that two or more events may appear here as one.

A couple of quick examples: During the invasion itself, all the men remembered having trouble getting off the beach. Dad wrote about engines burning out, Mr. Carlson remembers a large mine floating off their fantail, Mr. Irwin remembers the anchor getting stuck on a sunken landing craft, vehicle and personnel (LCVP), and Mr. Pillmore remembers the cable hanging up on the anchor winch. Since no one but Dad mentioned engines, I have left that out of the main story; had it occurred, loss of engines would have made an impression on the others as well. However, I have included the mine, the LCVP, and the winch because they're neither contradictory nor too similar, and they're the kinds of things that an individual would notice. Meanwhile, the possibility remains that, as different as they are, they are conceivably differing memories of the same event. Similarly, Dad remembered losing the counter-recoil spring off one of the 20mm guns, and Cromer remembered snitching parts from beached LCTs. Quite likely, these memories come from separate incidents, but they're so similar I have made one story from them.

The main point here is that I have tried to tell a cohesive story of men under combat and stress. I have tried to avoid stringing along fact after fact or anecdote after anecdote. My purpose is to record something of the contribution LCT sailors made to the war effort and what that contribution cost these particular men.

And one last note about a sensitive issue: Although mostly the men got along well, naturally several of the crew members were less popular than others were. In such cases, I have used the man's *name* in neutral or favorable contexts, but the man's *rating* in unfavorable settings. To use my Dad as an example, I would say that Carter kept yelling at the skipper, asking for permission to shoot back at the

Germans, and I would say that it was the ship's gunner's mate who was bad to play practical jokes on his shipmates. In the latter case I would not identify Carter as the gunner's mate.

Finally, this book is not intended to be the definitive history of LCTs. In fact, it's not so much the history of a single ship as it is the story of the men who kept her going through often-impossible conditions. Through the experiences of these men, I hope, readers will be able to see that these little ships, mentioned so obliquely by the historians of the Normandy invasion, played an important role in winning the war, a role that in no way ended with the initial assault. In that sense, LCT 614's history provides a glimpse into the overall history of these craft. The Normandy invasion, certainly the climax of their combat service, culminated a long and illustrious combat record accumulated by these craft. The 614's experience at Omaha Beach provides some understanding of the LCT's use in the European theater of operations, where the craft participated in the assault phase of an invasion and then subsequently in a support role. The 614's experience in China conveys something of the different way the craft were used in the Pacific. Mainly because of the long distances involved, LCTs rarely landed in the initial assaults on the islands, but they were in action soon afterward during the support and buildup phase of the invasions. Certainly, LCT sailors in the Pacific saw their share of combat, usually against Japanese aircraft. War correspondent Ira Wolfert reported that one Pacific LCT skipper claimed to have destroyed a Japanese midget submarine by butting it with his bow ramp, and at least one LCT engaged in a surface action against a Japanese craft. The 614's experience in the Pacific captures some of the uses of these craft in that theater—no combat assault, but some experience with air raids and keeping the fast-moving marines supplied.

But as it was for LCTs in general, D-Day and operations in Normandy constitute the real climax of this book. During his visit with his former skipper, Roy Carlson mentioned to Don Irwin how tricky memory was after fifty years. "But there's one thing we'll never forget," he said. "We'll never forget that we were there." The danger is not that the men who were there would forget but that everyone else will. Generations from now, someone might read Ambrose's or Ryan's books and wonder about those craft called LCTs. Navy records would tell them something of their numbers and sizes and shapes, but ships are more than machines; they take and give of the lives of the men who run them and fight them and paint them and scrape the paint off and paint them again. Without knowledge of these men and what they did, there can be no true knowledge of the LCT. That, finally, is why I wrote this book. If the story of the LCT is to be told at all, it needs to be told while the men who operated them are still alive—while the exploits of the little ships are still in living memory.

War correspondent Ernie Pyle put it best in his first dispatch from Omaha Beach: "I want to tell you what the opening of the second front in that one sector entailed, so that you can know and appreciate and forever be humbly grateful to those both dead and alive who did it for you."[2]

This is the story of some of those men.

■

Before beginning, some readers may need a few words of explanation about the confusing array of letters and numbers in this story. Beginning in 1920, the U.S. Navy gave each of its ships a hull number made up of type designation letters—CV for aircraft carriers, BB for battleships, DD for destroyers, etc.—and then a number. The system allowed most vessels to be identified by name and hull number for more specific identification, even when ships carry the same name. For example, World War II's famous USS *Enterprise* (CV 6) can easily be distinguished from the Cold War's famous USS *Enterprise* (CVN 65). For smaller vessels, however, especially the amphibious assault forces, the navy gave them only hull numbers. So the story that follows contains an embarrassing, and unfortunately inescapable, alpha-numeric jumble.

As will be told in more detail in chapter 2, the LCT was a small craft of about 140 tons and 120 feet long. American LCTs were of two varieties—the Mark 5 and the Mark 6. The designation was often included in parentheses after the LCT. Thus, this is the story of the USS LCT(6) 614.

Other types of landing craft are mentioned early: the 160-foot LCI(L), or landing craft, infantry (large); the 50-foot LCM, or landing craft, mechanized; and the 36-foot LCVP. The much larger LST (landing ship, tank) was some 330 feet long with a displacement of about sixteen hundred tons—comparable in size to a small destroyer. LSTs, by far the largest amphibious vessels of the war, often carried LCTs, LCMs, and LCVPs to destinations beyond the range of the smaller craft. Chapter 4 tells the story of the USS LST 291 carrying the USS LCT(6) 614 from New Orleans to Plymouth, England.

Readers who can follow that last sentence may now begin the story.

2. Pyle, "On the Road to Berlin," *Brave Men*, 247.

ACKNOWLEDGMENTS

The biggest chunk of my thanks for the information that makes up this book must go to the officers and men of the LCT 614 who patiently answered my many questions. Several of them looked over early drafts of these chapters, provided corrections, and added details. With these thanks must also come apologies for any errors that remain through my own obstinacy. I know I owe more than one of them an apology for reawakening old nightmares. I also regret that I took so long bringing this project to completion that far too many of them did not live to see their story in print.

The following people stayed in contact with me over several years, providing rich details about life on LCT 614: Frank Pequigney, Don Irwin, Roy Carlson, and George Pillmore.

These men gave me valuable details and insights, but for various reasons I lost contact with them after all too short a while: John Jarvis, Richard Gudger, Fred Kleen, William Cromer, and Nick Andin of the Atlantic crew; and Jack Banks, Francis Coffas, Glenn Dunnegan, and Paul DiMarzio of the Pacific crew. I must also mention here Buster Shaeff of the LST 291's crew.

Another major portion of my thanks goes to my family: my mother-in-law, Ruth Yarbrough, for helping fund my trip to Normandy; my siblings, Robert, Steve, and Betsy, for aiding my research and goading me to complete this book; my aunt Jerry Carter for her descriptions of life among the Carters in Etowah; and mostly to my wife, Catherine, and daughter, Julia, for putting up with my too many hours writing and revising.

This book would be much thinner (in number of words and quality of detail) without the able assistance of an entire crew of researchers and archivists at the National Archives and Records Administration, the Operational Archives Branch and the Ships History Branch of the U.S. Navy History and Heritage Command, and the National Personnel Records Center.

And, of course, many thanks to Dr. Elizabeth Demers and the many people at Potomac Books who brought this manuscript to life.

1

PEARL HARBOR TO BOOT CAMP

Luther "Luke" Carter

The Boy Scouts was everything to fourteen-year-old Luke Carter. His childhood in Depression-era east Tennessee offered no particular hardships; everyone was already poor before the Depression hit but it seemed to offer no immediate opportunity for adventure or excitement. The Boy Scouts filled voids in Carter's life that the youngster probably didn't realize were there.

When Luther "Luke" Eldon Carter was born on September 29, 1927, his parents had buried their first son, Winfrey, just three months earlier. Their first child, Ruby Lee, was alive and healthy, but Luke's arrival so soon after Winfrey's death seemed a blessing to the religious, and improbably named, Noah and Dove Carter. A younger sister, Jerry, followed Luke in 1930. Two years later, another son arrived named Danny. But Danny died in 1935, like Winfrey, barely short of his third birthday. His death left Luke the only son, cherished and guarded, between two sisters.

Home life for the Carters followed the rather strict norms of their Southern Baptist traditions. Luke and his sisters had to hide under the porch so they wouldn't get caught reading their comic books. Breaches of discipline resulted in spankings, usually with a switch cut from a hickory tree in the yard. In the most memorable incident, Luke pleaded with his dad to play ball with him, but Noah was sitting on the fence, chatting with a neighbor. In frustration, Luke bashed his dad in the legs with his bat. Noah came off the fence, pulled up a sapling by the roots, and administered the lesson.

Noah's job with the Louisville and Nashville Railroad provided a steady income, but it also kept him moving quite often. No two of his children were born in the same town. At the height of the Depression he found his work slowed; the railroads were still a crucial form of communication, but the slowdown in orders and production meant less freight to ship. To keep the family larders filled, Noah and Dove would plant and tend a vegetable garden. In the fall, Noah would hunt for squirrel, rabbit, and turkey (the story in the family was that during the Depression, he would work three days and hunt two). In fact, hunting became a tradition that persisted to the end of Noah's life. All through the 1960s and 1970s, the Thanksgiving turkey on the Carters' table hid a liberal peppering of No. 6 shot (not fun to bite onto), and each fall during hunting season, squirrel was a staple meat. Fried squirrel was fine, since most of the flavor was in the seasoning anyway. Dove Carter's squirrel and dumplings, though, hid a sometimes nasty surprise: Noah Carter liked to eat the brains (he said it helped him think like a squirrel), so it was not uncommon to dip in the ladle and come up with a gravy-covered squirrel's head. It was skinned and eyeless and had no meat to speak of, but Noah would crack open the skull for the delicacy inside. That particular eating custom did not survive into later generations of Carters.

Although life for Luke and his family was difficult, it also had its share of hospitality and humor. Through hunting and gardening, the Carters always had plenty to eat and enough to share. Because the family always lived near the railroad, hobos constantly showed up asking for leftovers; the family later found out that the hobos had marked their house as a place where they could be assured of getting food. (The hobos apparently made an impression on the Carters as well; in later decades, one of Luke's favorite songs to sing to his children was the old hobo Utopian ballad "The Big Rock Candy Mountain.")

Also, Noah was an inveterate prankster. Inspecting the tracks one day, Noah and a coworker happened to see a rattlesnake slither off the tracks and under a bush. As the coworker picked up a big rock and cautiously approached the bush, Noah picked up a twig, worked around behind the man, and poked him in the ankle. He was startled so badly that he ended up jumping into the bush with the snake. The prankster gene certainly was passed along to Luke, who had plenty of stories of childhood deeds: knocking over outhouses on Halloween, soaping rails right beyond the depot where the locomotive needed to gain traction, and other devilry that sometimes bordered on the felonious.

Apart from pranks, Noah and Luke also shared a fondness for gun collecting and trading. Noah favored Winchesters, especially the smaller-caliber lever-action rifles and the pump-action shotguns that he used in hunting. The back room of his house always carried the faint whiff of gun oil. Consequently, Luke grew up around guns and thought of them as a natural part of everyday life. Luke tended to prefer rifles, especially the 1903 Springfield, old percussion muzzle-loaders (they weren't in common use, but plenty of them were still around), and Western-style pistols, such as Colt six-shooters. In a mix of friendly competition and cooperation, when Luke would find a firearm like an old Smith & Wesson revolver chambered for .32-20, Noah would trade for a Winchester rifle of the same caliber.

Noah served as Luke's main source of male companionship, and although their relationship was strong, it certainly wasn't chummy by today's standards. Noah kept to the strict roles of fatherhood that the east Tennessee culture of the early twentieth century expected. Luke also tended to be the target of torment from his older sister, Ruby, and younger sister, Jerry, and he found it hard to make any kind of alliance within the family dynamics. Probably as a result of that separateness, Luke developed a lifelong love of reading. With fellow Tennessean and World War I hero Alvin York then at the height of his fame and popularity, Luke particularly liked stories of that war, but he read almost anything and everything he could find.

In the mid-1930s, Noah was promoted to track supervisor and transferred to the railroad town of Etowah, Tennessee. For the first time since Noah and Dove were married in 1920, the family had something like a hometown. It was near Noah's hometown of Benton, Tennessee, and therefore one set of the children's grandparents was fairly available. (The other set lived just across the nearby state line in Murray County, Georgia, but fifty miles was not an insignificant distance in the 1930s South.) The children were able to keep friends from one school year to the next, and Noah and Dove found themselves being quickly absorbed into the family of the First Baptist Church. But the greatest benefit to Luke was his membership with Boy Scout Troop 74. Now, with many other boys his age in his life, Luke made lots of friends and found plenty of outlets for his youthful, boyish energy.

That energy showed in how quickly he advanced. His friends from school introduced him to the troop, but it was his shooting and outdoor skills, coupled with his affability and natural intelligence, that smoothed his socialization into the group. Fittingly, his first two merit badges were Pathfinding and Reading, awarded in May 1941. That summer, he immersed himself in Scouting and attained the rank of First Class Scout on August 8, 1941. Exactly three months later, he earned

Star, the first of the senior Scout ranks. He lost no time beginning work toward his Life rank, and he had no doubt that he would earn the coveted Eagle Scout rank by the time he was sixteen. Of course, earning advancement in the Boy Scouts meant earning merit badges, and earning merit badges meant proving to the troop's Scoutmaster that he had qualified for them.

Just a month after earning Star rank, Luke went to his Scoutmaster's house after Sunday dinner to sign off on the Safety and Surveying merit badges—two of the five badges he would need for advancement. As is typical in the Southeast during late fall, a strong front had pushed away unseasonably warm weather and left the day sunny and crisp, so Luke sat with his Scoutmaster on the front porch, demonstrating his new knowledge and skills. It was pleasant enough for both of them until the Scoutmaster's wife came to the door and said they should come listen to the radio.

The Japanese had bombed Pearl Harbor.

The young teenaged Luke followed the war news as if it were a big football game. That first winter and spring the news was almost all bad, but then fortunes seemed to turn during the summer. In early June the U.S. Navy had stopped the Japanese advance across the Pacific at a little island called Midway. During that first summer of the war, Luke followed the news while continuing to rack up the merit badges. In August, Luke was promoted to Life Scout, the last stop on the way to Eagle. But in that same month, the American offensive began. America's first amphibious assault took place at Guadalcanal. In the Atlantic, the U-boat crisis seemed to have climaxed with the waning of the Operation Drumbeat offensive against America's coastal shipping. In November, the Russians held the Germans at Stalingrad, and the American landings in North Africa trapped German field marshal Erwin Rommel's troops against the British forces in Tunisia.

By Christmas, both Japan and Germany were clearly on the defensive on all fronts. By the spring of 1943, Rommel was all but defeated in North Africa and the invasion of southern Europe loomed in the near future. The Americans had begun advancing up the Solomons, and the Russian counteroffensive had gained momentum. Luke began to grow anxious. In only a year, the Allies had turned the war around and had begun winning. He would not be seventeen until September 1944, and he worried that the war could very well be over by then.

A week or so after Rommel escaped from Tunisia in March 1943, Luke had waited as long as he could stand. Although he had not quite finished his sophomore year in high school, he knew his height of a little more than six feet tall and his already weathered complexion would help him claim an additional year or more to his age, despite his lanky build. Picking a day when he knew his father would be out working on the tracks, Luke skipped school and took the train to Chattanooga, Tennessee.

Luke's first stop was the U.S. Marine Recruiting Station. Either because of a steady supply of volunteers or because the marine recruiter suspected something amiss, he told Luke the marines could not take him because of his teeth. That seemed absurd to the youngster. "I want to shoot them, not bite them," he protested to no avail. Next door was the navy recruiter. He persuaded another fellow there, Ed Worthington of Watauga, Tennessee, to stand in as his guardian and told the recruiter that he had just turned seventeen and was eager to get into the war. On May 21, 1943, with a completely fictitious next of kin and hometown listed on his record, fifteen-year-old Luther Eldon Carter became a swabbie.

When Luke did not return home from school that Friday, his parents didn't worry until late in the evening. After all, he often spent after-school hours with his troop members working on merit badges, especially on the weekends, but as afternoon turned into evening and on into night, they knew something was amiss. Early the next morning, Noah Carter checked with his friends at the railroad station and found out his son had gone to Chattanooga. He went home to pack and, along with his wife, went in pursuit of his son. Because it was the weekend, they found him before he shipped off to boot camp in Bainbridge, Maryland, and they told him they fully intended to reveal his fraudulent enlistment to the navy. Noah and Dove had already buried two of their sons, and they didn't want to see the last one risking his life in war unnecessarily. But he reacted in a way they did not anticipate: he cried. His tears showed them how sincere he was about staying in the navy. They went home without him and hung up a blue star in the window.

William Cromer

A bit farther south, in Thomaston, Georgia, William E. Cromer grew up in conditions much different than Carter did. Instead of no brothers, Cromer grew up immersed in brothers—not only his own, but also those of everyone else in the neighborhood. The Cromers were a large, bustling family that was fairly well established in the small community. They lived on the edge of town, near the railroad station, and although they had plenty of mouths to feed, their father had steady work in the cotton mill in town—work that meant that the Cromers never lacked for food throughout the Depression. So when the friends of the Cromer boys went hungry, as fortunes fell as a result of the Depression, they knew they could always find food at the Cromer table. So many people passed through that it would not have been a surprise if occasionally a total stranger, some hobo riding the rail through town, had wandered in and made himself at home. True, the boys often had to fix breakfast, dinner, or supper on their own, but that was never a hardship.

There in the small Georgia town, surrounded by family and friends, the war seemed distant to Cromer. He certainly felt no need to escape the confines of small-town life the way many other men did. For Cromer, the war did not present an opportunity but a duty. Cromer knew he had to go to war the way his mother knew she had to feed all the boys at her table, her boys or not.

Cromer was only slightly older than Carter was—in fact, pretty much the same age that Carter claimed to be. When he visited the navy recruiter, he was told that because he was seventeen he would have to enlist in the regular navy rather than sign on "for the duration" (as the even younger Carter had done in Tennessee). He fell for it.

Frank Pequigney

Much farther north, in the Bronx, New York, the war was already quite real to Frank Pequigney. During the winter and spring of 1942, he had seen torpedoed ships burning off Long Island. That summer, he and two friends spent a week at a beach house on the Jersey shore owned by the father of one of the friends. They had looked forward to a week of swimming and girls, but once there, they found the water covered in a film of oil and the sand coated in the stuff. Being kids, they swam anyway and found the oil almost impossible to wash off.

At the end of that school term, Pequigney was about to turn eighteen. He knew the draft would snatch him up as soon as he was of age, so he and a couple of friends bought into the advertising slogan: "If you'd rather ride than walk, join the Navy."

Roy Carlson

In the opposite corner of the country, Roy Carlson was already nineteen and working in the logging camps of the Oregon woods near Astoria. The war seemed quite distant to him and the Pacific Northwest, despite the fact that Japanese sub-launched balloon bombs had in fact landed in Oregon. Like Pequigney, he began feeling the draft wafting his way, and a friend suggested they join up. Carlson went along mostly out of curiosity. But he had already decided that if he had to join up, he was going into the only military service he had any experience with—the Coast Guard. He gave in to the peer pressure, talked to the Coast Guard recruiter, and ended up at the induction center. After his group was sworn in, the officer said, "Well, men, you're in the Army now." Carlson snapped back, "Like hell I am. I'm in the Coast Guard." Some intense negotiations followed, with Carlson threatening to go back to Astoria and the officer threatening jail time. Somehow they reached a compromise that he would go into the navy. Carlson was curious about what the navy was going to do with a logger.

Don Irwin

In the nation's midsection, Don Irwin was preparing for a career in advertising at Cornell College in Mount Vernon, Iowa. Despite his distaste for math classes, he majored in economics and minored in art, two disciplines he thought would bolster his position in the business world. A member of the varsity basketball team, he was working his way through college by waiting tables on campus. The Monday after Pearl Harbor, Irwin carried his tray into the kitchen in time to hear President Franklin Roosevelt's war message to Congress.

The talk among the men on campus had but one topic—not whether to join, but which branch of service to join. Most of Irwin's friends leaned toward the navy, which always had a soft, dry bed and hot food. Then one weekend, a friend of Irwin's who had graduated returned to Cornell from the midshipmen's school at Northwestern University. The new ensign sported immaculate dress whites, and the sight of that uniform made up Irwin's mind. Knowing that the draft board was about to catch him, he asked about the navy's V-7 program. If accepted, he would be allowed to graduate before reporting for active duty at the midshipmen's school at Columbia University. The catch was that he would have to change his curriculum to include eight hours of math courses. He passed the medical and application examinations, and after taking analytical geometry and trigonometry in the same semester, plus a summer school session for his major requirements, he was in. On August 1, 1943, Irwin reported to the Reserve Midshipmen's School at Columbia University in New York.

The Amphibs

All around the country during that turning-point year of 1943, men from all kinds of backgrounds found their way to the navy recruiter for various reasons—some well thought out and others on a whim. Richard Gudger came from a small farm in North Carolina and Frederick B. G. Kleen from an old established family farm in New Jersey. Woodrow Johnson came from the Boston area and John Jarvis from icy Minnesota. Nick Andin and Robert Clark hailed from upstate New York. John Dowling, Walter Stefanowicz, and Robert Long all came out of the nation's industrial midsection. But once in the navy, forces ranging from personal preferences, to world politics began knitting the lives of these men together.

During his seven weeks of boot camp at Bainbridge Naval Training Station, Carter did well enough on the battery of aptitude tests that he was allowed to sign up for a specialty school. He had grown up around guns, and having met Alvin York once or twice on the World War I hero's preaching tours through Tennessee, he naturally gravitated toward gunner's mate school. The additional training kept him at the Bainbridge Naval Training Station another five months, much longer than he would have liked, but the training seemed to guarantee that he would be part of the fighting navy. As he neared completion of his training, he and his classmates filled out the preference cards; Carter asked for destroyers. At first, the navy seemed to grant his request, assigning him to a four-piper destroyer escorting convoys across the Atlantic. Carter was so excited about his assignment that when he came home on leave he wrote it into the family Bible. But in early December 1943, just as his gun school class graduated, the men were gathered up one last time. "OK, men," the chief said. "You guys with names A through K are going to the amphibs." The needs of the service had been determined.

By 1943, the amphibious forces had already gained notoriety in the navy. World War II for the Americans had turned into a series of seaborne assaults in both theaters, and the variety of the specialized ships and craft that deposited marines on Pacific islands or soldiers on Mediterranean shores had gained some press. Despite its novelty, Carter and the others sent to the amphibs considered it the dreaded "Gator Navy"—a part of the navy that lacked the glamour of battleships and carriers, the in-the-thick-of-it battle tradition of cruisers, the excitement of destroyers, the intrigue of submarines, or even the anonymity of the fleet train of auxiliary vessels. In a way, the Gator Navy was the worst of all possible sea-going worlds because it had all the danger of front-line combat with none of the offsetting ability to catch headlines.

Young sailors found their way to the amphibs through a variety of foul-ups or bad luck. Pequigney, who surprised himself by doing better than anyone else in his boot camp company on the battery of tests, gave in to the pressures of his chief to sign up for quartermaster school. It seemed a bit odd to him; he couldn't drive a car, and now the navy was going to teach him to drive a ship. As it turned out, he was not a stellar student at quartermaster school and did not fulfill the potential of those test scores. The navy decided to send him where the ship he would be driving was intended to run aground.

Carlson found out what the navy does with loggers. After boot camp, he found himself back in the Northwest, maintaining and driving trucks at the motor pool at the navy's training center in Farragut, Idaho. Carlson didn't know, nor did anyone else for that matter, that the motor pool unit would later form the nucleus of a construction battalion company, or the famed "Fighting Seabees," of the Pacific theater. For that moment, the war that had seemed so distant to him in Astoria was even farther away, even though he was now actually in the navy. But while he was there he met John Jarvis, an affable fellow from the north woods of Minnesota, and they developed a fast friendship. To the straightforward Carlson, the friendship seemed an acceptable consolation for the navy's apparent decision to have him sit out the war in Idaho.

Cromer found that his enlistment in the regular navy brought him no benefits. If anything, he was even more subject to the dictates of the needs of the service than other men were. After boot camp, instead of a service school he went simply from one temporary duty station to another. For a nonrated enlisted man, temporary duty was not the navy's equivalent of limbo but of absolute hell. After weeks of picking up trash, cleaning heads (bathrooms), waxing floors, and doing other menial jobs, he was beginning to wonder if he'd even see a ship. Finally orders came for him to report to the Amphibious Training Base on Solomons Island, Maryland. He had no idea what the amphibs were all about, but at least it wasn't temporary duty.

For Irwin, things happened way too quickly. As a farm boy in Iowa, he had never seen a body of water larger than the Mississippi River, and the largest vessel he'd been on was a duck boat. At Officer Candidate School (OCS), he spent four months becoming a "90-day wonder" (the teasing, sometimes derogatory, term dates from the days of the twelve-week OCS program), thinking he was getting the full four years of the Annapolis curriculum squeezed into that time. More than a hundred men in his class of nearly a thousand bilged out of the school, but he made it through to his commission as ensign on November 24, 1943. Young Ensign Irwin found that the gold braid on his cap and shoulder boards gave him no more benefits than the two short white stripes of a seaman second class on Cromer's sleeve. Some of the men at the top of the class got to choose submarines or patrol torpedo (PT) boats, but almost all the rest of the men—some eight hundred or more freshly minted ensigns—went off to the amphibs.

In the spring of 1943, the word "navy" had connoted to these men images of battleships, carriers, cruisers, and destroyers. Now, as their lives began to intersect at a little island in the Chesapeake, they began to learn of a whole new fleet whose ship types were letters and whose names were numbers.

2

LCTs ENTER THE WAR

At about the same time that Carter ran off from Etowah to Chattanooga to join the navy, on the opposite side of Tennessee workers had already begun to assemble material for the vessel that would define Carter's navy experience. In Memphis, nestled against an inlet to the Mississippi River, the quarter-mile-long assembly plant at the Pidgeon-Thomas Iron Company had gone into full production of something called a landing craft, tank (LCT).

Amphibious warfare was really nothing new by 1943. Certainly the Romans and Vikings had mastered the art of the seaborne raid and on a few occasions (the Roman invasion of North Africa during the wars with Carthage, and the Vikings' settlements on Britain and even North America) showed they could sustain forces on the far shore. England's fight against the Spanish Armada was perhaps the most famous defeat of an invasion force. After a fashion, the decisive naval battle of the American Revolution had its amphibious element, as the French fleet under Admiral De Grasse prevented the British fleet from reaching Lord Cornwallis's army bottled up on the Yorktown peninsula. A little more than a century later, the marines' landing at Daiquiri, Cuba, in 1898 vaguely foreshadowed what that branch of the military would face in the Pacific in the 1940s.

But as the destructiveness and effective range of weapons increased, strategists and tacticians began to believe that amphibious warfare had come to an end. Much of that lesson came from the Gallipoli Campaign of World War I, when a relatively small Turkish army was able to contain the Allied invaders while they slowly unloaded from the transports. Many strategists argued that the lesson to be learned from Gallipoli was that large-scale amphibious assaults were impractical and doomed to failure, but the strategic situation of World War II dictated that, doomed or not, such assaults would be required. Military planners then tasked themselves with finding a way to overcome the tactical weaknesses that had hobbled the Gallipoli Campaign.

To a large extent, geography had as important a role in defeating the Allied troops on Gallipoli as had the Turks. The rugged peninsula provided natural fortifications for the defenders and no room for the invaders to deploy once they established a beachhead. In the future, planning for an amphibious assault would take geography into major consideration (but the lesson was almost forgotten at Tarawa and Anzio). Another major tactical weakness at Gallipoli was the lack of mobility. The infantry came ashore in the transports' lifeboats, and their vehicles, heavy weapons, and supplies had to be brought in on lighters. The awkwardness of the ship-to-shore movements slowed buildups and signaled preparations for attempted offensives, preventing the Allies from gaining any element of surprise or mobility over the Turkish forces. Later in the campaign, the British devised a special landing craft called a "beetle." The first specially designed amphibious craft, the beetles could carry five hundred men or forty horses, which could be easily landed over wide gangways extended over the bow. Their armored sides proved invaluable during the Suvla Bay landings in August 1915. Unfortunately, these craft were either unpowered or underpowered, so they had to be either towed or shipped to the landing site and then loaded over the side as with any other lighter. They offered nothing in the way of surprise or mobility.

So as early as 1940, Britain began designing special warships that could avoid the cargo-handling aspect of earlier assaults by bringing both men and matériel to the enemy's shore in battle order. The most celebrated of these ships were, in Winston Churchill's now-famous phrase, "those god-damned things called LSTs" (landing ships, tank). They were converted from shallow-draft tankers that had been designed for use around the Venezuelan oil fields of Lake Maracaibo. This led to the specially built Mark 1 LSTs, which followed the basic design of the converted tankers except for the inclusion of side ramps that allowed loading to lighters while simultaneously unloading across the bow ramp directly onto the beach. However, these large ships—at thirty-six hundred tons and four hundred feet long, they were about the size of a small cruiser—tended to beach relatively far from the shore and required a segmented bow ramp that could extend to more than a hundred feet.

The LST(1)s proved so unsuccessful that only three were built. The entire LST idea almost found itself scrapped. However, the British had been building smaller, more versatile craft since 1940, and they had fortunately proven their value in such hit-and-run raids as the one on Dieppe, France, in August 1942. The British designers therefore scaled down the LST(1)s, resulting in a vessel that displaced two thousand tons less but with no loss of cargo capacity. These lighter ships of shallower draft could beach higher onto the enemy shore and unload more quickly. At slightly more than 325 feet long, they were still sizable ships (decreasing from cruiser to destroyer size), and by this stage of the war, British shipbuilding facilities were fully contracted. The British handed the design over to the U.S. Navy, and the American-built LST(2)s became the wartime standard.

British LCTs

The smaller landing craft, tank, actually pre-dated the LSTs. The design of the LCT developed from the landing craft, mechanized (LCM), the only prewar landing craft that could land a tank. LCMs were versatile little craft, based vaguely on the Gallipoli beetles. In the late 1930s LCMs were much smaller than their ancestors were, but even at fifty feet they were a bit large for other ships to carry in numbers to an invasion site. The options were either to build or convert ships specifically to ferry LCMs to the far shore or to build a larger beaching craft that could cross on its own power. Both approaches were in fact taken, but shortly the more practical solution proved to be the larger beaching vessel.

LCTs entered service with the British as early as 1941, and some two dozen of the early LCTs took part in the Dieppe raid. With only two diesel motors, their relatively high freeboard, and a shallow draft, the early LCTs were notoriously hard to maneuver (a design problem never fully solved through all marks of LCTs); one British source even suggested that course changes were best applied in multiples of twenty-five degrees. Indeed, this lack of handiness contributed to the failure of the Dieppe raid. Subsequent marks of the LCTs were larger and powered by three motors, somewhat improving speed and maneuverability. The wartime standard for the Royal Navy became the Mark 4, a two-hundred-ton ship almost 190 feet long and 39 feet wide that could carry six forty-ton tanks, although to simplify production they had only two diesel motors. All LCTs featured a cellular construction that made them quite resilient to damage. One LCT(4) struck a mine and returned to port towing its severed and demolished bow section. This strength made the LCT one of the most indispensable craft for amphibious assaults.

American LCTs

When the United States entered the war, the scope of envisioned amphibious operations increased, and another theater opened up in the Pacific. Consequently, the need for LCTs became even greater. The design of the LCT(4), however, posed many problems for both the British and the Americans. Its size made it impossible to reproduce rapidly in large numbers, and the number of craft already contracted had fully engaged every possible railroad manufacturer and other structural steel firms. Like the LST, the large numbers of additional LCTs required would have to be built in the United States. That necessity posed other problems: the LCT(4) could not cross the Atlantic under its own power, and although it could be carried in sections as deck cargo, one LCT(4) would pretty much monopolize a freighter. In short, LCT(4)s could not be shipped across the Atlantic in the numbers needed.

The next step in LCT evolution, therefore, called for a smaller ship: 118 feet long, 32 feet wide, 140 tons, and half the cargo capacity of the LCT(4). The LCT(5) had three Gray Marine diesel engines instead of the two larger Davey Paxman diesels found in the Mark 4s. The three screws added a certain amount of dependability and perhaps a touch better maneuverability at slow speeds, but these smaller motors plus the bulkier beam-to-length ratio of the Mark 5 (3.6:1, as opposed to 4.9:1) reduced the maximum speed of the craft to eight knots. Like the larger LCTs, the Mark 5s could be carried as deck cargo in three sections, but the smaller craft could be bolted together by the craft's own crew using hand tools. The craft also carried two 20mm Oerlikon guns.

The design for the LCT(5) developed concurrently with that of the LST(2), which led to a "chicken or the egg" kind of origin. The British planners neither designed the LST(2) to carry the LCT(5) nor designed the LCT(5) to fit onto the deck of the LST(2). Rather, the two evolved together as a kind of binary vessel: the LST would carry its load transoceanic distances, and once at the far shore the LST would launch the LCT off its deck to act as a lighter. The designers also envisioned incorporating the LCT's sectional construction into its operational use. An LST could carry an LCT as deck cargo either intact or in three sections. This sectional feature gave rise to a plan to "marry" an LCT to an LST by launching the sections independently and assembling only the two forward sections that constituted the tank deck. The incomplete forward portion would then be moored to the mouth of the LST. Vehicles could then drive out of the LST onto the LCT sections and, from there, onto a complete LCT or other lighterage for further transfer to the beach. Once the LST was unloaded, the two would separate, leaving the LCT crew to bolt the stern section of their craft onto the forward sections and continue their inshore work while the LST returned to the near shore to reload.

This original concept of the LCT(5) as a glorified "ship's boat" for the LST never really worked in practice. Bolting LCT sections together under fire appealed to no one outside a naval architect's office. Apparently, amphibious forces in the Mediterranean attempted the "marrying" maneuver in an operational setting during the invasion of Sicily, but the bulky, unpowered forward section proved just too unhandy in an open seaway. Nor was it terribly practicable to carry an assembled LCT to the far shore on the deck of an LST, because the LST had to shift ballast to attain the ten- to eleven-degree list required to launch the LCT—a maneuver that could not be carried out if the LST also had a full internal load. Therefore, an LCT carried to an assault beach aboard an LST could not be available for the initial assault or even the initial unloading. The nature of amphibious operations in the Pacific dictated this procedure, but whenever possible, LCTs would be loaded at staging areas on the near shore and either sail under their own power or be towed to the far shore. Therefore it came about, through necessity rather than design, that the LCTs became the smallest units of the fleet that also served as their crews' home. PT boats, for comparison, operated from forward bases or from tenders that provided the sleeping, feeding, bathing, and recreational needs of the PT crews.

During 1942 and 1943, some one dozen U.S. barge, bridge, and other structural steel companies built almost five hundred LCT(5)s. About a third (169) of them went to the British under lend-lease agreements. Because the British already had an LCT numbering system in place, they added two thousand to the U.S. Navy hull number (thus, the USS LCT 2 became the HMS LCT 2002, the USS LCT 500 became HMS LCT 2500, etc.). Some of these craft, owing to manpower shortages, found themselves operational with American crews. This put them in the rather odd position of being British designed, American built, British owned, and American crewed.

As battle- and seaworthy as the LCT(5)s proved, the U.S. Navy lost little time tinkering with the design. The first five marks of LCTs all shared a common basic outline—a large open tank deck that, in the Mark 5, took up as much as 70 percent of the length of the ship, and the deckhouse and machinery spaces sited right aft. Even before Operation Husky proved that the idea of marrying an LCT to an LST didn't work in an open seaway, the navy had decided that a through-deck design might be more practical. Arranging the deckhouses along the sides of the ship would allow vehicles to drive onto the ship from the stern and not have to be backed on with all the slow, tricky maneuvering that move entailed. Also, LCTs could take on loads from LSTs simply by backing up to the LST's ramp. No doubt, too, someone hoped beyond hope that distributing the weight along a greater percentage of the ship's length would improve its handling. There's no evidence that any such miracle occurred.

The winning design for the LCT(6) came from the Manitowoc Shipbuilding Company, Manitowoc, Wisconsin, in July 1943. It used essentially the same hull (just slightly longer at 120 feet) and machinery as the LCT(5), but the superstructure consisted of four deckhouses distributed two to a side. This subsequently became the wartime standard for American-built LCTs. After building the lead ship in the class, the LCT(6) 501, Manitowoc Shipbuilding dropped out of the LCT program—as did four other firms that had built Mark 5s—leaving the construction of the other 964 LCT(6)s to eight firms scattered around the Great Lakes and along the Mississippi River: Bison Shipbuilding in North Tonawanda, New York (301 craft); Mare Island Navy Yard in Vallejo, California (166); Pidgeon-Thomas Iron Company in Memphis, Tennessee (156); Quincy Barge Builders in Quincy, Illinois (110); Darby Steel Corporation of Kansas City, Kansas (90); Kansas City Structural Steel of Kansas City, Missouri (49); Mount Vernon Bridge Company in Ironton, Ohio (46); and Missouri Valley Bridge and Iron Company, Leavenworth, Kansas (46).

The soundness of the LCT(6) design and construction is attested by the fact that two dozen or more of these wartime craft survived on the U.S. Navy's inventory into the 1980s. Re-designated as utility landing ships (LSUs) in 1949, several of these craft participated in the landings at Inchon in 1951. In April 1952, the craft were again re-designated as landing craft utility (LCUs) and referred to as the "501 class" rather than the "Mark 6." A flotilla of sixteen of them saw service in Vietnam. During the 1960s and 1970s, many of them were converted to yard craft (derrick barges, etc.), a role in which some of them may yet survive. Subsequent designs of LCUs followed the basic patterns of the World War II–era craft. The 1466-class LCUs, built in the early 1950s, were slightly larger and more accommodating LCT(5)s but had the Mark 5s' trademark deckhouse across the stern, while the 1610-class ships of the late 1950s and the 1960s (and still in service in the early twenty-first century) followed the through-deck design of the Mark 6s, except that the deckhouses were along the starboard side and the pilothouse sited forward.

LCT Construction and Layout

The first two firms to get LCT(6) contracts were Bison Shipbuilding in North Tonawanda (near Buffalo), which was to build LCTs 502 to 573, and Pidgeon-Thomas Iron Company in Memphis, LCTs 574 to 621. Both firms had been involved in the LCT(5) program, and in fact they had completed their orders well enough in advance to earn the army-navy production "E" award. As the earlier numbers indicate, these two firms remained the principal eastern U.S. builders of LCT(6)s for the rest of the war. Pidgeon-Thomas prefabricated the craft at its plant on Iowa and Main Streets and then transported the parts to a new facility (dubbed the Pidgeon-Thomas Navy Yard) on the Wolf River at the foot of Auction Street. The assembly line held up to twelve craft side by side, moving through the line from the shoreward end of the factory building to the water end. When completed, the craft slid out of the building sideways into the river. At its peak, Pidgeon-Thomas could launch an LCT every other day. The first LCT(6) rolled off the production line on July 22, 1943.

One of the reasons for the speed of construction was the fact that an LCT is little more than a number of hollow steel blocks welded together. Nine blocks, some thirty-three feet long by twelve feet wide by six feet tall, made up the hull. Most of these hull sections were further divided into voids that were sealed closed to provide reserve buoyancy. The second section from the stern contained the three Gray Marine diesel engines and diesel-powered electric generators. The section just forward of that contained fuel and lubricating oil, and the next section forward contained the freshwater tanks. The voids in one other section were left accessible for stowage of everything from ammunition to food to the crew's souvenirs.

As mentioned, the three-section hull design of the LCT required the Mark 6 to have four deckhouses (two to a side) rather than two (one on each side); the seam that joined the stern and midships sections ran through a four-foot gap between the forward and aft deckhouses on each side. The tank deck extended aft through a fourteen-foot space between the sets of deckhouses. The three main deckhouses were each twenty feet long by nine feet wide by seven feet tall. The after deckhouse on the starboard side was only twelve feet long. Removable catwalks connected the tops of the deckhouses, allowing the men to move around topside without having to go down onto the tank deck from the side. All the deckhouses had watertight doors along the forward bulkheads; vehicles or cargo could easily block the doors opening onto the tank deck from the side. The two berthing compartments (forward deckhouses) also had watertight doors in the after bulkheads.

The forward deckhouse on the port side held the principal crew's quarters, with four sets of three-tiered bunks and corresponding lockers. The six-foot-long bunks were suspended from the bulkhead with chains and could be triced up to provide a little additional shoulder room for the twelve men who lived there. The only creature comfort provided was a two-kilowatt heater forward and a one-kilowatt heater aft.

The deckhouse aft of the crew's quarters held the galley. A six-foot-long picnic table dominated almost the whole inboard forward quarter of this space. Just aft of the table was the coffee urn mounted on a countertop, and, aft of that, the sink and mess gear lockers were arranged above and below the countertop like kitchen cabinets. On the outboard bulkhead aft, across from the sink, sat the oil-fired galley range, and forward of that were the hot water heater, provisions locker, a large refrigerator, and, in the forward outboard corner, a hatch into the engine room. The outboard bulkhead held brackets for twelve loaded 20mm magazines and a small tank for the range's fuel oil.

On the starboard side of the ship, the larger deckhouse was divided by a curtain with the forward section designated as the officers' quarters. This area contained two bunks along the outboard bulkhead and a log desk, small arms lockers, a safe, and the medical kit along the inboard bulkhead. Aft of the curtain were another six bunks, three to a side. They were originally considered passenger accommodations for vehicle drivers, but as it turned out the crew thinned themselves out by claiming them for themselves. The officers' section got the two-kilowatt heater, and the crew section got the smaller one.

The short deckhouse on the starboard side aft contained the head. The one shower took up the forward inboard corner, and the bulkhead aft of that held a foundation for a vise and some "workshop" space. Two washbasins took up the after bulkhead, and the two toilets sat along the after outboard bulkhead. Also inside the head was the barber equipment, and in the outboard forward corner was another hatch to the engine room. Like the galley, the bulkheads in the head held brackets for 20mm magazines. The toilets and the shower were hand pumped and saltwater fed, meaning no hot baths for the crew of an LCT. The Spartan accommodations reflect the original design concept that LCTs would almost always operate with LSTs, a concept that rarely manifested itself in operation.

The pilothouse stood atop the head. This six-by-eight structure barely had enough room for three men. The quartermaster, or helmsman, stood on a wooden grating slightly forward and inboard of the center of the compartment. The throttles and other engine controls were on a panel in the outboard forward corner, and the inboard forward corner held the radio receiver and related equipment. The chart board (certainly not to be confused with a chart table) and communications gear, including the radio remote handset, took up the after outboard corner. Although designed for three men—the helmsman, throttleman, and navigator—in practice only the helmsman and the throttleman maintained stations there. The pilothouse also served as the station for the man on watch when the craft was not under way.

The LCT's pilothouse should not be confused as analogous with the bridge of a larger ship. As a holdover from the craft's British origin, the skipper's conning position, with a binnacle and voice tube communications to the pilothouse, was atop the pilothouse, fully exposed to weather and gunfire. The arrangement was similar to that of a submarine running on the surface; in fact, LCT skippers called the pilothouse the "conning tower," the same term used for the superstructure of a World War II submarine.

The only real "below" space on the LCT was the tiny, cramped engine room that spanned the width of the ship beneath the head and galley. Headspace in the engine room was only about five and a half feet. The three 225-horsepower Gray Marine diesels took up most of the space here. At each outboard end of the engine room was a separate compartment that held the diesel-powered generators for electrical power. The already cramped space also contained pumps that provided seawater for engine coolant and firefighting, rudder controls, electrical switchboards, and other engineering equipment. Like in the pilothouse, three men were supposed to occupy the space, but in practice only two men stayed below to supervise the operation of the machinery.

The craft's armament consisted of two 20mm guns in tubs made of quarter-inch armor plate on the forward ends of the berthing deckhouses. The 20mm fired a quarter-pound slug (LCT 614 carried only high-explosive incendiary and tracer rounds) at the rate of some 470 rounds a minute and was fed from a 60-round drum magazine that was twice as large as a man's head. Attached to the forward end of each gun tub was a ready service locker that held up to twenty loaded magazines; a dozen additional loaded magazines were stored in brackets in the galley and in the head. This placed almost four thousand rounds, about half of the ship's ammo allotment, in ready access. On large ships, such as battleships and cruisers, the 20mm had a four-man crew. The gunner aimed and fired the weapon, the loader changed magazines, the trunnion operator raised or lowered the mount to help the gunner aim high or low, and a phone talker relayed orders from fire control officers via sound-powered phones. On the LCT, only two men operated the mount—the gunner aimed and fired, and the loader wore the sound-powered phones and cranked the trunnion wheel as necessary.

Just aft of the port gun tub was an even more important piece of equipment—the anchor winch. The gasoline engine was housed in a big locker immediately aft of the gun, and the drum winch sat aft of that. The anchor cable stretched across the length of the galley roof to the anchor mounting built onto the after end of the galley. During combat landings, the anchor would be dropped astern a hundred yards before the LCT grounded at full speed in an effort to drive the ship as high onto the beach as possible. Once ashore, the LCT would keep pushing forward with the engines and maintain tension on the anchor cable to prevent the craft from broaching, or turning sideways in the surf. The vehicles rolling off the ship would lighten it enough so that reeling in the anchor would pull the craft off the beach. In short, if the anchor winch were inoperable, the LCT's beaching ability would be greatly impaired. In routine landings, however, the anchor was rarely used unless weather conditions threatened the craft with broaching or a shallow beach gradient required the crew to run the LCT ashore at full speed.

The only other usable spaces on the LCT (besides, of course, the tank deck) were the two lockers in the bow structures supporting the ramp. The port locker held the gasoline engine that powered the winch that raised the twelve-foot-wide by eleven-foot-long steel ramp. Lowering it was simply a matter of releasing a dog on each side of the ramp and letting it splash. During an assault landing, the starboard dog could be loosed while heading to the beach, but someone had to lie atop the port locker (with its ready access to the winch room beneath) and knock the last dog loose—not a popular assignment. The starboard locker held mooring ropes, wire towing cable, paint, and all the other basic nautical necessities.

The USS LCT(6) 614, among the first forty-eight LCT(6)s built by Pidgeon-Thomas, slid out of the end of the Auction Street assembly plant in early January 1944. On January 7, Lt. G. R. Faust, Ensign G. E. Grimshaw, and Machinist's Mate L. L. Garrett took the craft through trial runs in the Mississippi River off Memphis. The craft passed the trials, and, on January 9, the builder delivered the craft to the navy. Still, LCT 614 was far from being a completed naval vessel. Much of the everyday equipment necessary for running the vessel—everything from its two 20mm guns to spare parts for the engines to plates, cups, brooms, swabs, and paintbrushes—waited in crates lashed to the deck.

On January 10, the craft was ready to be taken down the river to New Orleans. To make maximum use of the few men available, a ferry crew would lash six LCTs together, three abreast and two deep, for the trip down river, with the aftmost center vessel acting as a pusher boat. The arrangement may have made efficient use of manpower, but it greatly diminished the craft's already minimal maneuvering characteristics; therefore, the ferry crew operated the craft only during the day. So even with the help of the river's current, the LCTs took almost a week to get from Memphis to New Orleans. And there, like everything else in the navy, it waited.

The LCT Goes to War

As LCT 614 was being designed, ordered, built, and delivered, LCTs were already in action. The first LCT lost to enemy action was the LCT(5) 21, which was still deck cargo aboard the freighter SS *Arthur Middleton* when it was torpedoed and sunk by the *U-73* off Oran, Algeria, on January 1, 1943. The LCT's crew of eleven men was killed in the attack. It was an inauspicious introduction to combat.

Apparently the first fully operational LCT unit in a war zone was the Pacific theater's LCT Flotilla Five under the command of Lt. Edgar M. Jaeger. These twelve craft—LCTs 58, 60, 62, 63, 156, 158, 159, 181, 322, 323, 367, and 369—supported operations at the close of the Guadalcanal campaign and then the leapfrogging operations as U.S. forces moved up the Solomons chain and up the coast of New Guinea. The first mention of LCTs in an amphibious operation in *The Official Chronology of the U.S. Navy in World War II* is on February 1, 1943, when five LCTs landed an army battalion behind Japanese positions on Cape Esperance, Guadalcanal. The landings met no opposition from shore, but later that day, aircraft attacked and sank the escorting destroyer USS *DeHaven* (DD 469), whose survivors were assisted by LCTs 63 and 181.

Elsewhere in the Pacific, owing to the large distances involved and the unfavorable beach gradients, the navy used LCTs principally in support of operations rather than in assaults. They showed up for battle helplessly chained to the decks of LSTs or ingloriously towed by larger craft and often took hours or even days to become fully operational. That does not mean that LCTs showed up only after the marines secured a beachhead. LCT sailors in the Pacific faced their share of shore battery fire and air raids, and several crews suffered casualties—occasionally even the loss of the entire craft—before they could get the LCT into the water.

On the other side of the world, LCTs saw their first combat in the European theater in July 1943 during Operation Husky, the invasion of Sicily staged from North Africa. Of the three American assault forces, only Rear Adm. Richard L. Conolly's Task Force (TF) Eighty-six (Joss Attack Force) had LCTs in any number. Of the sixty-six LCTs attached to the task force, all but eight were assigned to the initial assault (of the other two attack forces, TF Eighty-five had six craft and TF Eighty-one had none; a follow-up reserve group had five). These craft took on their loads in North African ports, battled through a Mediterranean gale to get to the target, and delivered their loads under fire without a single loss.

Here the Americans experienced firsthand what the British already knew: as frustratingly impossible as the LCT was to maneuver, it fully made up for that shortcoming by its ability to survive withering enemy fire and to land a significant number of troops and equipment. In action report after action report, U.S. commanders praised the LCTs' ability to land large cargoes of either assault troops or armored vehicles or bulk cargo. The ships' "turtle-like speed" drew constant dismay, but none of the other amphibious craft, from the stately LST to the humble landing craft, vehicle and personnel (LCVP), had the versatility of the LCT. The combat record amassed by LCTs in their earliest amphibious assaults led ultimately to the planners of the Normandy invasion demanding large numbers of these indispensable craft.

That versatility can be seen in the fact that, although the little ships excelled in the amphibious warfare for which they had been bred, they earned the title of "warship" through their combat actions in other modes of naval warfare. Before the twentieth century, the term "naval warfare" meant pretty much exclusively ships of the enemy nations slugging it out with one another on the open sea or projecting force onto an enemy-held shore in a combination of surface warfare and amphibious warfare in their classical senses. By World War II, navies also had to be adept at aerial warfare (including air-to-air and air-to-surface actions), antiaircraft warfare, naval gunfire support (using major seagoing warships to support amphibious operations and forces ashore), antisubmarine warfare, and submarine warfare. The LCTs had no role in aerial warfare or submarine warfare (although certainly at Normandy, and probably in other actions, many LCTs fulfilled their duties in a semi-submerged state), but they did participate or find themselves forced into all the other forms of naval combat.

Giving LCTs two 20mm guns was probably the naval warfare equivalent of giving an army officer or sergeant a .45 sidearm; its principal function was as a badge of authority and only secondarily served as a means of personal defense. The 20mms marked the LCTs as warships, but their short range and light projectiles were not going to decide the tide of any battle. Nevertheless, the LCT crews decided the navy had given them the guns for a reason, and by God they were going to use them.

In both theaters, LCTs found themselves often thrust into antiaircraft actions. Air raids on invasion beaches and on marshaling areas gave the LCT gunners plenty of opportunity to pop off a few dozen 20mm rounds. No accurate numbers are possible, but official records from all areas of LCT operations credit the little craft with downing enemy aircraft. In many instances, the aircraft had targeted a larger ship and ignored the smaller "barges" dotting the area to learn that only a few rounds from a 20mm can fatally damage most aircraft. For example, on April 20, 1943, LCT 33 was carrying cargo along the Algerian coast when a German Junkers Ju 88 made a bomb run on it. The first bomb missed, so the plane circled around to correct its error. This time the LCT gunners were ready for it. Hit by several rounds, the plane crashed in flames on the nearby coast, providing a rare confirmed kill that earned LCT 33 a commendation from Vice Adm. H. Kent Hewitt, commander of the amphibious forces in the European theater. Later, during operations off Salerno, LCT 33 reported that in twenty-five air raids between September 10 and September 29, its gunners expended a thousand rounds of 20mm ammunition. LCT 33's experiences are likely not unique, especially for operations in the Mediterranean, where the vast majority of LCT losses occurred before the Normandy invasion. However, the true number of aircraft kills by LCTs can never be determined. It is sure to be less than the hundreds that the LCT crews claimed and may even be less than the dozens officially credited by formal action reports, but the indisputable fact is that

LCTs did shoot down their share of Japanese, German, and Italian aircraft (and quite possibly a few British and American planes in the mix as well).

Another mode of naval warfare that the LCTs assumed as a natural extension of the amphibious operations was naval gunfire support. Part of the reason for the craft having 20mm guns was to provide some covering fire for the troops being landed. However, while the craft's broad beam made it a ship handler's nightmare, it also made the craft a relatively stable gun platform. As I will discuss in chapter 5, many LCTs were converted specifically for shore bombardment. Some of the larger British Mark 4 craft even got old 4.7-inch guns off damaged or used-up destroyers. But naval commanders in all theaters quickly learned that tanks and even field guns could fire with some accuracy from the deck of an LCT.

Certainly by no stretch of the imagination did any naval officer envision the LCT as a surface combatant, and yet on more than one occasion the LCTs found themselves in a classic naval battle against enemy ships. They mostly happened in the Pacific, when LCTs trying to get troops behind Japanese lines encountered Japanese barges attempting to reinforce or pull out the troops the Americans were trying to encircle. The Japanese Daihatsu-class landing craft, roughly the size of an American LCM and armed with 12.7mm machine guns, were the standard prey of the PT boats in the Solomons, but the LCTs accounted for several of them as well. On one occasion, LCTs 146 and 322 found themselves faced with several of the craft. The heavier 20mm guns and steel hulls of the LCTs outmatched the smaller guns and wooden hulls of the Daihatsus, and when the battle was over, American officers estimated more than fifty Japanese personnel had been killed, with only two men on the LCTs wounded.

And in at least one chance encounter, one LCT got the opportunity to engage in antisubmarine warfare. Pulitzer Prize–winning war correspondent Ira Wolfert wrote about one LCT skipper who claimed to have sunk a Japanese midget submarine. In his "LCT, I Love You" (*Saturday Evening Post,* January 8, 1944), Wolfert recounted Ensign "Cooky" Johnson's laconic description of the action: "Cooky claimed there was this Jap two-man sub looking him square in the eye. 'I lowered my ramp and charged,' Cooky said over a bottle of beer, 'and I butted him to death.'" The account has since been confirmed in the LCT veterans' group newsletter by Jack Johnson, who was then the skipper of LCT 182 and who later went on to command LCT Group Sixty-seven in Flotilla Twenty-three.

LCTs also accomplished feats of pure seamanship. One of the most dramatic was the epic voyage of LCT(6) Flotilla Thirty-one (Lt. Cmdr. C. V. Dilley), whose thirty-six LCTs steamed five thousand miles under their own power from Pearl Harbor to the Philippines in 1945. The voyage took them from the Hawaiian Islands to Johnson Atoll, Majuro, Eniwetok, Guam, Ulithi, Leyte, and finally Luzon—all at about 5.5 knots, and occasionally up to 6 knots, with the wind and seas behind them. After a few months in the Philippines, two of the flotilla's groups were ordered to Okinawa, a distance of only fourteen hundred miles. But this time a typhoon blew in, scattering the little craft all over the western Pacific. Their accompanying destroyer escorts finally rounded them all up, but many ended up steaming more than twenty-three hundred miles to reach Okinawa. That story deserves its own book.

So, starting in 1943, LCTs entered service and began quickly building their reputation as unmanageable "large creeping targets" that were nevertheless tough, versatile, and indispensable for modern amphibious warfare. As the men who would form the crew of LCT 614 found themselves being assigned to the strange world of the amphibious navy, they may have felt themselves robbed of the chance of being aboard the carriers and battleships and destroyers of the "real" navy. But they had no doubt that they would be in the real war.

3

SOLOMONS ISLAND

In December 1943, the same month that Pidgeon-Thomas Iron Company gathered the materials that would become LCT 614, Carter and some of the men who would become his shipmates began arriving at the U.S. Naval Amphibious Training Base (ATB) at Solomons Island, Maryland. Like Carter and Pequigney, many came straight from service schools. For other men who had, like Cromer, been berthed in temporary assignments since boot camp, the orders to amphibious training came as a kind of deliverance into the "real" navy at last. Few of the men came aboard with previous service afloat.

The base had been established in July 1942 as a temporary facility to train a couple of thousand men for the invasion of North Africa in November, but as training for one amphibious operation began to wind down, another pending operation required the training of another batch of men. The increasing pace of amphibious operations throughout 1943 coupled with the geared-up mass production of landing craft of all sizes convinced the navy to make the Solomons Island facility a permanent base. However, its beginnings as a temporary camp, plus the ever-growing demand for trained crews, outstripped ATB Solomons' facilities for training them until the fall of 1944. When Carter and his future shipmates arrived (between late 1943 and early 1944), the problems stemming from overcrowding were acute. Originally conceived to train two thousand men for a couple of months, the base eventually operated almost three years and trained as many as eight thousand men at any one time (that number peaked at more than ten thousand in the summer of 1944). By the time the navy deactivated the base in February 1945, it had graduated almost seventy thousand men. At the base's height of activity, the ten piers along the western edge of the peninsula were packed with landing craft "as tight as cigars in a box," one observer said.

Lack of real estate prevented expansion to relieve the overcrowding. The base occupied less than a hundred acres on the tip of a peninsula at the juncture of Back and Mill Creeks. The confluence of the rivers formed a lagoon that opened just inside the mouth of the Patuxent River, providing a safe haven for the landing craft but also forming natural boundaries that restricted the base's expansion to the west, south, and east. The only direction possible for expansion lay to the north, but farmlands and swamps blocked growth in that direction. Also, the navy's bureaucratic lock on the concept that the base's usefulness was almost over disinclined the government from expending the effort and money that such an expansion would require.

The most serious problem associated with overcrowding at Solomons was the supply of fresh water. Eventually the base had a daily demand of almost a million gallons of water. Engineers sank four wells into the sandy soil beneath the base, and fortunately the area was far enough from the brackish waters of the Chesapeake that backflow contamination was not a problem. However, the aquifers that supplied the wells were not water rich, and the wells took time to replenish. The men at the base often found themselves on water hours and learned to take "marine showers": water on to wet down, water off to soap up, water on to rinse off.

The other problems, as irritating and real as they were, actually served to prepare the men for their work on amphibious vessels. Inadequate berthing kept the Quonset huts and other "temporary" structures overcrowded; limited supplies taught the men to preserve, improvise, substitute, or do without; and having too many mouths to feed meant that the food, not the navy's best to begin with, got to the men with minimal preparation. These circumstances would be normal living conditions for the crews of the smaller landing craft once they began operating in forward areas.

The problems on the base were exacerbated by the fact that nothing off the base offered any relief. The town of Solomons itself was little more than a fishing village with a prewar population of around three hundred people. That shot up to more than two thousand once civilian construction workers started moving into town to help build the base and additional service industries moved in. Of course, the increased civilian population overtaxed the town's amenities even before liberty parties from the base invaded.

Nor was the area served by public transportation that could take the men off the peninsula. The men found themselves in the classic navy hell: no liberty, nowhere to go if they had it, and nothing to do once they got there. By some accounts, Solomons Island had one of the highest absent without leave (AWOL) rates of any base in the navy. It was easy for the men to gain the impression that the base was staffed almost entirely by "prisoners at large (PALs)" training fellow PALs. The men joked (I think) that even the base chaplain was a PAL. The brig, reserved for those guilty of the most serious offenses, had a waiting list.

Training Ashore

By 1943, the training station had established an eight-week curriculum for LCT sailors that included everything from basic seamanship skills, such as line throwing, mooring, anchoring, and navigation; basic navy skills, such as gunnery, aircraft recognition, damage control, and sound-powered phone procedures; and the basic landing craft skills, such as beaching, loading, and towing. The "graduation exercise" was supposed to be a full-scale shore-to-shore landing, complete with loading vehicles, navigating to the target area, and unloading the vehicles onto the beach. All of that was on paper; however, the actual experience of the men could be, and usually was, quite different.

In December 1943, the men received only three weeks of classroom instruction. Much of it was refresher training for skills introduced in boot camp; on a ship as small as an LCT, everyone needed to know basic deck seamanship and damage control. Later classes introduced the men to the workings of an LCT and the basic ideas of amphibious warfare. But having only three weeks to work with, all of this training was simply an introduction. The men had no time to practice or polish their skills.

After those three weeks, men of various ratings and specialties were grouped together into training crews. On January 6, 1944, the day before LCT 614 went through her trials, ATB Solomons formed Crew No. 5158, which would eventually become the nucleus of LCT 614's crew. On larger ships, men are formed into divisions that perform various functions of the ship's duties. Gunner's mates form the gunnery division, quartermasters and signalmen form the navigation division, boiler tenders form the boiler division, and so on. Each division has a full range of ratings from chief petty officers to petty officers to unrated men (called strikers), all under the command of an ensign or lieutenant junior grade (j.g.) as the division officer. Divisions with similar functions gather together to form departments with a lieutenant or lieutenant commander (perhaps even a commander on battleships and carriers) as the department head. For example, the gunnery, antiaircraft, and torpedo divisions would form the weapons department of a destroyer.

With twelve to fourteen men skippered by an ensign or a lieutenant junior grade, an LCT crew bore a superficial resemblance to a division on a larger ship, but the similarities quickly vanished. An LCT could afford only one specialty rating for each function that would be a department on a larger vessel. So Carter was the sum total of Crew 5158's gunnery department even though, as seaman first class, he was not yet an official gunner's mate. Similarly, Pequigney was the crew's one quartermaster. Only Robert Long, a signalman third class, was already a petty officer. What would have been the engineering department was made up of three firemen first class (the engineering equivalent of seaman first class): Walter Stefanowicz, the electrician (and therefore known by the universal nickname "Sparky"), and Robert Clark and John Dowling, the motor machinist's mates (motor macs). One other crew member was a steward striker, or ship's cook. William Cromer, Richard Gudger, and Woodrow Johnson rounded out the crew as unrated seamen ("deck apes").

Training Afloat

Once formed as a crew, these men were transferred to LCT(5) Flotilla One based at ATB Solomons. They spent only two weeks aboard a Mark 5 LCT. Their instructors accompanied them for only the first few days, showing them where the equipment was and how to operate it and supervising their first few times under way. Later the men were pretty much on their own. The craft they were assigned was fairly well worn from its training duties and having had so many different crews every two weeks or so. The engine room leaked (a perennial problem with the Mark 5s), and much of the equipment had not been properly maintained. On those January mornings, the men would go down to the piers and have to pump the voids and clear ice from engine intakes and the decks before starting off on the day's assignment.

At first, their assignments were as simple as clearing the docks, heading out into the river, and coming back. Later, the trips were a bit longer and more complicated. Maneuvering an LCT in the Patuxent River and the upper reaches of the Chesapeake Bay with no experience in a craft notorious for its bad handling made for some tense moments—similar to taking their first driving lesson in a dealer's lot filled with shiny new cars. They crashed into pilings, bumped into other craft, knocked over the locals' crab pots, and generally menaced everything that stood or floated within three feet of the water's surface. Sometimes they would head out at night and simply roam around at what seemed to Pequigney to be the whim of the instructor. Later assignments, once they were on their own, offered more challenging navigational problems, such as sailing across the Chesapeake to a site invisible from the base or down to the navy's gunnery range off Bloodsworth Island to practice on the 20mm guns.

Toward the end of their two weeks, they received an assignment to leave the base in the evening and sail down to Little Creek, near Norfolk, Virginia, to practice beaching. Pequigney laid out the course on the chart, complete with speed and time of course changes. The crew tried to follow the course as closely as they could, but by daybreak Pequigney realized they were totally lost. They edged over to the Eastern Shore, and everybody scanned with binoculars for a road sign or a town name on a water tower so they could figure out where they were. Fortunately, about that time, the Cape Charles Ferry came by on its way south. Pequigney knew it was headed to either Norfolk or Little Creek, so he followed it until he could tell their location.

Even though many of the men filled specific billets aboard the ship, they did not have the luxury of concentrating on that one task. Carter would have liked nothing better than to work only on the big machine guns and the variety of small arms aboard, but as one of the more highly trained individuals (a graduate of a service school, even if not from high school) aboard, he became the backup helmsman and radio operator. Pequigney taught him some rudimentary navigation, such as how to take the bearings of two objects ashore to find the ship's position. For more complicated shore-to-shore navigation, Pequigney had a shortcut: "Use the chart to figure out what direction your destination is, and then steer south of it. Once you reach shore, head north till you get there." Signalman Robert Long taught Carter the basic workings of the radio and helped him brush up the Morse code and semaphore he had learned in Boy Scouts.

Working as a team also allowed the men to get to know one another. All of these men were young, and only a few of them had actually graduated from high school (that winter was to have been Carter's junior year). Stefanowicz stood almost six and a half feet tall and had a solid build. Fortunately, he was also a bit of a clown, always joking around and punching people on the shoulder. The men soon called him the "Mad Russian." Dowling was an easygoing fellow from the Buffalo area, always willing to help out. His main interest was in the ship's big diesel engines. Gudger—mountain bred like Carter—was an athletic southern farm boy who kidded Pequigney unmercifully about not knowing how to drive. His experience on the farm had made him quite good with his hands, whether working the ship's tackle or any other form of small machinery. Cromer loved to talk and had plenty of adventures about his childhood and adolescence to serve as fodder for his stories. Like the other southern boys, he tended to be a good shot, especially with pistols. Clark was probably the quietest man on the crew, preferring to work with his hands. All high-spirited young men, they quickly meshed into a cooperative crew.

Officer Training

Ensign Don Irwin did not train with the men who would later become his crew. Officers training at Solomons formed their own crew, primarily because they needed to know the full operational requirements and capabilities of the craft they would later command and because they required some special training in conning the craft and in coordinating landings. The separate training had the added advantage that the crew did not see their future skipper being as bungling a trainee as they were.

Much of Irwin's training involved sailing an LCT(5) back and forth between Solomons and Little Creek. It involved plotting the course on the charts, getting the craft under way in the afternoon and steaming all night through slushy ice and crab pots. For a while, he lived on the LCT. The tiny heaters did little to warm the compartments. On the contrary, the bare steel bulkheads and overheads became thoroughly chilled on those windy January nights, and the relatively warm air inside the compartment readily gave up its moisture on contact with the steel. The condensation dripped all night, and Irwin often woke up to a cold, damp rack with water deep enough on the deck to slosh around. The trainees soon learned to keep shoes and all other articles off the decks. During those sleepless nights, he bitterly remembered why he had joined the navy—soft, dry beds and hot food.

Conditions ashore weren't much better. The Quonset huts also sweated, being heated by small coal-burning stoves that everyone was too tired to stoke at night. By 2:00 a.m., the fires had long burned out and the ashes turned cold. The men shivered under their blankets until finally someone, usually a southerner who could stand the cold no longer, would go out into the night and bring in wet coal. Of course, with the ashes themselves cold, the stoves resisted relighting. The men used any form of paper they could find as kindling and even resorted to using fuel from cigarette lighters.

Toward the end of his training, Irwin was conning the LCT into the base at Little Creek through a narrow channel between stone jetties. The entrance to Little Creek was more open to the Chesapeake than the harbor at Solomons Island had been, and this day featured typical blustery Chesapeake weather. As the unwieldy craft entered the channel, the LCT encountered a tug heading out. The instructor sized up the navigational problem and the weather and took the conn from Irwin. Just as the LCT and tug began to pass, a stiff gust of wind caught the LCT's bow and pushed it into the tug's side. The corner of the ramp tore out big chunks of wood from the tug's side, but apparently the glancing blow did not start (or separate) any of the tug's wooden seams to cause a leak. Still, the tug's skipper had a few choice words to relay to the LCT crew. Irwin could not suppress a chuckle, but it was a clear lesson that no mere human could safely steer an LCT.

Forming the Crew

On January 22, 1944, the men were transferred out of LCT Flotilla One and sent down to Camp Bradford, another amphibious training base near Norfolk. Here the officers were finally matched up with their crews, and all got their assignments to a particular craft. Irwin and Crew 5158 drew LCT 614, but the crew was not yet complete, having only nine men. Nick Andin—a scrappy seventeen-year-old from Dunkirk, New York—showed up at Camp Bradford fresh out of the boot camp at Sampson, New York. He came to the crew never having gone through any of the training at Solomons Island. Irwin and his men were told that their craft was now waiting for them in New Orleans and that all they had to do was get down there, get hoisted aboard an LST, and then be off to England to join the invasion of Europe. The two firemen they would need to round out the ship's complement would meet them in New Orleans.

Roy Carlson and John Jarvis had gone to the receiving station in New Orleans having no idea what they were being asked to do. They had been pulled straight from the motor pool at Farragut, Idaho; sent to Norfolk, where they sat around a few days; and then went to New Orleans. Neither of them had ever been on a naval vessel of any description and for sure had no idea what an LCT was. They certainly had received no training about amphibious craft or their operation. To help round out the feeling of disorientation, Carlson's seabag, containing all his uniforms and personal gear, had been lost somewhere in the shuffle.

Finally, at the receiving station in New Orleans, a chief petty officer came in with blank orders. "OK, men," he said. "This is one time in the navy you're going to get your choice. I have four LCTs here that need men, and you can choose which one you get." It was rather an empty choice for Carlson and Jarvis, having no idea what the chief was talking about. All they knew was that they wanted to stay together. "Let the other guys have their choice," Carlson said. "We'll take whatever's left that needs two men." That led them to LCT 614.

When the rest of the crew arrived in New Orleans on January 31, they learned that matching up with their LCT was not going to be as easy as they had thought. Because the LCT was not yet fully operational or assigned to a flotilla, they could not simply report aboard the 614 and start to work. Instead, they were to report to the LST that would take them and their craft across the Atlantic, LST 291, but she was away from New Orleans, undergoing her "shakedown" exercises and operating out of Panama City, Florida. Without a ship in port to report to, the men looked forward to extended liberty in New Orleans.

The receiving station was also where Jarvis and Carlson became members of Crew 5158; however, their introduction to the crew did not have a smooth start. As they were settling in at the berthing compartment at the receiving station, the men who had trained together stood to the side, sizing up these newcomers. While both Jarvis and Carlson were of average height, Jarvis had dark curly hair and a stocky build, and Carlson was fair haired and slimmed by his years in the logging camps. Some of the guys suggested to Sparky, the Mad Russian, that he should go over and find out what these two new men were like. The big electrician went over to them and gave Jarvis two quick punches to the shoulder, then two more. A rather short man, Jarvis had no idea what this big fellow was up to and decided to back off. Carlson had watched what he was doing, and when Sparky came over to him and punched him the first two times, he was ready when the second set of punches came his way. Grabbing Sparky by the wrist, Carlson twisted around and threw him to the deck. He straightened up and turned to the other men standing there. "Any of you other guys want to try me out?" Soon, the two new men became full members of the crew. To Carlson's surprise, he learned that, apart from the skipper, he was the oldest man among them.

Since he still didn't have his ship yet, Irwin thought that under the circumstances he didn't have to worry too much about his men. They were technically under the command of the receiving station, and apparently they were going to be stuck in New Orleans for at least another week. There on the Gulf Coast in early February, the seasons had already started to change to spring, a welcome relief from the cold Chesapeake. Irwin thought that, with the unexpected time on his hands and with the nice weather, this would be the perfect time and place to marry his college sweetheart. Once the crew left New Orleans, they would be on their way overseas with no time for marriage ceremonies. He called his fiancée and made the arrangements, and soon she was on the train headed south.

The next morning, Irwin walked into the headquarters of the navy receiving station and just happened to notice his name at the top of a set of orders being typed by a yeoman. Peeking over the man's shoulder, Irwin saw that he and his crew were being ordered to hitch a ride on LST 294 to Panama City, where they would board LST 291 for the last week or so of the ship's shakedown. That put quite a damper on Irwin's plans. He scrambled to wire his fiancée to tell her the wedding was off, but she was already on her way. He explained the situation to her parents, and they were able to get word to her before she had left Iowa. The couple's hopes for a wedding before he left the States had pretty much evaporated. As far as he knew, once the ship left New Orleans it would have very few stops before England.

Finally at Sea

Crew 5158, now nearly at full strength, boarded LST 294 on February 3 and got to Panama City three days later. When they arrived, the LST 291 was still at sea, going through various exercises, but after only a few hours' wait the 291 steamed into the harbor and anchored. About eight o'clock that Sunday evening, Irwin and his twelve men transferred by boat and reported aboard the 291.

LST 291 had been built by the American Bridge Company near Pittsburgh and launched into the Ohio River on November 14, 1943, almost seven weeks after being laid down. Commissioned on December 22, the ship had to sail the entire length of the Ohio River and much of the Mississippi to reach open sea, a distance of almost two thousand miles. At the commissioning ceremony, Ensign A. G. McNair took command of the big ship. A mustang officer, McNair had been a chief petty officer before receiving a wartime commission to command landing ships. Just two hours before Irwin and the 614's crew arrived on the 291, McNair received a promotion to full lieutenant, skipping over lieutenant junior grade.

A newly commissioned navy ship does not go immediately to the battle fleet; it must first go through shakedown. This exercise puts not only the ship and its new equipment through various tests to ensure that all works properly, but it also allows the crewmen to familiarize themselves with their new ship and to form a cohesive unit. Shakedown cruises differ from trials in that they are much more thorough and that the ship's company, rather than navy representatives, take the ship through its paces.

Once on board the 291, Crew 5158 learned that they were not to be merely passengers on a pleasure cruise, they were also to be on full duty as part of the 291's crew until they reached England. That put Irwin and his men in a fairly awkward position. Technically a crewman of the 291, Irwin had no official responsibility for his men while on the ship; instead he was just a very junior officer who filled in, standing quarterdeck and bridge watches. Once the 614 was hoisted aboard, however, it would need some work to maintain it and to start getting some of its equipment installed. Irwin wasn't sure if he had the clout to demand that he retain some command over his crew to get that work done. As it turned out, the 291 was such a new ship that its organization was still confused enough to allow Irwin some authority over his men.

Catching the last week of the 291's shakedown cruise, the 614's crew got almost as much training as they had received at Solomons Island. Over the next five days, they followed a routine of going to sea each day for the planned exercise and then returning to anchorage that evening. Some mornings, fog would delay their departure from St. Andrews Bay, but it never prevented them from sailing. They went through beaching exercises, gunnery drills, tactical maneuvering exercises, night beaching and night antiaircraft firing exercises, and even formation surf beaching.

Most of the men drew watch stations at the guns. That was what Carter expected anyway, but Carlson wondered how a motor mac truck driver ended up on a 40mm gun crew on the bow of an LST. Pequigney was soon standing watches in the pilothouse, and the other men drew watch and workstations somewhat appropriate to their rates and training.

During that week, Irwin had his first run-in with McNair. Apparently McNair found young Cromer's uniform not up to standard. Usually, the navy chain of command dictated that the captain would inform the department head, who would inform the division officer, who would inform the division chief petty officer, who would inform the man. But McNair still had too much of the chief in him and started dressing down Cromer on the spot. Irwin stepped up and said, "Captain, this is my man. I will take care of this." The intervention apparently impressed McNair, because afterward the 614's crewmen were not totally swallowed up into the 291's complement.

On February 12, the ship had its final battle problem, sort of a shakedown graduation exercise. Cmdr. E. J. Strickley, representing the LST training command, and the skipper and senior officers of LST 509 came aboard as evaluators, and for three hours that afternoon the ship went through every exercise imaginable: gunnery, abandon ship, man overboard, engineering emergencies, and full power runs. That the inspection took only a few hours indicates how well the ship and crew performed. They returned to St. Andrews for final debriefing and to drop off the inspection team, and at eleven o'clock that night they pulled up anchor and headed for New Orleans.

The next day, as the 291 steamed toward New Orleans, was a Sunday, so a touch of holiday routine flavored the 614's crew's first real taste of life at sea. To them, it seemed they were on their way to war at last. They only had this one stop to pick up the LCT, and they were off. But what seems simple enough to navy men never quite works out.

The LST entered the Mississippi River about six o'clock that evening and right after midnight anchored off the navy's ammunition depot south of the city. Just before dawn the ship edged over to the pier to unload the ammunition left over from the shakedown—some three thousand rounds of 20mm and almost nine hundred rounds of 40mm. It took only thirty minutes, so by the normal time for turn-to (8:00 a.m.) on February 14, the ship was moored at the Todd-Johnson Dry Dock.

Loading for War

During this visit to New Orleans, McNair permitted his crew as much liberty as the workload would accommodate. The LST had not gone there to make a liberty call but to prepare for its voyage to war. Nevertheless, McNair knew this would be the last extended stay in any American port, and he thought the men deserved as much time as they could get. The 614's crew was quite happy to be able to revisit the liberty spots they had discovered during their short stay at Algiers Naval Station. The visit coincided with the traditional festivities of the weeks preceding Mardi

Gras. The Fat Tuesday celebrations themselves were toned down because of the war, but neither the civil government nor the navy could cancel the long traditional party atmosphere that preceded Ash Wednesday, providing the men with some of the best liberty they had seen during their short navy careers. But Carlson's luck still had not turned. When he got back to New Orleans, the navy still had not found his seabag, and on top of that, he got a Dear John letter from his girlfriend back in Oregon. Disconsolate, Carlson bummed uniforms from his shipmates and spent his time in New Orleans as drunk as he could make himself.

While the sailors worked and played, shipyard workers set up the wooden framework on which the 614 would ride on the deck of the LST. Because the 614 would eventually have to slide off the ship, the cradle had to be flat. To provide the necessary grip, the yard workers welded nine or ten bits of steel angle iron along each side of the LST's deck to provide footing for the wooden shoring that would hold the LCT in place. Corresponding bits of angle iron had already been welded along the LCT's hull, protruding about four inches. Once the LCT was in place on the cradle, all the men had to do was wedge the shoring into the brackets and then chain the craft down.

On February 17, the 291 moved through the Industrial Canal to the Florida Avenue wharf to pick up LCT 614. The process of putting one small ship atop another ship happened fairly quickly. A tug towed LCT 614 into position near the bow of the LST, and a crane on the wharf lowered six large slings. Men hooked the slings into lifting lugs built into the LCT, and the crane lifted the 614 out of the water, maneuvered the 112-ton craft over the deck of the LST, and settled it onto the cradle. Once in position, the men secured the LCT with chains and hammered the shoring into place. The whole process took less than an hour, and soon the LST was on its way back to the Todd-Johnson Dry Dock.

For the next two days, the ship's company prepared the ship for sea, taking on almost 80,000 gallons of fresh water and various other stores. But the day of hardest labor was February 21. On the evening of February 20, the ship moved down to the Shell Oil dock to take on a cargo of more than 200,000 gallons of fuel oil. That took much of the midwatch of February 21, and after breakfast the ship moved again to the navy supply depot. For a relatively small ship like an LST, taking on supplies requires the participation of almost every man on the crew. The navy calls it an "all-hands evolution." Trucks bring pallet after pallet of boxes and crates filled with canned food, powdered food, some fresh vegetables and milk (these destined to run out or spoil very early in the cruise), and gunnysacks of fresh meat. The men form a long daisy chain from the pier to the ship's refrigerators and storage compartments and then pass each crate, box, or sack one at a time to its designated spot. The work moves along fairly quickly, but it is relentless and monotonous and tiring. For LST 291, this morning's work took the crew about three hours—less time than a man would normally spend on watch but so exhausting that it already seemed like a full day's work.

That done, however, the ship moved once more to the navy ammunition depot. There the crew experienced another three-hour all-hands evolution while taking on almost forty-five thousand rounds of 20mm and more than seventeen thousand rounds of 40mm ammunition. To men already tired from handling the supplies, saving the heavy ammunition boxes for last seemed more like punishment than work. For safety reasons, the ammunition could not be passed man to man, as the food had been; instead the men had to pick up the heavy metal boxes and carry them one by one down to the magazines. The last of the boxes was not stored in the magazines until 10:00 p.m.

As soon as the ammo handlers had finished their work, the skipper ordered the engines started. Within thirty minutes, the ship was headed down the Mississippi for the open sea. On the way down the river, Irwin had a chance to chat with one of the river pilots. He had been impressed with the skill with which the pilots moved the big LST up and down the river, even on the darkest nights. As the conversation moved along, Irwin said that he was going to be the skipper of the LCT lashed to the deck. The pilot laughed. He said that he'd never had any trouble piloting one of the three-hundred-foot-long LSTs because their flat bottoms were really not that much different from those of river boats. But once he was piloting one of the little LCTs and ordered right full rudder; the helmsman cranked the wheel hard left and promptly beached the craft on the riverbank.

Around dawn the ship anchored off Pilottown, Louisiana, for a few hours to drop off the river pilot and to wait for a channel pilot and the tide. They were soon under way again, and by 10:30 a.m. they were clear of the sea buoy and off to New York. They were on their way to the war at last.

4

LONG, SLOW TRIP TO WAR

No matter how good a liberty port is—and New Orleans is one of the best—the first day or two on the open sea almost always has a refreshing effect on the crew. Few sailors would admit as much. The underway hours are, if anything, longer. On top of the normal routine of ship's work, at sea in wartime a crewman stands three and sometimes as many as four watches a day, whereas in port a sailor stands one or two watches every two or three days. (The seagoing navy day consists of six four-hour watches, although the 4:00 p.m.–8:00 p.m. watch is usually broken into two two-hour "dogs.") Working conditions are also more demanding at sea. The engines make the inside of the ship hotter, the constant wind makes the weather decks colder, and often the sailor has to contend with unrelenting motion in addition to the task at hand. In port, a sailor has the promise of a few hours off the ship, with time for beer, roaming, and new faces. At sea, the sailor rarely has time to himself, the edges of the deck demark nonnegotiable boundaries, and the faces don't change.

True, being in port has its subtle psychological pressures as well. The ship sits in muddy, sometimes polluted, water often unruffled by any breeze. In port, watches are incredibly boring and tedious; the sailor doesn't so much help operate the ship as simply occupy an assigned place for an assigned number of hours. Dockside, the ship lies under a blanket of noise from machinery on the pier, steam escaping from other ships and pipes and sewers, and people working. And being anchored out is probably worse than being moored, for there's a greater sense of being isolated from the shore when it's over there, and we're over here. But probably most nagging, in its way, is the sense of not getting anywhere. Usually, however, the sailor doesn't notice these things. He goes about his work and looks forward to a few hours' liberty at the end of the day, something he cannot look forward to while at sea.

So although the sailor has every reason to prefer long stays in port over long stays under way, that first day at sea touches something deep in the human psyche that longs to peek over the horizon, to hit the elements head-on, or at the very least to avoid all-hands working parties loading ammunition. On that first day at sea, the men stand at the rails, look out at the sea, breathe in air that doesn't stink, and relax. Pity it doesn't last. After just a week at sea, the routine, constriction, and lack of sleep begin to take their toll.

The crew of the 291 had been on shakedown a month or more, and the 614's crew had joined them only for that last week. The routine during that time—lift anchor, head out for the day's exercises, return to port that evening, and anchor for the night—never gave the men a true sense of being at sea, of pointing the ship to a distant port. Now they were done with the training and the milling around. They were at sea. In a vague, general sense, they all knew what lay ahead of them: around Florida and up the East Coast to New York; then to Boston to catch a short convoy to Halifax, Nova Scotia; then a long convoy across the Atlantic to England to participate in the invasion of Europe. Everyone knew the invasion was set for that spring, so they all felt an urgency to get there before they missed it and not to linger in an ocean that still hid German submarines.

In 1942, as Pequigney knew firsthand, the submarines had ranged almost unchallenged up and down the East Coast and into the Gulf of Mexico, sinking whichever ships they wanted. By February 1944, the submarine threat had all but ended in the Gulf, and it had eased considerably along the East Coast. March 1943 is generally considered the time that the tide of the U-boat war had turned, but now, almost a year later, some U-boats were still out there. The men aboard the 291 knew that once they entered the Atlantic, the farther north and east they sailed, the greater the threat they faced.

LST 291 left New Orleans on the morning of February 22—Mardi Gras day— and headed south. That afternoon she joined up with LST 56, and the two ships closed the coast of Florida to be better protected by aircraft patrols, the only escort these ships would have. On the evening of February 24, the ship set its first wartime general quarters as a precaution as it transited the Florida Strait and entered the Atlantic. Three days later, off North Carolina, the little formation grew by the addition of the LST 509 coming out of Morehead City on her way to Norfolk; she stayed with them only a day. The ships hugged the coast so closely that when they crossed Diamond Shoals off Cape Hatteras, the skipper stationed a man on the bow with a lead line to take soundings. During the midwatch on February 29, the ship entered New York Harbor and by breakfast was moored to Pier 51 in the North River.

The four nights the ship stayed in New York were devoted to liberty calls. The advantage to which the men took this liberty is indicated by the simple statistic that over this time seven men of the 291's crew overstayed their liberty, two of them so long that McNair declared them deserters. Playtime ended on March 4, when tugs lugged the ship over to the navy supply depot in Bayonne, New Jersey, to make the final preparations for the voyage to England. At eight o'clock the next morning, the crew began loading the ship with general cargo. For this convoy, LST 291 was going to be more of a freighter than a warship. Instead of tanks and jeeps and DUKWs (amphibious trucks) and other military vehicles, the giant tank deck was filled to capacity with pallets full of crates and machinery. Day and night for the next four days, forklift trucks carried the cargo into the tank deck and placed it in position. During this time, the off-duty section continued to get some liberty, but the on-duty section helped load and store the cargo.

Irwin also understood that this was his last chance, as skipper of the 614 rather than as a junior officer on the 291, to get supplies his little ship would need later. Pidgeon-Thomas had included a list of the equipment stored in the crates on the LCT's deck, so Irwin went over that list carefully and then requisitioned everything else he thought the 614 would possibly need: tools and spare tools, paint and more paint, mooring lines, wire cables, fenders, lube oil, lightbulbs, pens, logbook pages, and on and on. He also requisitioned a number of classified publications that he thought he might need. Soon every void on the little craft was crammed with these items. Some of the men on the crew wondered where the equipment in the crates would go later. Others wondered whether the filled voids would affect the ship's buoyancy.

On March 7, the 291 took on board its first load of passengers: two navy doctors and thirty-eight enlisted men. Most of the men were hospital apprentices, the medical corps' equivalent of seamen first class or seamen second class. Aspiring to become pharmacist's mates once they made petty officer status, they were assigned routine nursing duties. Soon the rumor spread throughout the ship that they had doctors and nurses aboard. Surely the presence of women would pique interest during the Atlantic crossing, but the men never could figure out in which officers' quarters the nurses stayed.

Unscheduled Shipyard Visit

When LST 291 left Bayonne on March 8, the men felt that they were truly on their way to the war. They knew they were on their way to Boston to catch the next convoy to Halifax. The Boston-Halifax convoys, coded "BX," sailed as soon as enough ships had gathered to make a convoy, so everyone expected to spend only a day or two in Boston. From Halifax, they would catch the next slow convoy to England. The 614's crew thought that they would be launched from the LST and on their own within two or three weeks.

The 291 headed up the East River to exit New York through Long Island Sound rather than through the harbor itself. McNair, who was from Yonkers, knew his family would be somewhere near Hell Gate to watch the ship leave, so as they neared the Triborough Bridge he relieved the pilot of the conn. Three minutes later, the ship crashed into a rock only 160 yards south of the bridge. Fortunately, the ship gave the rock only a glancing blow and did not stick on it. McNair returned the conn to the pilot and dispatched damage control parties to assess how badly his ship was hurt. Soundings indicated that the ship was taking on water in only one of the midships ballast tanks on the starboard side; the void, as luck would have it, was designed to be filled with water anyway. The ship continued on its way, unimpaired by the grounding.

A flurry of radio traffic indicated that the 291 had probably just earned a trip to the drydock. Moreover, as the workers would not have time to repair the ship before the next BX convoy, the crew would have to wait around in Boston for more than a week. The pilot, William Wayman, kept the conn all the way to Boston. The ship anchored off the Cape Cod Industrial Canal in the predawn hours and then spent much of March 9 transiting the canal. By 5:30 p.m., the ship was moored in Charlestown Navy Yard.

For men who thought they had already pretty much bid farewell to the United States, the delay in Boston was not unwelcome, but it was a bit irritating, even embarrassing, to McNair and the senior officers. (An officer said to me once, while our destroyer was stuck on the muddy banks of the Suez Canal, "It's a sad, sad day when a warship runs aground.") Irwin, however, felt no such empathy with the ship's reputation. Even before the ship pulled in, he decided to make the most of the delay and asked for a ten-day leave to start as soon as the ship pulled in. To his surprise, McNair granted his request. They pulled into Boston late the following afternoon, and Irwin made no delay telegraphing his fiancée of his leave and of their unexpected chance to marry before he left the states. With no time for trains, Irwin flew to Iowa and back, a trip that easily cost him more than a month's pay.

The morning after docking a diver went over the side to assay the hull's damage. Early that afternoon, tugs came alongside and pushed the ship into the drydock. By 2:30 p.m., the ship was completely out of the water. Yard crews worked through the night to patch the hull and finished before noon the following day. In less than twenty-four hours, the ship was again waterborne, but the quick repair work was mostly to make the most efficient use of the limited drydock facilities. Ships were constantly coming into Boston with torpedo or weather damage from their duty out in the Atlantic, and the drydock was too valuable to have it tied up by some mustang LST skipper who couldn't keep his ship off the rocks. The crew had nothing to do now but wait.

Irwin's matrimonial leave meant that he could no longer run interference for his crew. By this time, Carlson's one uniform was getting a bit worn, and his constant bumming of dungarees and liberty uniforms had become annoying to others in the compartment. Finally, one of the chief petty officers called him out. "Carlson," he said, "if you don't buy another seabag, I'll transfer you ashore and you'll have to stay there."

"Fine," Carlson said. "I'll be happy to stay right here. I don't have any money to buy a whole new seabag. Anyway, the navy lost my seabag, and so the navy can get me another one." The chief arranged a special liberty and requisition so Carlson could go ashore and fill out his seabag. Finding uniform items in Boston was easy enough, but the seabag itself wasn't. So after Carlson drew the uniforms and took them to a tailor shop to have the two red stripes of a fireman apprentice sewn on, he had to go out and find something to carry them in. Later, when he got back to the ship, he said to Jarvis, "I think I'm the only man in the navy going to war with a suitcase."

That weekend, when they should have been sailing to Halifax, the men had one of the best liberties so far in their short navy careers. One of the men hooked up with a young woman who had plenty of friends, and Carlson and Jarvis got blind dates. The date worked especially well for Carlson, and he continued to see her every chance he got over the following few days. After the ship left, he kept up a running correspondence with her for two years through the end of the war. When he was discharged, he flew back to Boston and married her.

On Friday, March 17, the 291 took on another load of passengers for the trip across the Atlantic. The group included six navy men of a training unit and three army officers and thirty soldiers of a Signal Corps unit. This brought the ship's cargo to some seventy military personnel (in addition to the ship's complement of fifteen officers and two hundred men), 200,000 gallons of fuel oil taken on in New Orleans, and several thousand tons of general cargo loaded over four days in Bayonne.

Carter, Pequigney, and Long, the 614's signalman, made up the LCT's unofficial bridge crew. Fortunately, they were also on the same watch section, and they drew liberty on the 291's last night in Boston—St. Patrick's Day. Even in wartime Boston, it was the perfect night to celebrate their last night in the States, even though they knew at least a few of them would likely not return. A photograph taken of them that night shows a chummy threesome. That threesome was not destined to last long.

Halifax

On the morning of March 18, LST 291 took station as the third ship in the third column in convoy BX 100, the hundredth wartime convoy to sail from Boston to Halifax. While forming up, the ships milled around at five knots and then increased speed only to seven knots for the trip north. The trip took no longer than running from New Orleans to Panama City, getting to Halifax on March 20. On this trip, though, the crew battled cold and heavy seas all the way. It was only a taste of what they would experience later. Late that afternoon, the ship passed through the boom defenses of Halifax Harbor; it was a grim reminder of how close to the war they were getting.

The stay in Halifax became a literal plague on the crew. The day after they arrived, the 614's crew lost its first member. Long, who had helped Carter and Pequigney celebrate St. Patrick's Day, came down with a disease that the ship's pharmacist's mate couldn't treat, and he was transferred ashore. Standard procedure at the time was to transfer seriously sick members of the crew off the ship so that there would be no administrative mess if the ship sailed before his treatment was complete. Long's illness was serious enough that he was transferred to the U.S. Naval Observer in Halifax for treatment. In short, Long was gone.

Over the next couple of days, the ship began preparing for its transit of the Atlantic. On March 23, two Royal Canadian Navy officers came aboard the ship to calibrate the gyrocompass, a task that required the ship to moor out into the harbor for a few hours. Returning to the Arcadia Sugar Refinery dock in Dartmouth, the unwieldy LST had no tugs maneuvering it, and the still rather inexperienced Pequigney had the helm. As they approached the dock to moor port side to, the pilot ordered right full rudder. For some reason, Pequigney started turning the wheel hard left. The quartermaster of the watch, standing right behind Pequigney, knocked him out of the way and took control of the ship. Fortunately, on an LST the rudder engine does not react immediately to the helm, so the quartermaster's quick action saved the ship from crashing into the dock.

That afternoon back at the Arcadia Sugar Refinery dock, the ship replenished its freshwater tanks with some nineteen thousand gallons (the ship's crew used about seven thousand gallons a day). Over the next few days, the ship took on a few additional passengers for the voyage and worked on the engines, making final preparations for the convoy. On March 27, one of the ship's hospitalman apprentices became sick and was transferred off. Later that afternoon, after taking aboard two more passengers, medical authorities in Halifax slapped a quarantine on the ship—scarlet fever.

The next day, one man was transferred off the ship for treatment, and twenty-one others, including the remaining men of the 614's crew, were sent to the hospital for observation and any necessary treatment. In the hospital, the men had no more liberty than they would have had on the ship, but at least they had windows and could see the town. Besides, the hospital had real nurses—and fairly real food. For a week, the men sat around, played cards, wrote letters, and stared out the windows.

On April 4, just as the week of observation was ending for the guys in the hospital, another four men, this time including two of the army passengers, went to the hospital for their week-long observation. That meant at least another week's delay before catching a convoy. As those men were going in, the other men came back—all except Jarvis, who for some reason had to stay another week. When they got back to the ship, they found that it had been moved out into the harbor to a mooring buoy; they never knew whether this was part of the quarantine or simply to free up docks pace. They also found that the ship was using this additional week of being stranded to get ready to go to sea. Barges came alongside to deliver more than eighty thousand gallons of water—in addition to the daily topping off of the tanks for normal consumption. The ship also moved to the Royal Canadian Navy gun wharf, where the fire mains could be drained and purged, the main engines tested, and the magazine sprinkling systems checked. Finally, on Saturday, April 8, medical authorities declared the ship healthy and lifted the quarantine. Of course, it wasn't going anywhere yet because it still had men in the hospital.

The day after the quarantine lifted (which happened to be Easter Sunday), additional LST crew members started coming aboard, having been kept waiting ashore until the medical board cleared the ship. It was not until the next day that Jarvis and the other four LST crewmen who had remained in the hospital came back, giving the ship its full complement once more.

That evening, the latest BX convoy pulled in fresh from Boston, this one with six LSTs, and joined six others that had arrived the week before. The arrival of all of these LSTs, one of which moored to the side of the 291, renewed the crew's hopes that they would join the next convoy out of Halifax. One of the ships in that group, LST 535, had almost the exact opposite experience from that of the 291. Whereas the 291 had left New York more than a month earlier, getting delayed in both Boston and Halifax, the 535 had left New York on April 8 (the day the 291 shook off the quarantine), caught convoy BX 103 the following day, and arrived in Halifax on April 11. The next convoy across was scheduled to leave on April 16; the 291 crew wondered what would delay them next.

As it turned out, the convoy was delayed a day when the group of Royal Navy ships that was to escort them across the Atlantic reported that it would need an additional day to work back up to operating status. These five ships arrived in Argentia, Newfoundland, battered and exhausted from their westward voyage escorting another convoy and could not turn around in the time allotted for the scheduled departure. The 291's crew took small comfort from the fact that the entire convoy, not only they, had been delayed this time. Finally, just before noon on April 17, LST 291 got under way to join up with England-bound convoy SC 157.

Convoy

SC 157 was a fairly typical 1944 convoy. In addition to the thirteen LSTs, the convoy had fifteen British cargo ships, nine U.S. cargo ships, seventeen cargo ships of other Allied or neutral countries, five British tankers, and three tankers from Allied countries. Two other freighters were to sail from St. John's. The initial escort consisted of five Royal Canadian Navy vessels: three Flower-class corvettes (HMCS

Dundas, *Timmins*, and *Brantford*) and two minesweeping sloops converted for escort work (HMCS *St. Boniface* and *Brockville*). The senior officer of the escort was in HMCS *St. Boniface*. The two ships from St. Johns had another minesweeping sloop as escort, HMCS *Red Deer*. None of these escorting ships was of more than a thousand tons displacement. At first glance, the tiny Canadian naval vessels seemed a weak escort for the sixty-four ships of the convoy. But by 1944, merchant ships were practically naval auxiliary fighting vessels.

One of the major problems facing naval planners early in the war was how to provide merchant shipping with sufficient air cover. Aircraft had proven invaluable against all threats to the convoys. Not only could aircraft spot submarines lurking at periscope depth, but they could also patrol for surface raiders and even defend the convoy against air attack. Early in the war, the Royal Navy fitted some merchant ships with a fighter plane on a catapult; the plane could be flown off to attack approaching bombers or to help the escorts locate an attacking submarine. The system had its limitations: since the catapult-armed merchant ships had no recovery apparatus after his flight, the pilot had to parachute out or ditch his plane near a ship that could pull him from the water.

So the Royal Navy came up with the merchant aircraft carrier (MAC), a bulk cargo ship or tanker that had been decked over so it could fly off and recover aircraft. They were not the small escort carriers converted from merchant ships (those were operated by the navy and designated as "CVEs") but merchant ships with merchant sailor crews that continued to carry merchant cargoes. Since they had no hangar space or even elevators, the ships could accommodate only four aircraft operated by Royal Navy aircrews. As it happened, the MACs soon had their roles taken over by the escort carrier (the famed jeep carriers), which could accommodate more aircraft and had hangar facilities. The already converted MACs continued in operation, but once a sufficient number of CVEs were on hand, the development of the MAC program ended. SC 157 had two of these merchant aircraft carriers: the British bulk cargo ship *Empire MacAlpine*, which was carrying grain and was the lead ship of a class of these vessels, and the Dutch tanker *Gadila*, carrying navy fuel. *Gadila* had the historical distinction of being the first ship under the Netherlands' flag to operate aircraft off of a flight deck, although, as did her British counterparts, she operated under the merchant flag with a civilian crew rather than under the naval ensign.

In addition to the merchant aircraft carriers, several of the convoy's other merchantmen had military capabilities. Two of the convoy's tankers were fitted out as escort refueling ships. These ships had underway refueling rigs, making them similar to the fleet oilers that accompanied the tasks forces in the Pacific and allowed them to remain at sea for extended periods. The relatively speedy British freighter *Accrington* carried no cargo but did have aboard extensive communication gear and additional lifeboats and life rafts; she was the convoy's rescue ship, the one vessel in the convoy that had permission to drop out of line and assist torpedoed ships or take off their crews. A couple of other cargo ships carried fairly sophisticated radio direction-finding equipment to help locate German submarines, and most of the other ships had been fitted with an old World War I–era 4-inch or 3-inch gun and carried a navy Armed Guard unit to shoot the thing. Clearly by this stage of the war, the concept of a convoy being a collection of defenseless merchantmen only minimally defended by a few scraped-together naval escorts was totally outdated. SC 157 had a vague resemblance to a carrier battle group.

That being said, the convoy did also have its share of rusty old tramp steamers. One of them had experienced almost as much trouble joining up with the convoy as LST 291 had. The American-owned, Panamanian-registered freighter *Colin* was a motor vessel of some six thousand gross tons. She had been armed with an old three-inch, 50-calibre (3"/50) single-purpose gun and four modern 20mm guns that were manned by fourteen Navy Armed Guard personnel commanded by Lt. j.g. Simon R. Navickas. *Colin* had a relatively light load—some four thousand tons of sulfur and seventy tons of mail and general military deck cargo—so she also had ballast tanks filled to improve her trim. She left New York on March 5, but her motor broke down during her approach to Boston. After getting the machinery fixed, she left for Halifax in the same BX convoy as the 291. She was able to catch the next transatlantic convoy, which sailed on March 29 (the day after the 614's crew went into the hospital); however, only two days out with that convoy she suffered another motor breakdown and had to straggle back to Halifax. After a two-week delay for repairs, she was once again poised for the crossing. This time, her crew hoped to make it all the way across.

After leaving Halifax on April 17, the ships spent five hours milling around at five and a half knots, forming up. The convoy deployed in thirteen columns of normally five ships each (two columns had fewer ships), a disposition that avoided giving a submarine off to the side a long target. The LSTs took stations along the rear of the convoy, an arrangement that allowed the warships, with their better radars and communication gear, to keep watch over the convoy. LST 291's position was the fifth ship in the tenth column. The merchant aircraft carriers and the tankers took up positions scattered in the middle of the convoy, and the freighters with less critical (i.e., expendable) cargoes went to the sides. The convoy commodore, B. W. L. Nicholson, was a retired Royal Navy officer who held the Distinguished Service Order. During World War I, he had been the executive officer of the armored cruiser HMS *Cressy* when it was sunk by U-9. He ended the war as the executive officer of the battleship HMS *Orion*. He flew his pennant from the British refrigerator ship *Empire Pibroch*, stationed at the head of the seventh column. The senior naval officer was Capt. J. D. Shaw, commander of LST Flotilla Seventeen, whose flagship was LST 517, the fourth ship in column eight. Captain Shaw was also the most senior LST officer in the Atlantic fleet; after the invasion, he was designated to take command of all American LSTs operating on the Normandy coast. The convoy escorts then took up their assigned positions ahead of the convoy.

Because the convoy had so few escorts, the corvettes took positions dictated by a U-boat's most likely direction of attack. To stage a daylight attack, submarines would try to get in front of the convoy and then submerge and stop to lie in ambush. At night, submarines would operate on the surface, using their higher speeds and low silhouettes to get in among the ships. For those reasons, the convoy escorts would take station ahead of the convoy during the day to form a sonar sweep for lurking U-boats, and at night they would fall back to the sides. Consequently, dawn and dusk tended to be the times of greatest danger for the convoy as the escorts shifted positions.

Also at these times, the big surface ships lost their protective covering of darkness and could be silhouetted against the glow of sunrise or sunset, whereas the low-profiled U-boat could still take advantage of the gloomy visibility right on the surface. The tradition of dawn stand-to in the Royal Navy dated from the days of sail, when the crew of a warship, blinded by night, had no idea what the morning would reveal to them. Even in 1944, with the ships' extensive electronic sensors, the procedure made sense enough to retain, so the warship crews went to general quarters at sunrise and sunset. This was so routine, though, that the men were told that these precautionary general quarters would be announced over the ship's intercom and that the alarms would sound only for an actual alert. On that first evening at sea, the convoy barely had time to form up and assume its base speed of seven and a half knots before the ships set their first wartime general quarters. It served as an unnecessary reminder that they were now truly in the war.

The planned route was to head east to a point just north of the Azores and then arc north around the northern coast of Ireland. A secondary route, the straggler's route, ran north of the main route. Any ship that lost contact with the convoy or could not keep station would steam independently along that path. The ships' crews considered banishment to the straggler's route as a death sentence, especially for these slow merchantmen, since they would have no escort or accompanying ships to distract the U-boats' attention. Once the convoy reached the Irish Sea, it would break into four groups. The biggest group, nineteen of the merchantmen, would continue north to Loch Ewe on the northwest coast of Scotland, where they would regroup into coastal convoys destined for ports on England's east coast or into other convoys to the Mediterranean or Murmansk. Another group of eleven ships would break off and go into ports along the Clyde River near Glasgow. The third group of fifteen merchantmen would go to the mouth of the River Mersey in the Liverpool area. The thirteen LSTs and six merchantmen were to continue south to the Welsh port of Milford Haven near Cardiff.

Weather

The weather on those first few days at sea was typical of late winter in the North Atlantic—cold, rough, and wet. Luckily for Pequigney, he stood wheel watches in the pilothouse, where he was at least out of the wind. Other members of the 614's crew stood watch in the open gun tubs. Carlson drew duty as a phone talker in the forward 40mm mount, which protruded over the LST's bow doors. During his first watch that night, he called the bridge. "How about a little relief here," he said. "I need to go to the head."

"Stay at your post," he was told. "Pee in your pants if you have to, but stay at your post." When he came off watch, his clothes had frozen solid from the spray of the blunt bow.

Irwin stood junior officer of the deck watches on the bridge. He spent most of the time on watch peering through his binoculars and trying to pick out the small blue stern light on the ship ahead of them. Even when he could see it, the light was so dim he had no idea if they were keeping station, creeping up on it, or dropping behind. Much of the time he couldn't see it at all, and after getting off watch he felt as though his eyes had poked through the binoculars and gotten stuck.

Irwin's problems were exacerbated by the fact that the ship ahead of them—the *Elisabeth Dal*, a British freighter loaded with sugar—had her own problems keeping station. Engineering troubles slowed her to the point that she could not maintain the convoy base speed of seven and a half knots, even with a stiff following wind, and at dawn she was almost always off station. The convoy commodore finally threatened to send her and the 291 out on the straggler's route. The commodore apparently expected better sea-keeping skills on the part of the American Navy crews and sent a short but pointed message to McNair: "You are a bloodhound, not a mouse. Keep in position or I'll send you on the northern route." McNair wasted no time gathering his officers and chewing them out. Irwin felt even more pressure, having to pay attention not only to the *Dal* but also to the rest of the convoy. Despite the inexperience of the LST crews and the rickety machinery of the merchant ships, the convoy arrived at the first checkpoint, a spot just off the Grand Banks called the "Western Ocean Meeting Point."

There, on April 20, the navy command in charge of the convoys, known as Tenth Fleet, sent word to the convoy that it could expect bad weather ahead and that as soon as the ocean escort group arrived later that morning, the convoy should begin its arc to the north. In mid-morning, the Royal Navy escorts relieved the smaller Canadian escorts, which returned to pick up other convoys (the slow speed of the convoy can be judged by the fact that the corvettes—Churchill's famous "cheap and nasty" escorts not built for speed—reached St. John's the next day). Four of these Royal Navy ships—HMS *Inglis*, *Louis*, *Moorsom*, and *Mounsey*—were former American destroyer escorts that had been transferred to the Royal Navy and reclassified as frigates. The fifth ship of the group, HMS *Strule*, was a River-class frigate and slightly larger than the former American ships. The two freighters from St. Johns also joined that afternoon, bringing the convoy up to sixty-four ships escorted by five frigates. As soon as the new ships had settled into their positions, the convoy wheeled north.

The more northerly route they were taking was very close to the one taken by RMS *Titanic* thirty-two years earlier. And of course, the convoy had its own encounters with icebergs. At nine o'clock on the morning of April 21, an iceberg passed through the middle of the convoy, some two miles to port of LST 291. The daylight passage served to warn the lookouts to be especially alert at night. At 4:30 a.m. the next day, the general quarters alarms went off. This was no drill. Men scrambled to their battle stations in whatever they could grab, some of them slipping on the icy decks in only their socks. At his assigned gun, Carter could see brilliant flashes ahead lighting up the sea and reflecting off the low clouds. He thought that one of the ships had been torpedoed and was exploding. Just a few minutes later, though, the ship ahead of them moved out of the way, and they could see an iceberg directly in front of them, with one of the frigates playing a searchlight on it. Apparently either the convoy commodore or the escort senior officer had decided that the danger of the iceberg at that moment far exceeded danger from U-boats and risked the lights. The 291 had to maneuver to avoid the iceberg, but once they were safely around, McNair allowed the men to go below a few at a time to dress. As a precaution in case the light show had attracted attention, the ship remained at general quarters until after dawn.

All that day and into the evening, the weather deteriorated steadily. By nightfall the convoy was battling the outer edges of the storm it had moved north to avoid. The flat-bottomed, shallow-draft LSTs were horribly uncomfortable in the storm. Almost everyone aboard became seasick and moved about as little as possible. The bluff bows kicked up as much water as they deflected to the sides; the long welded sides warped and occasionally sprung leaks; and in particularly long swells the screws would come completely out of the water, giving the ships a worrisome shudder. Half of the men expected the ship to sink and half hoped that it would.

Toward dawn on April 23, at the height of the storm, the main seacock on the U.S. freighter *West Nilus*, the lead ship of the twelfth column, gave way, flooding the engine room. With the ship slowed and in very real danger of sinking, the convoy commodore ordered her to turn back to St. Johns and detached the American freighter at the end of the column, the *Wolverine*, to escort the *West Nilus* in case she needed to be towed or her crew needed to be taken off if she began sinking. Later that same day, the heavy seas knocked loose the cargo of another American freighter, the *Meanticut*, and with a steep list she limped back to St. John's with the *West Nilus* and *Wolverine*, making only six knots.

The *Meanticut's* station had been in the eleventh column immediately to port of the *Wolverine*, so all three ships that had dropped out of the convoy were from the 291's side. In the reduced visibility of the storm, the men on the 291 could not see what was happening on the port wing of the convoy, but it seemed reasonable that it was getting as bashed as the starboard wing. By dawn of April 24, the storm had let up, but the convoy had so scattered that lookouts on the 291 could spot only a handful of ships. The convoy spent much of that day reforming.

MV *Colin*

One of the ships that had gotten scattered was the luckless *Colin*. That dawn, her lookouts could see only a couple of the ships from the convoy, so she speeded up to try to regain her position and the safety of the convoy. Of course, it was at that time that her steering gear broke down, and she had to come to a full stop to make repairs. By the time she was under way again, the convoy had completely disappeared, and after a full day's steaming *Colin* had still not caught up. The master of the *Colin* had to admit that his ship had become a straggler, and he headed north to the designated straggler's route. After the trouble his ship experienced even getting into the convoy, he had no intention of returning to Newfoundland, and now that he could steam at his ship's best speed, he thought that with any luck the *Colin* could reach the United Kingdom before the convoy. The navy's Armed Guard unit was now the ship's only protection. The navy men augmented the ship's lookouts, one on each of the four 20mm guns and one aft on the 3"/50. That man could not shoot the gun by himself, but if a submarine did attempt a surface attack, he could at least get the gun ready while the other men scrambled to their stations.

The next day, April 26, was one of those days when, under different circumstances, it would have been fun to be at sea. The sky was cloudless though windy, and at a sea state 3 the waves are choppy and whitecapped but not so large that they make shipboard life miserable. That afternoon, at position 054:16 N, 31:58 W, *Colin* was still headed north to the straggler's route, with the wind and sun both to port. The whitecapped waves masked the tracks of two torpedoes. At 5:50 p.m., the torpedoes struck simultaneously, one well forward in hold number 1 that started a fire, and the other well aft in hold number 6 that ruptured the side, causing massive flooding. The explosions ruptured fire mains and steam pipes, wrecked auxiliary engines, tripped the main electrical circuits, and knocked both the compass and the radio transmitter to the deck. One merchant sailor panicked at the sudden damage around him, and he jumped from the ship, never to be seen again. Others of the crew tried to get the radio working and sent out an SSS signal, a special SOS signal that specified the ship had been attacked by a submarine. They got no response and were unsure whether the radio was working or whether anyone had received the signal. Meanwhile, Navickas and his men readied their guns, but they had no targets to shoot.

Within ten minutes everyone aboard knew the ship was sinking. The master ordered the engines secured (shut down) in an effort to lessen the chance of fire and directed the crew to abandon ship. The navy men stayed at their guns while the ship's crew lowered the two lifeboats and rafts, and the officers collected confidential codes and publications and threw them over the side in a weighted canvas sack. Fortunately, punctured both forward and aft in the holds, *Colin* was settling on an even keel, allowing boats on both sides to be launched safely. By 6:15 p.m., the crewmen were well away from the ship, and the navy Armed Guard men escaped in a small painting dingy. By 6:30 p.m., the main deck was already awash, but once the gun crew left the ship the submarine wasted another torpedo that struck dead amidships. *Colin* broke in two and sank even as large chunks of the ship continued to fall around Navickas and his men. Only the man who had panicked and jumped ship died; the most serious injury among the fifty-three survivors was a cut lip.

As the crew struggled to form up the boats and rafts to keep them together, the submarine surfaced and approached one of the boats. The men got a good look at their attacker and later identified it as a 740-ton Type VII, the standard type of U-boat. An officer who spoke very good English—one of the crew said he had an Oxford accent—asked the name and tonnage of the ship but offered no assistance. (Earlier in the war, submarine captains would often give survivors in the boats the heading to the nearest shore.) The U-boat disappeared to the west, into the glare of the setting sun.

The *Colin*'s survivors were now alone well out in the North Atlantic. With night approaching, they scrambled to round up the rafts and lash them together so they would not be separated during the night. They had a cold night ahead of them in open boats on a windy, choppy sea, and they had no idea whether their distress call had been heard. Also, having been sunk between the convoy route and the straggler's path, they could not count on a ship spotting them as it passed. It was not a situation that encouraged hope.

Fortunately their SSS call had been picked up and relayed to Tenth Fleet headquarters. The British Admiralty detached two prewar Canadian destroyers, the *Skeena* and *Qu'Appelle*, from the screen of another nearby convoy to hunt for the U-boat, and the Royal Navy frigates *Bentley* and *Affleck* to search for survivors. The destroyers did not find the U-boat, but the frigates found their target, pulling all fifty-three survivors from the water only twenty hours after the *Colin* sank.

Landfall

From the point of view of the men aboard LST 291, Convoy SC 157 was taking a beating. All four ships lost on account of the storm had come from the two columns to starboard of the 291, and with the poor visibility hampering the view of the convoy that stretched into the gloom to port, everyone assumed the far side of the convoy had suffered similar losses. On a few occasions, the men at their routine dawn general quarters stations could see columns of smoke rising above the horizon behind them that they took to be victims of U-boats, perhaps even from their own convoy. They could almost feel the convoy shrinking around them, thereby increasing their chances of taking a torpedo. None of them harbored any hopes of survival if they did get hit; if the 200,000 gallons of fuel oil failed to incinerate them, the cold waters of the North Atlantic would freeze them in ten minutes. Such fears, while not totally unfounded, were somewhat exaggerated, as the experience of the *Colin*'s crew showed. Of course, the men on the 291 knew only that the *Colin* and the other missing ships were gone.

This relatively gradual transition into the war had differing effects on the men. Some grew a bit quieter and more thoughtful. Others joked more. The 614's cook talked more belligerently, bragging about what he was going to do once he had the chance to fight back. The others paid little attention to him. They knew he was afraid, but of course they were all afraid.

On April 30, the convoy reached position off Oversay, Ireland. With a following wind and sea, the convoy had averaged almost eight knots and, quite surprisingly, had shaved a day off its estimated sailing time. At 2:00 p.m., the convoy commodore detached the thirteen LSTs, which broke off and headed down the Irish Sea in a single, long column. For much of the next day, May 1, the LSTs had the welcoming sight of protective land all around them. It was Roy Carlson's twenty-first birthday. His two presents were that the sight of land meant he had survived his first participation in the Battle of the Atlantic and that he could now vote.

Late that evening, the LSTs anchored in Milford Haven, Wales. Their only business there was to wait for one of the nightly convoys around Cornwall to the southern ports. That didn't take long. The next night, less than twenty-four hours after entering the harbor, LST 291 was under way again in a convoy code-named "Gather." That trip took another twenty-four hours, and by 10:30 p.m. on the evening of May 3, the ship was safely anchored in Plymouth, England. The next morning, the ship moved to the Cattedown Wharf in Plymouth and began discharging its cargo of fuel oil. Having thus lightened the ship, the crew prepared to launch LCT 614.

At 5:30 p.m. on the afternoon of May 4, the 291's engineers began shifting ballast from port to starboard. It tended to be a slow process. The object was to heel the ship over but on a relatively even keel fore and aft; after all, the crated general cargo still filled the LST's tank deck. While that was going on, others of the crew began loosening the chains and knocking the shoring away from the hull of the 614. Some two hours later, the ship had attained the proper list of ten and a half degrees to starboard. The last of the shoring was knocked away, and LCT 614 splashed into the waters of Plymouth Harbor. The flat bottom of the LCT directed much of the splash back toward the LST, keeping the two ships from colliding. LCVPs acting as tugboats nudged the LCT to the wharf in front of the LST, and immediately Irwin and his men were detached from the bigger ship.

One problem remained: the 614 still lacked a signalman. Irwin had been asking for a replacement, but none had been sent. Finally, McNair asked his newest signalman, who had reported aboard just after the quarantine was lifted, if he would like to volunteer to go with the LCT crew. Having had no time to get attached to the 291's crew (or perhaps having had enough time to see what kind of a skipper McNair was), he accepted the offer. Frederick B. G. Kleen was a regular navy signalman third class from New Jersey who had enlisted as early as 1942. He had been on an assignment to escort some sailors to the brig in Boston, and from there he was supposed to get a few days' leave. Instead, he found himself being ordered to Halifax with a couple of other sailors, and he ended up assigned to the 291. As he got to know the LCT 614's crew, the story soon circulated that his family had a horse farm, so he became a sort of go-between for the southern boys who had all been raised on or near farms and the northern big-city boys. Like Carter, Kleen read constantly, and he sported a pipe rather than the ubiquitous cigarettes smoked by the rest of the crew.

Finally, almost four months after delivery from the builder, the USS LCT(6) 614 entered the service of the U.S. Navy.

5

THE NEAR SHORE

Once they were on their own, the men had a frenzy of work to do. They had been able to do some maintenance and preservation work while the 614 sat on the 291's deck, but they couldn't get equipment pulled out of the crates and installed. The men spent the first couple of days in Plymouth getting the little ship working. That first evening aboard their new home was moving day, as the men brought aboard their gear, selected their racks, and then uncrated and set up the mattresses and bedding. As the two senior enlisted men, Kleen and Pequigney took the racks just aft of the skipper's compartment, separated only by a canvas curtain. The other men selected bunks in the crew quarters on the port side of the ship.

Also of immediate concern, the food and water had to be stored and the oil-fired galley range set up. The motor macs got the generators working to supply power to the heaters, lights, and other electrical equipment. The next day, the crew focused on uncrating and stowing all the other gear that sat in boxes on the tank deck—everything from the ship's 20mm guns to the life raft and firefighting pumps and hoses to brooms and mops and cases of toilet paper.

On May 6, the crew loaded its complement of almost eight thousand rounds of 20mm ammunition from the 291. For the next day or so, Carter did little else but load up drum magazines and hang them on the bulkheads or store them in ready service lockers attached to the front of the gun tubs. Sparky, Johnson, and Jarvis helped him, since they needed to know something of the workings of the gun, and other members of the crew pitched in as they could. The routine way to load a magazine is for every third round to be a tracer. Carter decided it might be fun to load one of the magazines with nothing but tracers. He marked the magazine and made sure it got placed at the top of the ready service locker near his gun.

Slowly the little LCT began to get into shape, and the men began to settle in to their responsibilities. For the rated men—Carter, Pequigney, Sparky, and Kleen—that was a natural progression, except that while in port Pequigney took on the role of the ship's de facto yeoman and did the paperwork. Signalman Kleen, with his ubiquitous pipe, helped with the paperwork and message traffic while getting the radio, blinker, and signal flags set up. Sparky ranged all over the little ship with his voltmeter and screwdrivers, checking out everything electrical. The two motor macs gravitated toward their personal interests: Dowling wanted to tend to the big diesels, and Clark liked taking care of the small gas engines. Johnson helped Carter with the guns and became the principal first aid provider. The rural southerners Gudger and Cromer found common ground with the steel town Yankee Andin in their ability with hand tools and tackle, so they took on various duties as deckhands. Jarvis and Carlson, both nonrated firemen second class, helped out with the engines, motors, and generators.

The anchor winch posed a bit of a problem. Neither Clark, despite his interest in small engines, nor Dowling could light off the engine. Even if they could, the system of levers that controlled the anchor clutch and drum baffled them. They had both trained on anchor winches at Solomons and had even gone through a few beaching evolutions, but their time at Solomons had been so short and now seemed so long ago that they had forgotten everything. Finally, after a couple of fruitless hours of their trying to remember, Irwin turned to Carlson. "You're a motor mac striker. Get up there and see what you can do."

Carlson hesitated. "I haven't had any training on an LCT, and besides, I'm just a fireman second."

"Doesn't matter," Irwin said. "Get up there and see if you can do anything."

Carlson climbed up to the winch and studied it for a few minutes. He soon realized that it wasn't much different from the drum winches he was used to in the logging camps. He started the engine, walked the anchor down on its cable a few feet, and then brought it back up. "That's yours," Irwin said. Carlson looked around at the exposed position, above and behind the port gun tub.

"Hell, you didn't give me much," he muttered.

After a few days, the crew got the ship operational and chugged up the Hamoaze—the first time LCT 614 had been under its own power since its trials four months earlier—to Saltash, just under the big railroad bridge that is one of the main landmarks in Plymouth. There, on May 9, the men were officially assigned to LCT Flotilla Twelve. The flotilla skipper, Lt. Cmdr. William Leide, told Irwin that his craft would eventually be part of LCT Group Thirty-five, but currently the group commander, Lt. Dean Rockwell, was on special assignment. Leide made some effort emphasizing to Irwin and the crew that the invasion was not far away at all and that they had very little time to get the ship ready and over to Portland Harbor to load up.

At Saltash, the men had a few base amenities, such as a mess hall and a post exchange, for the first and almost the only time of their stay overseas. They also had access to various machine shops, which helped them make some last-minute alterations to their craft. One was the addition of mulock ramps, or two hinged steel grid works welded to the end of the ramp that allowed the craft to land vehicles in deeper water. The men—mostly Irwin, Kleen, and Pequigney—also had to contend with administrative matters, such as distribution of codes and flotilla-level procedures and regulations.

Portland Harbor

Toward the middle of May, the 614 made its first sea voyage under its own power, sailing with half a dozen other landing craft along the coast to Portland. The distance was not great, some one hundred miles, but at five knots it would take a full day. The voyage also included a "dash" across Lyme Bay, where just three weeks earlier German E-boats had attacked a group of LSTs practicing for the invasion, sinking two, damaging a third, and killing more than seven hundred men. The men on the 614 knew of the attack, and they understood that this short convoy would be about as dangerous as the Atlantic crossing was. They timed the trip so most of it would be during daylight hours (the air umbrella over southern England by this time restricted German aircraft and E-boats to nighttime operations), and all the craft made it across without incident.

Portland Harbor is a large artificial port protected by long concrete seawalls that enclose an anchorage under the shelter of Portland Bill. Before the war, it was a sleepy little anchorage, known primarily as a repair facility and torpedo station. The Royal Navy's major southern facility was to the east in Portsmouth, with a secondary base to the west in Plymouth. Portland generally served as home port for nothing larger than destroyers. By late May 1944, all that had changed. The anchorage was almost filled to capacity with landing craft of all descriptions. The larger ships, from cruisers and destroyers to LSTs, were anchored individually, and the LCTs, LCIs (what the British called landing ships, infantry), motor launches, PT boats, and other small craft were anchored in nests of three or four ships. The USS *Ancon*, flagship of the Omaha Beach assault force, was there, along with several attack transports. Looking at the crowd of shipping, the men of the 614 thought that certainly a bomb dropped anywhere into the harbor would be bound to hit something.

Soon after LCT 614 arrived in Portland, the crew received reinforcements. Ensign George Pillmore reported aboard about May 20 as second officer, a billet that corresponded to the executive officer slot on a commissioned warship. He had been an NROTC student at the University of Colorado, but the need for junior officers had become so acute that the navy commissioned his class a year early. Like Irwin, Pillmore had been training at Solomons Island and had in fact already been given his LCT crew and orders to the Pacific. Suddenly, though, Pillmore found himself among some ninety ensigns plucked from the training group, packed off to New York, and shipped unceremoniously aboard a troopship to Liverpool and from there to Saltash. Most of the men were divvied up among the LCTs as second officers, and Pillmore drew duty with Flotilla Twelve and the LCT 614. Unfortunately, the LCT had just sailed for Portland, so Pillmore took the train to Weymouth.

Pillmore brought with him three men. Francis J. Kelly, from Chicago, was a motor machinist's mate third class and as a petty officer took charge of the ships' engines and machinery. Chester Wajda from Massachusetts and Lemuel Taylor from South Carolina were unrated seamen who would help out as deckhands. Everyone knew these extra men were not to fill empty billets, although there was enough work to go around. These men were there so the crew could take casualties and still fight.

With the crew at full strength, the men attended to the matter of battle stations. For many of the men, the battle stations came with their responsibility on the ship. As skipper, Irwin conned the ship from his station on top of the pilothouse, and Kleen was beside him to man the blinker light and flag hoist. As second officer, Pillmore had no station but acted as a kind of cargo officer, roaming the ship, making sure Irwin's orders were executed, and getting the army personnel and vehicles off the ship. Inside the pilothouse, Pequigney was at the helm, and Kelly, as the ranking motor mac, operated the three throttles. Carter, the gunner's mate, chose the port 20mm as his station because that gun had the widest arc of fire—from off the starboard bow around to port to astern—and therefore seemed the one most likely to shoot. Three other men were needed as gun crew, so Sparky took on the job of loader for Carter, Johnson became gunner for the starboard mount, and Jarvis was his loader. Just aft of Carter's 20mm gun tub, the anchor winch had already become Carlson's baby. Dowling stayed below with the engines, and Clark operated the ramp winch from inside the port bow locker. The rest of the crew, nonrated seamen, took on various duties as deckhands. Wajda and Gudger stood near the ramp directing vehicles off; in their exposed positions, they would be armed with the ship's two Thompson submachine guns. Cromer, as one of the smallest and nimblest men on the ship, had the unenviable task of crawling on top of the port bow locker to release the dog that dropped the ramp. Andin and Taylor worked the deck aft, releasing vehicles from their tie-downs, directing traffic, and helping get the anchor in and out of its housing.

Planning

Irwin and Pillmore began attending a series of briefings that explained to them the overall plan, the precise location, and the exact part they would play in the invasion. These briefings took place in a large hall where hundreds of officers gathered. Irwin and Pillmore realized that they were getting the same information as battleship captains, and they felt reassured that nothing was being withheld from them. In fact, the LCT skippers were being flooded with so much information that Lieutenant Commander Leide complained about the lack of secure storage space for the documents.

The overall plan of the invasion of Normandy is so well known that it needs little repetition here. The code name "Operation Overlord" applied to the overall invasion and the development of a beachhead inland. After an airborne assault to secure the flanks of the main invasion area, the Allies would come ashore over five beaches: Utah and Omaha for the Americans, and Gold, Juno, and Sword for the British and Canadians. In order to distribute forces evenly and logically over the beaches, planners had also subdivided the main beaches. Since Omaha Beach was to support a two-division landing, it was divided in half; the First Division would land on the eastern half of the beach (designated O-1), and the Twenty-ninth Division would take the western half (O-2).

Five roads led off the beach through breaks, or draws, in the bluffs. The draw on the western end of the beach held the road to Vierville, the next two held the roads to St. Laurent, the largest draw led to Colleville, and a small draw at the eastern end of the beach led off to Cabourg. Naturally the first waves of assault troops were to capture those draws, and their placement dictated additional subdivision. Charlie Beach lay just to the west of the Vierville draw (designated D-1); Dog Beach stretched from the Vierville to the first, and main, St. Laurent draw (D-3); Easy Beach straddled the secondary St. Laurent draw (E-1); and Fox Beach covered the rest of the beach to the east, including the wide, joint opening of the Colleville and Grand Hameau draws (E-3 and F-1). Each of these beaches (except Charlie) had a Green and Red sector to the invaders' right and left (west and east). Dog Beach also had a White sector in the middle. These subdivisions, however, were of unequal width. The O-2 "half" of Omaha contained Charlie, Dog Green, Dog White, Dog Red, and Easy Green sectors, while the O-1 half had Easy Red, Fox Green, and Fox Red.

The navy's role, Operation Neptune, had three objectives: getting the troops and their equipment onto the beach, supporting them with naval gunfire, and keeping them supplied. The warships—battleships, cruisers, destroyers, frigates, minesweepers, torpedo boats, and Coast Guard cutters—would shepherd the landing craft across the channel and then provide gunfire support. The beaching craft and transports would take the men and their equipment from the near shore to the far shore and onto the French beaches. Once the beachhead had been established, uncounted numbers of supply ships would maintain the flow of food, machinery, ammunition, weapons, fuel, and everything else an army needed.

Rear Adm. J. L. Hall commanded Assault Force O, which consisted of the two main assault groups (O-1 and O-2), a follow-up group (O-3), and a smaller detachment to land the Ranger units assigned to destroy the battery atop Pointe du Hoc. Hall had more than 550 ships and craft under his command (and some 200 or more of the uncountable LCVPs and landing craft, assault [LCAs] carried by the transports and LSTs). The bombardment and escort groups brought the strength of Assault Force O to two battleships (*Arkansas* and *Texas*), three light cruisers (two French and one British, while the American heavy cruiser *Augusta*, flagship of the American naval forces, operated in Assault Force O's area), and thirty-two destroyer types. Coastal warships—PT boats, submarine chasers, motor launches, and Coast Guard patrol boats—accounted for almost a hundred of the warships, a number that included the Royal Navy's entire inventory of six steam gunboats. At the bottom end of the naval spectrum, a motley collection of some fifty-eight powered barges had been gathered to carry fuel, water, workshop facilities, or even kitchens (to feed the LCVP and LCM crews).

The LCT crews found themselves participating in all three of Operation Neptune's missions. Indeed, the importance of LCTs to the Normandy invasion can be seen in simply the sheer numbers of these craft and their various uses throughout all stages of the assault on Omaha Beach. Apart from the many LCVPs and LCAs that were to carry the infantry's rifle teams ashore, the LCTs were by far the most numerous craft in the invasion fleet. Some comparative numbers:

Beaching Craft assigned to Assault Force O (from Operation Order BB-44)

LSTs	24
LCI(L)s, including landing craft, headquarters (LCHs) and landing craft, control (LCCs)	41
LCTs	147
LCMs	36

Most of these vessels had duties to fill during specific chronological stages of the invasion. The LCVPs and LCAs were crucial craft during the early part of the assault in getting the spearhead troops ashore. The plan was that once those troops had secured a beachhead, the LCVPs' troop-landing function would be taken over by the larger LCI(L)s, which could bring in large numbers of troops (each LCI[L] could carry almost a full-strength company, as opposed to the thirty men—an understrength platoon—on the smaller craft). The big LSTs were to anchor offshore in the transport area and send their contents ashore on LCVPs, LCTs, and DUKWs. The LSTs themselves were not scheduled to beach until D+1 or D+2, or the first and second days after D-Day.

In contrast, the LCTs participated in every stage of the assault. They carried their men and equipment from England to the far shore, landed them onto the beach, and provided gunfire support and antiaircraft cover. Perhaps the LCTs' functions can best be illustrated by the planned assault in the O-2 sector, the one to which the LCT 614 was assigned. The loads of the craft in the various waves show the speed with which the planners envisioned the assault developing.

The first LCTs of Group O-2 in action on D-Day were to be the craft carrying the Duplex Drive (DD) amphibious tanks. Lt. Dean Rockwell's "special assignment" (the reason Irwin could not meet his group commander when he first arrived in Saltash) was to train all the LCTs involved in launching DD tanks, including those used at Utah Beach. During the assault itself, sixteen LCTs of Force O were to launch the DD tanks six thousand yards offshore so that they could land at ten minutes before H-Hour and support the engineers clearing the obstacles and the first infantry units ashore. Of these craft, eight under Rockwell's direct command (LCTs 535, 586, 587, 589, 588, 713, 591, and 590) each would carry four tanks of the 743rd Tank Battalion to the beaches of the O-2 assault group. The eight assigned to the O-1 half of the beach (LCTs 537, 549, 598, 599, 600, 601, 602, and 603) were under the local command of Lt. j.g. J. E. Barry and would carry tanks of the 741st Tank Battalion. After launching the DD tanks, the LCTs were to return to the transport area for a second load. They were the only LCTs scheduled to make two landings on D-Day.

The first LCTs that were supposed to actually land in the O-2 sector were the eight LCT(A)s (2227, 2273, 2275, 2124, 2050, 2307, 2229, and 2075) that were to hit the beach at H-Hour. They each carried two tanks and a tank dozer (a Sherman tank fitted with a bulldozer blade) that were to lend direct support to the engineers clearing obstacles, and they each towed an LCM filled with explosives and other gear for the gapping teams. These LCT(A)s were American-built LCT(5)s that had been delivered to the British, who fitted the pilothouse and gun tubs with armor plating. For this assault, they had been reassigned to American LCT flotillas and were manned by U.S. Navy personnel.

The first wave of "normal" LCTs in Assault Group O-2 was scheduled to land an hour after H-Hour (H+60). These eight craft carried infantry of the 116th Regiment as well as soldiers and vehicles of the Sixth Engineer Special Brigade, whose task was to clear tank traps and mines from the exits off the beach. (The plan, of course, was that by this time the beach itself would be cleared of obstacles.) Of these eight craft, one (LCT 569) was to land on Easy Green, three (LCTs 704, 703, and 622) were to land on Dog Green, and four (LCTs 614, 613, 612, and 536) on Dog Red.

Hard on the screws of these eight ships were LCTs 775 and 705, which were to land tanks of the 743rd Tank Battalion and infantry and engineers on Dog Green at H+70. Twenty minutes after they hit, five LCT(5)s (197, 364, 332, 207, and

29) were to land the 58th Armored Field Artillery Battalion on Dog White Beach. These craft carried the M7 Priest self-propelled cannon, which were intended to cover the breakout off the beach.

A massive wave of twelve LCTs (27, 214, 147, 153, 776, 149, 616, 80, 615, 30, 294, and 244) was to land at H+120, or two hours after the landings began. The principal load of these craft was the 467th Antiaircraft Artillery (AAA) Battalion, whose job was to secure the defense of the beachhead. These craft also were to bring in antitank and cannon companies, headquarters units, and additional engineers. The nature of these loads indicates that the planners hoped that within two hours the beach would be ready to be developed as a support and staging area.

Three hours after the invasion began, LCTs 714, 767, 2297, 570, and 617 were to bring in a hodgepodge of follow-up units, including units of the 743rd Tank Battalion, 58th Armored Field Artillery Battalion, 467th AAA Battalion, Fifth Ranger Battalion, combat engineers, air support units, forward observers, and a barrage balloon detachment. These units would continue to consolidate the beach into a staging area for the push inland and to provide reinforcement of the assault troops, which by this time should be a mile or two inland.

At H+215, Rockwell's eight craft were to make their second landing, this time carrying combat engineers, barrage balloon detachments, and the 81st Chemical Battalion. And within thirty minutes after that, the remaining six LCTs of Assault Group O-2 (LCTs 571, 572, 573, 813, 665, and 666) were to have brought ashore further barrage balloon units, engineers, and the 967th Quartermaster Service Company. At this point, about five and a half hours after the initial landings, the assault phase should have been completed, and the operation order called for Leide to take the LCTs of Flotillas Twelve and Twenty-six to the British Gold area, and the remaining LCTs were directed by the operation order to "assist in unloading other ships and craft as directed initially by Assault Group Commander, then by Naval Officer In Charge, Omaha."

In addition to these craft assigned to routine LCT functions, Assault Force O's Gunfire Support Group (Task Group [TG] 124.8), under the command of Capt. L. S. Sabin, comprised primarily converted LCTs. This group was to lend support to the bombardment group of battleships, cruisers, and destroyers, and as planned twenty-one of these LCT types were to operate not as beaching craft but as warships.

Seven of these craft were landing craft, flaks (LCFs), British-built LCT(3)s armed with a variety of two-pounder (roughly the equivalent of the American

40mm) and 20mm antiaircraft guns. Like the LCT(A)s, the British LCFs had been reassigned to American flotillas and were manned by U.S. Navy personnel. They were to anchor off the line of departure and provide close air defense for the beaching craft, which were to be at this point out from under the umbrella of the fire support ships. The relatively wide beams of the LCTs made these craft fairly stable gun platforms, but they lacked any sophisticated detection or fire control equipment. Because these craft were to anchor in predetermined spots to facilitate their air defense mission, they also acted as guide ships, providing navigational aid to the beaching craft and directing them to the proper beaches.

Another five craft, also converted British LCT hulls, carried the respectable armament of two 4.7-inch naval guns removed from old destroyers. The landing craft, guns (LCGs), based on the larger LCT(4) hull, were remarkable little warships, with their guns mounted in a superfiring arrangement in armored gun tubs. A World War I–era visual range finder mounted on the pilothouse provided local fire control, and a contingent of Royal Marines operated the guns. These craft, veritable miniature monitors, were able to get closer inshore than the destroyers and shoot directly at targets on the beach, but their low-angle naval guns and lack of proper communication gear for long-range indirect fire made them useless after the fighting moved inland. These craft also carried a formidable array of up to ten 20mm guns, which added to local air defenses off the beaches.

The simplest of the LCT conversions were the nine LCT(R)s, which were LCT(3)s that had been decked over and fitted with rocket launchers. These craft could fire eight hundred to a thousand rockets onto the beach, saturating an area of some 120,000 square yards. The rocket launchers were fixed on the false deck, meaning the only "fire control" available was to point the craft in the desired direction and place it at a fixed range off the beach. In practice, the effect of these craft was more to encourage the invading troops rather than to destroy defensive positions. These craft carried only one full set of reloads, so after two full, albeit dramatic, salvos, they would have to withdraw for rearming or have their false decks taken down so they could return to normal LCT duties. Whereas the LCF and LCG conversions were permanent, including either welding the ramps closed or fitting the vessels with relatively ship-shaped false bows, the LCT(R)s kept their ramps operational and could be reconverted quickly. Thus the latter retained their LCT designation and numbers.

The Gunfire Support Craft also had under temporary command the eighteen LCT(A)s assigned to Assault Groups O-1 and O-2. Joining this group, but not under the command of Captain Sabin, were the five LCT(5)s of the H+90 wave carrying the self-propelled guns of the 58th Armored Field Artillery Battalion. These craft played a hybrid role—first sitting off the beach at designated stations to allow the army tanks and self-propelled guns embarked on them to fire over the ramps and onto the beaches, and then beaching at their designated times (H-Hour for the LCT[A]s) to land the vehicles to cover the obstacle-clearing teams and the troops pushing inland. Although LCTs as gun platforms were stable compared to PT boats and motor gunboats (MGBs), the army gunners found them much less stable than a land mass. During the invasion, the fire from these craft hit very little but drew considerable attention from the German gunners.

As described earlier, the army's initial objective on Omaha was to capture the five exits off the beach, or roads of varying degrees of quality that had been cut through the draws in the bluffs behind the beach. The westernmost of these draws, exit D-1, led to the village of Vierville-sur-Mer. Because this draw boasted a paved road to the beach from Vierville and because the bluff to the west of the exit commanded the whole beach looking east, its defenses were perhaps the most developed, including at least one 88mm gun. A mile to the east was the little seaside village of Les Moulins, at the mouth of the draw leading inland to St. Laurent, exit D-3. It, too, had good roads off the beach and was heavily defended. Exit E-1, the draw a bit more than half a mile farther to the east, had only a dirt trail leading out of it, but because it was in almost the exact center of the beach, the Germans had placed several strong points on its bluffs. On the extreme eastern end of the beach, where exits E-3 and F-1 connected on the beach, another good road led off the beach to Colleville. The bluffs here commanded the beach looking westward; therefore, they had been heavily fortified in similar fashion to the Vierville draw. Since the smaller F-1 draw had only a dirt trail leading off in the direction of Cabourg, the Germans had placed only a few machine guns and mortars there.

Lt. Cmdr. William Leide, commanding officer of LCT Flotilla Twelve, had been placed in charge of all fifty-six LCTs in Assault Group O-2: thirty-two LCT(6)s from Flotillas Twelve and Twenty-six, fourteen LCT(5)s from Flotilla Eighteen, the nine LCT(A)s from the Naval Gunfire Support Group, and LCT(5) 413, which supported the Ranger landings on Charlie Beach. Going up the chain of command from there, Assault Group O-2 was commanded by Capt. W. O. Bailey in the transport USS *Charles Carroll*, and his deputy commander, Capt. W. D. Wright, was in LCH 86 (a converted LCI). Rear Adm. J. L. Hall flew the flag of Assault

Force O in the command ship USS *Ancon*, and Rear Adm. Alan G. Kirk commanded the Western Naval Task Force (the mostly American ships assaulting both Omaha and Utah beaches) from the heavy cruiser USS *Augusta*. The chain of command from Ensign Irwin to Admiral Kirk had very few links.

The 614's Assignment

The LCT 614 was assigned to land with the H+60 wave on Dog Red Beach, to the west of Exit D-3 in front of Les Moulins. The crew would land vehicles and men of the 149th Combat Engineer Battalion and some infantry from the 116th Regimental Combat Team (RCT, or essentially, a heavily reinforced infantry regiment). The plan was that most of the assault's tanks—the DD tanks and the tanks from the LCT(A)s—would go ashore at H-Hour. The 614's wave, landing an hour later, was to bring in engineering units to help get the assault off the beaches and over the bluffs. Irwin and Pillmore were fairly happy with their assignment. The LCT 614 would participate in an important phase of the invasion, and their landing would be early enough that, if all went well, they would be clear of the beach relatively soon. Once they withdrew from the beach and anchored in the rendezvous area, they could sit back and watch.

Their sense of satisfaction, though, was tempered by their realization that the importance of the assignment carried with it an equal degree of danger, and they had an appreciation of their own inexperience. Capt. W. D. Wright, deputy commander of Assault Group O-2, allayed some of those fears slightly during a briefing. He told the officers of the landing craft going in early in the day that they had little to fear. First, Allied bombers were to pound the bluffs overlooking the beaches. Then, the battleships and cruisers would shoot up defenses on the beach itself, and destroyers would be just offshore for called fire support. "We're going to be throwing everything at them but the kitchen sink," Wright told them. "Hell, we'll throw that in as well."

Wright also stressed the importance of keeping to the landing schedule as tightly as possible. The army had created the schedule and had drawn up the loads for each landing craft based on what its needs would be at any particular time. The navy's job, and the job of each of these skippers, was to ensure that every load got to the proper landing zone at the proper time. The 116th Regimental Combat Team had not been in combat before, and although the troops were eager to get into the fight, some soldiers might be reluctant to leave the comparative shelter of the landing craft. The skippers were to force the men off the boats, at gunpoint if necessary. Failure to get men and equipment ashore could be grounds for a general court-martial.

At the flotilla level, Lieutenant Commander Leide tried to impress on his LCT skippers that their craft would be needed as much, if not more, in the days following the invasion. Yes, get the loads to the beach at all costs, but avoid unnecessary heroics. In particular, the LCTs were not to shoot their 20mm guns except in direct self-defense. Most craft would be going in well after the assault troops had started to land, and indiscriminate firing would endanger American soldiers already on the beach or working up the bluffs. Just as important, shooting draws attention from the enemy, thereby endangering the lives of the crew as well as the availability of the craft for buildup operations. Getting off the beach was as important as getting to the beach. Once retracted, they were to anchor in the rendezvous area and wait for further orders. Most of the craft from Leide's flotillas were to report to the British commander of the Gold assault area the next day.

Myriad other briefings followed the general talks. They were briefed about weather conditions, enemy defenses, convoy routes and position keeping, sailing times, rendezvous areas, and dozens of other fine points concerning the invasion and their part in it. They were given maps, navigation charts, code tables, landing schedules, and planning documents. Lieutenant Commander Leide later said that the LCTs were perhaps a little too well informed about the operation and that keeping up with the flow of documents was a "superhuman task." Like all LCTs, the LCT 614 had only one small safe in the officers' quarters where secret information was supposed to be kept. The number of documents so swamped the little craft that Irwin and Pillmore found themselves opening up void tanks under the deck to store confidential and secret material there, where it was largely forgotten.

A break in all this preparation came on May 25. The word spread around the invasion force that an important person would be viewing the ships from the deck of an American PT boat. Irwin and Pillmore got the men on the 614 topside in their dress blue uniforms in order to render proper honors when the craft passed. The men enjoyed the break in painting and greasing and storing, but they wondered what all the fuss was about and who the high-ranking officer standing in the bridge of the PT boat was. Only later did they learn the "officer" was King George VI, who had lunched with Admiral Hall and others on the flagship *Ancon* and then reviewed the invasion force.

Air Raids

After their brush with royalty, the men of the 614 settled down to getting the ship in shape to take on its load. It seemed odd to the men that the Luftwaffe had not targeted Portland. The crowd of anchored shipping would have been easy to pick off, akin to shooting a load of buckshot into a box of skeets. A concentrated, determined raid could easily have crippled the invasion fleet. They had experienced a few air raids in Plymouth, but they knew during those raids that they had little to worry about, that the bombers were after port facilities and supplies and the warships out in the harbor. Here, however, they knew they were not only within the target area, but as a member of the invasion fleet, they were part of the target itself. The few raids they experienced in Portland, though, were by a small number of planes. The men assumed that either the British were correct when they claimed to have severely crippled the Luftwaffe during the Battle of Britain three years earlier, or the Germans were hoarding their planes for a massive attack on the shipping off the invasion beaches.

That assumption was tested during a fairly large air raid on the night of May 27–28. Carter and Johnson manned the guns, even though the small ships were under strict orders not to shoot. Carter had Sparky put in the magazine filled with all tracer rounds, but no good excuse presented itself for him to shoot it. The rest of the crew made ready to get under way quickly if needed. Searchlights crisscrossed the sky, and soon the larger ships and antiaircraft batteries ashore began shooting. A moment later, bombs began exploding almost randomly around the harbor. Getting shot at directly is terrifying, yet usually the person under fire could do something about it—if only to keep his head down and pray. This business of waiting for a random bomb to fall—and even a relatively small bomb would make short work of an LCT—was worse precisely because of that impersonal feeling of helplessness and randomness. The men knew the situation was totally in the hands of luck or the will of God or whatever forces of fate they happened to believe in. The experience so shook the 614's cook that he developed an absolute phobia about air raids that would plague him, and thereby the rest of the crew, once they got to France.

Pequigney got caught in an open boat during the raid. He had gone ashore to collect charts and other material and was on his way back in total blackout conditions. The bomb explosions were dangerous enough, but even more dangerous to these men were the sharp bits of shrapnel from the antiaircraft bursts falling around them like hail. The boat scurried from one LST or LCT nest to the next, and men lucky enough to see the number of their craft would scramble out of the boat. Pequigney and several other men never saw theirs. Finally, the boat crew decided the bombs and shrapnel had become absolutely too threatening, so the boat's coxswain took them to the nearest LST to wait until daylight.

When morning came, the men were astonished to see that the raid had accomplished relatively little. The harbor was not choked with burning and sinking ships as they had expected. However, in addition to regular bombs, the planes had also dropped time-delayed bombs and mines. All that day, a Sunday, explosions went off throughout Portland Harbor as the shipping returned to its work, and some twenty landing craft, including several LCTs, suffered damage when they detonated the mines or happened to be too near an exploding bomb. For a while, all unnecessary water traffic came to a halt while minesweepers patrolled the harbor. The men of the 614 endured a rather tense day as the nest of three LCTs swung around on its moorings; the men never knew when, or if, the currents would push them into a mine or over a bomb. By evening, though, the explosions had mostly stopped, and the business of preparing for the invasion resumed. On June 1, troops and vehicles began filing into Portland, and one by one the LCTs and other beaching craft nosed in to take on their loads.

But before the ships loaded up, the crew had one more ceremony to hold. On June 1, the men who had fulfilled their qualifications officially assumed their new ranks. With everything else going on, the ceremony couldn't be elaborate, but Carter, Pequigney, Johnson, and Stefanowicz joined Kleen and Kelly as petty officers.

Loading and Waiting

With all the briefings and meetings over, there was little left to do but load up and wait. About June 2, the LCT 614 nudged up to the "hard" in Portland that had been built especially for the loading of landing craft. The hard was a paved area with the optimum gradient that allowed LCTs to beach right against the shore and drop their ramps on dry land so that vehicles could drive directly onto the ship. The paved slope also allowed the craft to land and retract without using the anchor. First the jeeps and their trailers backed aboard, a fairly touchy operation that required almost everyone to help. It led to the 614's first injury. Pequigney was on the ramp helping to direct traffic. Stepping aside as a jeep rolled aboard, he stepped through the grating on the mulock ramps and, fortunately, fell backward rather than to the side or forward, avoiding breaking his leg. As it was, he did suffer a badly scraped and bruised leg. It was a painful injury, but he continued with the work at hand.

Once the five jeeps and their trailers were in place and tied down, two bulldozers rolled up the ramp. These large, armored D-8 dozers had racks built over the driver's compartment packed with TNT. Apparently, some of the jeeps' trailers were also filled with demolition equipment. One good hit, and the craft would be blown to bits.

Next came the men. The jeep drivers and bulldozer operators and technicians belonged to units of the Sixth Engineer Special Brigade. Most of the men and jeeps were from the 3565th Ordnance Company, whose job was to salvage and repair vehicles on the beach. The rest of the jeeps and the bulldozers belonged to Companies A and C of the 149th Engineer Combat Battalion, whose task was to clear exit D-3 of mines and tank traps so that subsequent assault troops could get off the beach. Finally came the combat infantry troops—two lieutenants and men of the Third Battalion, 116th RCT. In all, sixty-five men crowded among the vehicles on the tank deck.

After loading up, Irwin edged the 614 over to Castletown pier to top off with fuel and water, and then headed out to the anchorage to wait. The LCT had been designed to accommodate twenty people, and now it had more than eighty men—both passengers and crew—crowded aboard. The heads were in constant use, as were those of the other 240-odd LCTs of Assault Force O. Plus those of the LCIs, the LSTs, and the transports, command ships, and warships. The warships' heads discharged directly into the sea, which is fine when the ship is under way, but in the little enclosed harbor, the water quickly became uninviting. It's little wonder that many men came away from Portland with the impression that England was a dirty place.

The 614's crew tried to accommodate the soldiers as best they could. The soldiers had their own rations and had been told to sleep in or under their vehicles or wherever they could. However, the LCT's tiny galley was always crowded, and the three-gallon coffee percolator was brewing as often as it was ready to serve. The cook at first tried the best he could to prepare a few short-order items or soups or stews, but soon he had to give up altogether under those circumstances and left the soldiers to live off their C and K rations.

Out of compassion for the soldiers, the crew tried to make them as comfortable as they could but without giving up their bunks. The soldiers slept in whatever space they found. A few could sleep on the deck inside the galley or the crew's quarters, but most had to sleep out on the tank deck—on the vehicles, under the vehicles, between the vehicles, and under tarpaulins. Deck space became valuable real estate, and the soldiers milled about on the top of the deckhouses, behind the pilothouse, in and around the anchor winch, in the bow lockers, and even in the gun tubs. A favored space was well aft, sheltered from the wind by the deckhouses and warmed slightly from the engine room, where the diesel generators were always running. The least favored space was well forward, for although the ramp and bow lockers provided some protection from the wind, standing water always collected in the dip in the deck just behind the ramp. Of course, nowhere on deck provided any protection from the rain.

The men struck up a few casual friendships with the soldiers. Carter especially enjoyed talking to the infantrymen about their weapons. One evening in the crowded galley, in an apparent fit of bravado, one of the soldiers pulled the pin from a grenade. Most of the swabbies cleared out, but Carter knew that as long as the man held down the lever, the grenade's fuse would not ignite. Regardless, a few tense moments passed before the man put the pin back in.

The talk stayed superficial and lighthearted. The 614's crewmen certainly felt cramped by the presence of so many soldiers, yet they all knew that many of those men would die within the next few days. A feeling of sheepish embarrassment settled over the ship. The crew's accommodations were anything but luxurious, yet they had blankets and relatively clean sheets and pillows and slept inside away from the rain and wind. The heaters in the quarters were inadequate, but they helped take some of the chill out of the damp English air. Worst of all was the knowledge that they would be leaving these men behind on the beach. Certainly the soldiers were not being abandoned or marooned, and the hundreds of ships carrying thousands of troops testified that these men would not be left alone. Still, none of the sailors envied the soldiers' job, and none of them begrudged giving them whatever comfort they could.

Waiting is certainly a mainstay of military life; in fact, "hurry up and wait" became probably the most used, indeed useful, cliché of the war. Fortunately for the men crowded on the landing craft, this wait did not take terribly long.

6

OMAHA BEACH

At 3:00 a.m. on Sunday, June 4, the LCTs, minesweepers, and other slow or advance craft began sailing from Portland. The ships formed up just outside the harbor and began their voyage to France. Once LCT 614 had settled into the convoy, Pequigney turned the wheel over to one of the other men and went below to rest his scraped leg and to catch what sleep he could. He knew that night and the following day would be long and trying.

Just after daybreak, however, patrol craft began running along the lines of ships signaling "Post Mike One," or return to port. The threat of bad weather on June 5 had led Eisenhower to delay the invasion by a day. In the scramble to get back to port, many craft that had sailed from Plymouth and were destined for Utah Beach ended up further crowding the anchorage in Portland. Later that afternoon, Pequigney woke up and went out on deck, only to find himself back in Portland. "Jeez," he said. "Did I sleep through the invasion?"

By 3:30 a.m. on June 5, the LCTs were again under way. This time, getting the unwieldy LCTs into position was complicated by the presence of the Assault Force U vessels anchored among the Assault Force O ships, plus the fact that more Assault Force U ships, for some inexplicable reason, began entering the anchorage against the signals. Lieutenant Commander Leide was supposed to direct his LCTs from an impromptu flagship, British motor launch (ML) 153, and two of his three LCT group commanders (apart from Lt. Dean Rockwell, who was off with the LCTs carrying the DD tanks) were aboard ML 189. For more than four hours, Leide scurried about in ML 153, trying his best to sort out his craft from the milling herd, as he called it. By that time, the craft had gotten out into the channel and into the full force of the weather that had caused the delay of the invasion. Leide finally had to concede that the LCTs would never be in proper sailing order.

All that day, the men on LCT 614 watched the ships of the force around them and the endless flights of bombers and fighters overhead. Although the sight of so many ships and planes encouraged them, occasionally they happened upon some reminder of the danger that lay ahead: various bits of flotsam, a couple of ditched aircraft, and once a capsized LCT(5). On top of those unsettling sights, most of the soldiers, and a few of the sailors, were seasick (it was the first time the 614 had been under way in the open sea), a feeling that did little to ease the tension they all felt.

Carlson noticed a young soldier sitting on the deck as off to himself as he could get, crying and looking at a photograph. Carlson sat beside him and asked to see the picture. It was of the man's wife and three daughters. "That's a damn fine woman," the soldier said.

"I'm sure she is," Carlson said. "And those are fine-looking girls, too." The two men sat together without saying anything else for a long time.

As evening approached, Pillmore told Irwin that he would take the conn that night. He knew Irwin would need his rest for the following morning, but he also knew he was not going to get any sleep that night. He wanted to be alone on the conn to have time to think. Like Pillmore, all the men had their secret thoughts and tended to turn inward as much as possible on that crowded ship. Some were able to sleep while others had to stand watch. Few said anything that night.

On the trip across, Leide had nothing but trouble trying to keep his LCTs in formation. The two motor launches assigned to him and the group commanders had also been assigned a place in the convoy's screen, and Leide had constant difficulty gaining permission from the convoy commanders to leave station so he could check on the craft under his command. When the convoy reached the transport area and Leide had some freedom of movement, he discovered that the LCTs, which were supposed to be four abreast in a column eight miles long, were straggled out over more than twenty miles. Fortunately, the craft assigned to the leading waves were roughly in position and ready to head toward the beach, leaving him some time to marshal the remaining craft. But to make matters even worse, Leide was ordered to give up one of the MLs to Assault Group O-3, so his group commanders had to transfer to his craft in rough weather in the dark. Leide now had only one small ML with which to direct and control more than fifty lost and unmanageable LCTs that were commanded, for the most part, by inexperienced skippers. Getting shot at suddenly seemed the easy part of the day ahead of him.

The First LCT Waves on O-2

The ships of the invasion fleet began reaching their stations about 3:45 a.m. The transports and LSTs turned right toward their assigned anchorages, and Lt. Dean Rockwell began deploying his sixteen LCTs in position to launch the DD tanks. Eight of the craft moved on to the O-1 sector of the beach, and Rockwell's eight craft headed in to the Dog Green and Dog White sectors on the far west end of Omaha Beach. In one of the most famous LCT exploits of D-Day, Rockwell, aboard LCT 535, soon determined that the water was too rough to launch the tanks, so after conferring with the army officer in command, he decided at about 5:00 a.m. to take his craft inshore and launch the tanks directly onto the beach.

At 5:45 a.m., the craft turned toward the beach. LCT 535 landed first at 6:29 a.m., and the others were ashore by 6:35 a.m. Coming in at low tide in front of the line of obstacles, five of these craft experienced textbook landings—dropping the ramps, landing their tanks within three or four minutes, then retracting quickly. Fire from German shore batteries and machine guns was heavy, and the skipper of LCT 586, just to starboard of the 535, reported getting rocked by many near misses. LCTs 589, 588, and 591 also reported no trouble beaching, unloading, or retracting; in fact, the 589 reported being on the beach only three minutes.

On Dog White, LCT 587 got stuck on a sandbar. The first tank went off into six feet of water, and when the second tank rolled perhaps a bit too cautiously off the ramp, a shell hit it. The skipper ordered the craft to retract, and he shifted position a few yards to land the last two tanks in shallower water. The 587 was finally able to get off the beach at 6:45 a.m., reporting no casualties among the crew and no serious damage to the ship.

The LCT 713, landing on Dog Green, also had a difficult time, striking a sandbar directly in front of the large gun battery in front of the D-1 exit. The commander of the lead tank took fifteen minutes to decide whether to drive off the ramp or inflate the skirts in case the water was too deep, but by the time he inflated the skirt and drove off the skirt had been damaged and did not fully inflate. The tank sank immediately. The LCT's crew rescued the tankers before pulling off the beach and coming in again some 150 yards to port. This time the three remaining tanks landed smoothly, but the 713 was the last to retract at 7:10 a.m., after spending thirty-five or forty minutes on the beach. As it started to turn to seaward, a shell hit and started a fire. The crew quickly brought the fire under control, and none of the crew was wounded.

The LCT 590 suffered the worst in this wave. Landing at the west end of the line, its tanks went ashore in good order, and the gunners on the 590 began returning fire, which brought additional attention to the craft. It was raked by machine-gun fire and hit several times by shells that killed three of the crew and wounded two others. Most of the men killed and wounded were members of the gun crews. The hits also damaged the LCT's ramp badly enough to prevent it from making its second trip to the beach.

The eight LCT(A)s scheduled to touch down at H-Hour were much less organized. These craft, weighted down with armor plating and slowed by the LCMs each towed, suffered tremendously from the weather even before they reached the transport area. LCT(A) 2229 never made it across the channel. The ship started to flood at about 4:00 a.m. while still well out in the channel. Once the engines failed, a patrol boat came alongside and took off the army engineers and navy demolition personnel but left the crew and the other soldiers aboard. By 5:00 a.m. the ship was far behind the convoy when it sank, taking down both officers, four members of the crew, and three army personnel. LCT(A) 2229 was perhaps the first LCT lost on D-Day.

Only five of the surviving LCT(A)s reached the beaches on time. LCT(A) 2075 experienced perhaps the most textbook landing, reporting no trouble beaching or landing its tanks and no casualties among the crew. LCT(A)s 2227 and 2050 reported beaching on time and getting their loads off but had some trouble retracting. The 2050 didn't get off the beach until 7:20 a.m., and the 2227 suffered several hits and lost its bow ramp. LCT(A) 2124 had a particularly rough experience. It made the trip across the channel with no damage and was able to land slightly later than scheduled on Dog Red. The two tanks went ashore immediately but drew fire from a gun emplacement to port. The tank dozer stayed aboard and returned fire for ten minutes, apparently silencing the emplacement. During that time, however, an emplacement to starboard containing a 47mm anti-tank gun opened up on the 2124, hitting it at least ten times. With its fuel tanks punctured and the anchor shot off, it finally retracted at 7:05 a.m. and lay to in the transport area. The next morning, it broke loose from its moorings, and as the craft drifted toward the beach the crew worked frantically to get under way. Finally the engineers found a fuel tank that had not been contaminated with salt water, and they linked that tank to two of the engines, which provided enough power to keep the LCT under control.

LCT(A) 2307 also landed only slightly late on Easy Green but had a particularly difficult time even getting to the beach. On the evening before D-Day, a wave smashed in the bulwark on the starboard side, partially swamping the craft. Still, it was able to keep station and beach approximately on time (6:40 a.m.). At that point it came under heavy fire and succeeded in landing only one tank. The commander of the remaining tank refused to leave in such deep water, and the tank dozer could not get around the second tank. The skipper, Ensign B. T. Geckler, tried to move closer to shore and then tried to retract so he could beach at another site. By then, though, the ship had been damaged, two crewmen wounded, and the ramp disabled, so Geckler decided not to attempt a second landing. As he backed toward the transport area with his one remaining engine and his ramp dangling, another LCT(A) took him in tow. About 6:00 p.m., the 2307 capsized and sank with the tank and tank dozer still aboard. Admiral Hall later criticized Geckler for not wrecking his craft on the beach in an effort to get the remaining equipment ashore.

The two remaining LCT(A)s had such trouble that they did not even reach the beach until several hours later. The skipper of one of these craft, Lt. j.g. J. S. Rhoades of the LCT(A) 2275, experienced horrible luck. First, on the trip across the channel, the starboard-side engine room began leaking, and he lost that engine. Underpowered, listing to starboard and with three feet of water on the tank deck forward, the 2275 could make a top speed of only four knots by the time it reached the transport area. (Rhoades later reported to Captain Sabin that at that point he had to give up his plans to capture a German E-boat.) The 2275 finally made it to the beach around noon, but it was further damaged by machine-gun fire. Despite four efforts to beach in shallow water, it was unable to get the tanks ashore and headed back to the transport area. The ship was able to land that afternoon at low tide (about 4:00 p.m.), but the engines finally conked out and it had to be towed off the beach by LCT(A) 2273, which was also not having a good day.

Like many of its sister ships, the LCT(A) 2273 experienced flooding on the way in. (The Mark 5 LCT was notoriously leaky to begin with, but the LCT[A] conversion made matters worse with the added weight of the armor and a British idea to cut away the port bulwark to allow side loading. The first-wave LCT[A]s' assignment to tow an LCM for the gapping teams further exacerbated the problems, slowing them and creating more strain on the hull sections.) The 2273 arrived in the transport area about 11:00 a.m., but by that time the situation on the beach was so bad that the craft was told to wait. It finally went in at about 4:00 p.m. with the 2275, landed its tanks, and towed the 2275 back to the transport area. But that evening, the leaks worsened (perhaps the strain of towing the other LCT), and it broke up and sank.

LCT 614 on Dog Red

The H+60 wave arrived in the transport area in much better order. At about 5:30 a.m. on June 6, the 614's crew started going to their battle stations. Because half the crew were already at their underway watch stations, which were also sometimes their battle stations, there was no sounding of the klaxon or running about. The men on watch below simply came up when they were ready and relieved the men at their stations.

Since about 3:45 a.m., Carter had been on watch at the wheel. Peering through the little slits that served as windows or out the door, latched open to provide air, he had seen the invasion begin to shape up. At first he saw nothing at all; the blacked-out ships revealed nothing of their presence that he could see. After a few moments, though, he began to see a few tiny blinking lights on buoys left by the minesweepers as they cleared a channel to the beach and then red, green, and white flares from the control craft marking the beach landing zones. Shoreward, over the horizon, bombs flashed like summer lightning. By about 4:30 a.m. a gray light let him see the other LCTs, but they soon dispersed so that the 614 had only three companions. LCT 613 had the lead, LCT 536 was the wave guide in second position, and then LCT 612 followed by 614.

As Pequigney came up to take the wheel, the battleships and cruisers began opening up with their big guns at targets ashore. Because of the narrow channels that the minesweepers had hurriedly cleared, the LCTs had to chug past the gunfire support ships, and the concussion from the 8-inch guns of the *Augusta* felt worse than the bombs that had fallen around them in Portland. Carter stood for a moment to watch the shooting; the smoke drifting away from the ships struck him as nonchalant. He then went below to get into his battle clothing of a blue coverall treated with a sticky substance that was supposed to protect him from the flash of a nearby explosion or from poison gas if the Germans decided to use it. He then picked up his helmet, life jacket, and gas mask. Before going up, he rummaged through C and K ration boxes in the compartment, looking for snacks, and ended up stuffing his pockets with chocolate bars.

Topside, Carlson was standing watch in the gun tub, and Sparky was already there, eating crackers and orange marmalade. As Carlson went below, Carter and Sparky began getting the gun ready. "How do you feel, Sparky?" Carter asked.

"Kinda shaky," he replied. "How about you?"

"The same," Carter agreed.

About the time the gun was ready, Carlson came back, his pockets bulging with cigarette packs. Carlson noticed that the shoreline had finally become visible.

"Mornin'," he said. "So this is France, huh? Take me back to Oregon."

With his bulky life jacket on, Carter needed the help of both Sparky and Carlson to strap himself into the mount. Once in, he told Sparky to go ahead and put tension on the magazines in the ready service locker in case they needed to reload quickly. As Sparky worked on that, Irwin shouted down at him from the conning tower: "Sparky! Put on your life jacket."

"I can't load with the thing on," Sparky replied.

But Irwin insisted. "Put one on. You might get blown into the water."

To Irwin, standing on the conning position on top of the pilothouse, things on the beach seemed to be going fairly well. All the shooting he could see came from Allied ships; no shooting seemed to be coming from the beach. As Irwin conned the ship, keeping an eye on LCT 536, the wave leader, Pillmore scanned the shore with binoculars, trying to find their landing area. Since they were supposed to beach just to the right of the Les Moulins draw, exit D-3, he thought it would be easy to identify. But now, in the gloom and smoke and distance, he had trouble picking it out. But there was still time.

To get to the line of departure, the 614 and other landing craft had to sail around the *Augusta*, past the French light cruisers, and then form up in front of the battleship *Arkansas*. The blast from *Augusta's* 8-inch guns jarred the LCT, and the sharp reports of the light cruisers' 6-inch guns hurt the ears of the men on deck. But just as they rounded the *Arkansas*, the battleship loosed a broadside from its 12-inch guns. The blast and noise rattled the little LCT and hurt the men on deck. Carter thought that, had they been any closer, the concussion from the big guns could have easily flipped the little craft over. Irwin, perhaps even more exposed on the conn, turned around at the painfully horrendous sound and thought he was looking straight down the muzzles of the battleship's guns. From his vantage point atop the wheelhouse, Kleen could easily see the big shells arching over them on their way to the shore.

About 6:30 a.m. they received the word to head to the line of departure. With the incoming tide, the LCTs made good time down the line of ships and reached the position sixteen minutes early. They milled around, watching the firing, until finally Leide radioed the order to beach. Irwin ordered Kleen to sound the beaching signal—five short blasts on the horn—and shouted down the voice tube to Pequigney to come about on a southerly heading. The three LCTs to starboard—703, 622, and

704—continued west and headed for Dog Green at the very end of the beach. LCT 569 held back, ready to go in on Easy Green to the east of the Les Moulins draw. The 614 was then exposed on the right side of the wave; suddenly Carter thought they were a much better target.

At first, the hour-long trip to the beach was quiet. Pillmore located the correct area of the beach and pointed it out to Irwin. He then left the conn to supervise getting the vehicles ready for landing. Irwin thought that Captain Wright had been correct when he said that the bombers and battleships would clear the Germans from the beaches. When shells started exploding in the water ahead of them, Irwin's first thought was that the ships behind them were shooting short. He needed a moment to realize the 614 had finally come under mortar and artillery fire. He also began to see that the promised gaps in the obstacles had not been blown. He ordered reduced speed and began looking for a way through.

With Irwin stuck on the conn piloting the ship, Pillmore roamed the deck, making sure everything went according to plan. When they turned to head for the beach, they exposed themselves to a quartering sea that made the ride all the more uncomfortable for the crew and the soldiers. Many soldiers stood in the jeeps and bulldozers to see where they were headed, and Pillmore saw Andin, Gudger, and Cromer clearing the tie-downs and chocks from the vehicles. Since they were about finished, he told Cromer to loosen dogs on the ramp and take his position on the port bow locker. Resembling a Wild West hero hitching up his gun belt, Cromer tucked his hammer into his belt and headed forward. Andin worked his way aft to loosen the anchor in its bracket, and Gudger grabbed a Thompson sub-machine gun from the compartment and went to the ramp to direct the traffic off.

Pillmore climbed back up to the pilothouse. By now the LCT was drawing some rifle and machine-gun fire. He stayed near the door to the pilothouse and called up to Irwin that the ship was ready to beach. Irwin had finally picked out what seemed to be a path through the obstacles, ordered full speed ahead, and then told Carlson to drop the anchor. Carlson released the catch, but nothing happened. "I said drop the anchor," Irwin shouted.

"It's stuck!" Carlson called back. Pillmore ran across the catwalk to see what the problem was. "I dunno," Carlson said. "We've never dropped the anchor before." Pillmore was taken aback a moment.

"You mean you have never dropped this anchor the whole time you've been on the ship?" Pillmore asked.

"No, sir," Carlson replied. "As far as I know, this anchor hasn't been dropped since this boat was built."

Pillmore bit off a curse. He was going to need some help, and fortunately the giant Stefanowicz was at hand. "Sparky, get back here," Pillmore ordered. He and Sparky began pulling the cable from the reel hand over hand while Carlson manually kept the reel rolling. Several tense moments passed under fire in the exposed area around the anchor winch before the anchor bit into the sandy bottom and enough cable came off that its weight took over and the drum began paying out freely. Pillmore ran back to the cover of the pilothouse, and Carlson and Sparky jumped back in the gun tub with Carter. Only later did Pillmore realize that those men probably saved the ship, but of course, it was still early in the day.

The 614 neared the obstacles, catching up to a line of LCVPs carrying the bulk of the 116th RCT's Company M, which was also trying to find a way through. The congestion of men and equipment drew increased mortar and machine-gun fire plus aimed artillery fire. The distinctive rip of an 88mm gun firing from the Vierville draw occasionally punctuated the hiss of the antitank rounds.

"God, look at those shells," Sparky said.

The soldiers on deck began to move toward the ramp, ready to move off. The soldier Carlson had befriended the day before came up to the gun tub and sat down facing Carlson. But before he said anything, a chunk of shrapnel banged against the back of his helmet, saving Carlson's face. Without saying anything, he climbed back down on deck.

Despite the intensifying small arms fire and mortar explosions, the men stood at their battle stations, ready to get the soldiers and vehicles off the ship as quickly as possible once the ramp dropped. Johnson, manning the starboard 20mm, glanced over at Carter from time to time and wondered whether they were going to shoot even without orders. Neither Carter nor Johnson thought that standing while strapped to their guns and drawing fire was the way to go to war. Jarvis, Johnson's loader, had even less to do with the guns not in action. He stood beside Johnson, crouched behind the tub's shield, scanning for targets. A tracer round zipped through his life jacket, puffing out a small cloud of the filler material. He jumped and shouted, "Jesus Christ!" In the tension, Carter and the others found themselves laughing at Jarvis.

The ship pushed through the obstacles, scraping against the hedgehogs and knocked a Teller mine off one of the posts. Irwin shouted course changes to Pequigney in such rapid succession that the quartermaster could do nothing but spin the wheel around. About 7:20 a.m., actually some ten minutes early, the LCT grounded a hundred yards away from the beach. Irwin thought they were still too far out, so he delayed ordering the ramp dropped. That left Cromer, lying on top of the starboard bow locker with his hammer, fully exposed to small arms fire and shrapnel from the shells. From his vantage point he could clearly see the wreckage of men, vehicles, and landing craft on the beach.

An LCVP coming in between the 614 and the 612 took a mortar or antitank round directly on its ramp. As the craft sank, the survivors jumped overboard and screamed toward the 614 for help. Machine guns opened up on the men in the water, and Carter and Carlson saw several of them roll over slowly. Other men scrambled for what safety they could find. Carlson saw several men gather behind a floating post that had broken off an obstacle. A shell hit the post, and when the spray and smoke cleared Carlson saw nothing there. Other men found cover behind the intact obstacles, many of them mined. Some of them were so close that Carlson could see the details of the large Teller mines with their pins slanted seaward, waiting for a bump.

Irwin's ability to maneuver to avoid the obstacles and get around the sandbar was severely restricted by the anchor cable payed out behind them. All four craft had landed just to the east of their assigned positions, with the 613 and 536 landing in front or just to the east of the draw and the 612 and 614 coming ashore at its western edge. Because the Germans had positioned their guns to fire along the beach rather than out to sea, the 612 and 614 were in a more direct line of fire than the other two craft. The 612, in fact, was between the guns and the 614. When the 612 slowed to thread through the obstacles and sandbars, it caught at least three shells. One exploded in the galley, but the others knocked out all three engines and the two generators. The 612 was totally dead in the water, but fortunately only one man was wounded. They hoisted the breakdown flag, began fighting their fires, and waited, under fire, for help. Carter watched the smoke rising from the 612 and began to wonder whether the fire from the gun that got them would shift to the 614. He hoped the 612 and the smoke rising from her would shield them.

Apparently the sandbar was not as much of a problem farther to the left. Irwin noticed, with a mixture of envy and frustration, that the two craft on the far left of their section were having an apparently easier time than the 614 and 612 were. The wave leader, LCT 536, was able to land its load and retract after only a few minutes. Once that craft regained the rendezvous area, Leide assigned it to take the place of LCT 590, one of Rockwell's LCTs carrying DD tanks that had taken a hit and was not available for a second load as planned. LCT 613, on the far left of the wave, retracted a short time later and came over to tow the 612 to safety. This left the 614 temporarily the only LCT on the Dog Red sector. Irwin knew his only two choices were either to retract and beach again farther to the left or to wait for the rising tide to lift him over the sandbar. He could see that the tide now was coming in fast, and knowing that the troops had been told to come in on a particular beach for a reason, he decided to wait for the tide.

Soon, though, the H+70 and H+90 waves began coming in on top of them. The craft in these waves had not been dispatched in an orderly fashion, and several craft from the H+60 wave, such as the 614, had not been able to retract. As a result, the craft began to crowd along the beach, making navigation inshore almost impossible. The larger LCTs and LCMs could only slowly work through the obstacles, and many waited just off the obstacles looking for a way in. By the time these craft began picking their way through the obstacles, the next wave of landing craft came in. Only the little LCVPs had the maneuverability to wend through the obstacles, but many of these plywood craft suffered damage from rifle and machine-gun fire and sank or broached, adding to the congestion.

Into all this came the first wave of four of the even larger LCI(L)s, two off to port and two immediately to starboard. The big guns shifted their fire to them, but machine guns kept up a steady fire at the 614, keeping the men pinned down wherever they could find cover. Mortar rounds continued to land all around them. The lead LCI(L) off to starboard, the 91, slowed at the line of obstacles and began taking hits. It backed off a bit and began nosing through again, only to begin burning and then to explode so violently that Carter and the others felt the blast. "My God," Carter said. "They took it in the magazine." The second craft, LCI(L) 92, rammed through the obstacles farther to the right, struck mines, broached, and began burning.

After several minutes, Irwin knew he wasn't going to get closer to the beach anytime soon, and the fate of the two LCIs made him realize staying on the beach was suicidal. He could see men wading ashore from the craft around them, and even some craft behind them were letting their men out. He decided to risk it. Irwin ordered the ramp dropped, and Cromer whapped the last dog with his hammer. The ramp splashed down, and Cromer lost no time rolling off the locker and ducking into the winch compartment with Clark. Yelling, "Let's go!" the lieutenant in charge of the men ran off the ramp and dropped into water up to his armpits. His second in command and several of the men followed. Carlson saw the soldier he had befriended looking up at him, crying, and repeating, "Oh, God. Oh, God. Oh, God."

The appearance of infantry drew the attention of at least one machine gun. A few quick bursts zeroed in on the ramp and hit several of the soldiers, two of whom fell on the ramp. The other troops stopped their advance and pulled the wounded men back on deck. One of them had been shot squarely in the stomach, the round just missing a rifle grenade. The other apparently suffered a painful but shallow wound to the back. With both of their officers now off the ship, the men showed no particular desire to move out. Irwin signaled to Pillmore to get the vehicles moving. The soldiers pressed themselves against the steel bulwarks to get out of their way.

The bulldozers rumbled off first, and some of the infantry followed behind them for protection. Other soldiers already in the water also bunched up behind the vehicles, not realizing that they were not only putting the steel of the dozers between them and the guns but also the dozers' load of TNT. The dozers made it almost to the water's edge before a large shell exploded between them and set them both ablaze. Fortunately the near miss did not provide the shock necessary to set off the TNT.

Next, two of the jeeps tried to land, but the driver of one was hit and the other jeep apparently swamped in a shell hole and drowned out quickly. The second jeep's driver struggled through the water for cover behind an obstacle. Irwin realized he would need to get the LCT even closer to the beach if the remaining jeeps were to get ashore successfully, so he sent Pillmore down to tell the remaining drivers and soldiers to wait a bit before heading to the beach. That was one order they had no trouble obeying.

The men on deck could see dead soldiers everywhere. A row of them lay in the surf, washing ashore with the rising tide. Others lay scattered on the beach, especially along the line of shingle. Still others floated in the water around them, some with only their legs in the air. When these men hit the water, they had inflated their life belts, but their heavy packs had flipped them over, drowning them. Carter stared, fixated on a dead soldier rolling with the waves just in front of the open ramp. They could see very little activity on the beach besides burning vehicles. One man caught their eye, who was walking calmly along the beach as if on a holiday stroll. They all thought he was shell-shocked. This could have been Col. Charles Canham, commander of the 116th RCT. He and others of the headquarters staff landed in an LCVP on Dog White about the same time as the 614. He and Brig. Gen. Norman Cota, the deputy commander of the Twenty-ninth Infantry Division, walked along the beach in opposite directions—Cota westward and Canham east—

urging the men to move inland and looking for opportune spots to scale the bluffs. Cota's efforts at the D-1 exit are now legendary in Twenty-ninth Division histories.

Again Irwin started shouting a flurry of engine orders and heading changes, trying to work the little craft through the obstacles and sandbars to the beach itself. If anything, the mortar and machine-gun fire grew even more intense. To Carlson, the shrapnel and bullet splashes looked as thick as raindrops on the water; instead of keeping tension on the anchor cable as the craft backed and twisted, he stayed in the gun tub. The starboard gun tub, perhaps because of its closeness to the pilothouse and conn, took more than its share of fire. Jarvis had already narrowly dodged one bullet, so he and Johnson pulled back to the cover of the pilothouse. Even Irwin, up on the conn, realized that his position was untenable, with the bullets zipping past and shrapnel buzzing around his head like angry bees. He and Kleen climbed down from the conn, and Irwin latched open the door to shout orders into the wheelhouse.

By this time, Carter realized he wasn't going to get an order to shoot. He wiggled out of the gun's straps in a Houdini-like accomplishment, considering that earlier both Carlson and Sparky had to strap him in around his life jacket.

"Sorry you couldn't shoot," Carlson said.

"That's OK," Carter replied. "I'm kinda glad to sit down a bit." The short conversation drew Sparky's attention to Carlson.

"Are you pulling in that anchor yet?"

Carlson thought the answer was obvious, but he managed a simple no.

Carter wasn't the only one who was frustrated at not fighting back. Gudger, who had no traffic to direct off the ramp, picked up a Garand rifle from one of the wounded soldiers and walked aft. "Skipper, I can see Germans up on the bluff. I can get them with this rifle. Let me shoot."

"Hell, no," Irwin said. "You start shooting that thing and you'll just draw more fire down on us."

Wajda, who had been on deck with Gudger directing traffic, climbed into the gun tub with Carter, Sparky, and Carlson. "Hell, I'm not staying up there. I'm staying here." Just as he climbed in, a shell exploded nearby and shrapnel from it clinked against their helmets. Carlson thought that for the second time that morning, his face had been saved by someone else's helmet. The four of them, basically a third of the ship's crew, lay as flat on the deck as they could manage inside the gun tub that was only seven feet in diameter. They stared at each other wordlessly, their eyes round and bloodshot, their lips white and tense. Carter thought of those carefree days with the Boy Scouts on the bank of the Hiawassie River in Etowah. Another third of the crew—Irwin, Pillmore, Kleen, Jarvis, and Johnson—clustered in the scant cover behind the pilothouse.

Another shell exploded off the starboard quarter. Jarvis, who was standing next to Irwin, suddenly spun around and began to crumple onto the deck. Irwin caught him and lowered him. Jarvis's face was already covered in blood, and Irwin was sure that he was killed. But as soon as he and Johnson got Jarvis straightened out, he regained consciousness. A piece of shrapnel had caught him just below the eye and cut him as cleanly as a knife. Johnson took him below to bandage the wound. Soon the word spread around the little ship: Jarvis got it. No one knew how bad the wound was, and all wondered who would be next.

The LCTs of this wave, going in after the German defenses were fully active but before naval gunfire had begun to take effect, suffered the highest number of casualties among the LCT sailors. In the 614's group, only the 612 suffered disabling damage, although all the craft had taken hits of various calibers. Three LCTs had gone off to the Dog Green sector, immediately in front of the D-1 draw at Vierville (the beach sector where Company A of the 116th—the Bedford Boys—suffered so badly when they landed at H-Hour). Two of those three LCTs took severe hits. LCT 703 struck mines that knocked out her engines, and before other LCTs could pull her off, several shells struck her, setting her afire and swamping her. She lay off the beach burning for the rest of the morning. LCT 622 also took several hits and casualties, but she was able to remain in operation. The 622's skipper suffered shock as a result of the hits, and Leide later sent him back to England. The second officer, Ensign W. H. Nordstrom, took command. Like the 614's Ensign Pillmore, Nordstrom had been aboard less than two weeks.

By now, LCT 614 had been on the beach not the three minutes as expected but almost an hour. The mortar and small arms fire had not let up in the least, and the water around them was filled with landing craft and men. Irwin knew that the tide was coming in because he had been watching the progress of two men holding on to the wooden post of an obstacle. One man had his arms around the post, the other held onto the first, and all the while bullets splashed around them and splintered the wood. Between the bullets chewing up the post and the tide pushing them toward the top, they would soon run out of cover. All this time, Irwin was ordering the craft backward and forward, letting the tide wash them to the left and testing whether the tide had come in enough so they could get over the sandbar.

At that point help arrived in the guise of a destroyer that ran in just a few hundred yards offshore and began an old-fashioned shoot-out with the guns on the beach. With the destroyer drawing the fire of the guns, the smoke from the burning LCIs and LCTs to starboard masking the fire of the mortars and small arms, and the fact that no men or vehicles were leaving the 614, the fire directed at the ship slackened slightly. The men could do a bit more than simply press themselves against the deck.

The screams of the men in the water had become intolerable. Pequigney could hear them clearly through the open door, and through the slit windows in the wheelhouse he could see how crowded the water was off to starboard. With the ship maneuvering back and forth and edging its way to port, Pequigney knew its propellers had to be chopping up many men in the water.

What he could not see was that Kleen, who had a good vantage point from behind the wheelhouse and who had little to do since Irwin was handling most of the radio traffic, had also spotted many men in the water around them and had called out to Carlson, Carter, Sparky, and other men topside. They clambered out of the gun tubs and threw lines to the men to bring them alongside the ship. There, Gudger, Cromer, Andin, and others on deck pulled them aboard. Soon they had rescued quite a number of men, some wounded and others simply stranded when their craft sank out from under them. Two of the men were the crew of an LCVP from the transport *Charles Carroll*. When they were dragged aboard, Irwin could see they were absolutely blue from their exposure to the cold channel waters. These men were so grateful for being rescued that they started emptying their pockets and giving everything they had, including their .45s, to their rescuers.

As proud as Irwin was that his men were risking themselves to save others, he also knew that they were exacerbating a problem he was growing more worried about. They had been on the beach for well over an hour now and landed essentially nothing. He knew he was doing his best to work in so that he could get the rest of the jeeps and the infantrymen ashore safely, but he also knew that he was disobeying orders by risking his ship and by not forcing the men off. Now he had even more men aboard that he was not forcing off. As an officer, he knew he was to display initiative, but what did that mean? Was he to force the army men off the ship to keep up the pressure of the attack even for the few minutes it would take to get them killed? Or did it mean he was to think of the men's safety, so that when they landed they could do some good? Of course, the longer he kept the soldiers in safety meant the longer he kept his own men and his craft in danger. But officer or not, he knew he couldn't force the men off the ship into the face of that withering fire.

The situation had grown frustrating to everyone. They couldn't land their troops and vehicles, they couldn't shoot back, and now they had rescued everyone within a line's throw of the ship. There was nothing left to do but provide target practice for the German gunners. Finally Sparky yelled, "Skipper, let's get the hell out of here!" Others took up the shout, and now Irwin wondered if, on top of his other worries, he was going to have to quell a mutiny or join it for he was as ready to leave as they were.

Finally, Pequigney yelled out of the wheelhouse door, "Skipper, listen to this." Over the radio, Leide and Captain Wright were ordering all landing craft to stop beaching operations and to return to the transport area to await further orders.

Confusion and Reprieve

As early as 8:30 a.m., the few beachmasters who had been able to set up shop on Omaha had begun to request the control craft to stop dispatching landing craft to the beach. These requests had some effect, but not until about 9:00 a.m. did enough information reach Admiral Hall to convince him to back up the beachmasters' requests. At 9:25, Leide had ordered the ML to approach the beach so that he could see the situation firsthand. What he found was an absolute mess. He saw for the first time that the obstacles had not been cleared, completely wrecking the schedule of landings. LCTs belonging to both the O-1 and O-2 assault groups were inextricably mixed and milling well within range of the shore guns, looking for ways in and out of the obstacles and mines. He realized that he needed to regroup the craft at the line of departure and take things from there. He immediately started ordering craft to delay landing or to pull off the beach and return to the transport area for further orders. Other unit commanders were taking similar actions, and by 10:00 a.m. there was a general call to stop landing on Omaha and to withdraw the craft that were still trying to struggle through the obstacles. Leide stayed off the beaches until about 11:00 a.m., trying to round up his LCTs and establish some semblance of order.

When Irwin got the message from Leide to retract, he wasted no time. "Up ramp! Pull in the anchor! All astern full!" Carlson ran to engage the anchor winch, but suddenly the men on deck yelled at him and pointed aft. A large naval mine was floating right behind the ship, its horns pointing menacingly at them.

"Carlson, what's the matter?" Pillmore asked. "Is the winch bound up again?" Carlson merely pointed at the mine. After a few minutes, it floated away, and Carlson engaged the winch. Backing through the obstacles, even with—or perhaps because of—the help from the anchor, proved even more difficult than getting through them to the beach. They had drifted quite a bit to the east, and the anchor cable had pulled against several obstacles. Irwin had to keep a bit of way on to prevent the cable from pulling them into the obstacles.

He couldn't avoid all of them, however. Suddenly the ship jarred to a halt and a violent vibration shook them for a few moments. Some of the men on deck looked under the stern and saw they were hung up on a submerged steel hedgehog that had caught them on the port quarter. To make matters worse, word came up from the engine room that the port engine had started running free and had to be shut down. The vibration they felt had come from that engine revving up; apparently the obstacle had knocked off the port screw. Irwin ordered ahead full on the remaining screws, and by moving back toward the beach and to the right they worked off the obstacle and got clear of it. A quick check with Dowling down in the engine room assured Irwin that the obstacle had not holed them, so they began backing off again, this time more slowly and keeping a sharp lookout for underwater obstacles.

Getting the stern-mounted anchor up on a backing LCT was always a tricky business. Usually, the bracket housing kept the anchor well clear of the screws while dropping or raising it, but while under fire the temptation was to keep the ship moving as fast as possible. Moving astern, there was the chance of the anchor washing beneath the ship and fouling a screw or rudder. So as the angle on the cable steepened, indicating they were nearing the anchor, Irwin ordered all stop so that only the tug of the anchor winch kept them moving away from the beach. When the cable was up and down, instead of lifting the anchor off the bottom the winch began to strain heavily.

The anchor was stuck.

Ordering Carlson to shut down the winch, Irwin felt a sudden rush of panic. So close to getting off the beach, now they were again sitting ducks for the German gunners and far enough off the beach to make an inviting isolated target. There was no way to know what the anchor had snagged or what to do to free it. Cutting the cable would essentially disable the craft, since it needed the anchor to retract from the beach. Backing with the anchor down risked fouling a screw. Moving forward would likely only hook the anchor more firmly into whatever was holding it, but that seemed the safest option. Irwin ordered all ahead full and hoped for the best.

The craft began to move forward, and the cable angled aft, indicating the anchor was at least off the bottom. Still Carlson could reel it in only slowly because of the strain on the winch. Finally the anchor came in sight with a large portion of a blasted LCVP hooked onto it. Irwin ordered a sharp turn away from the beach, and the wreck broke clear of the anchor. They were safely under way again, after more than two hours.

They still had three jeeps aboard, a portion of the infantry, and a bedraggled group of rescued soldiers and sailors. Many of these men were weaponless, several were wounded, and almost all of them were dispirited by their experience and what they had seen on the beach. These men were not an effective fighting force. Because he still had a load, Irwin did not pull all the way back to the rendezvous in the transport area but anchored slightly seaward of the line of departure. Kleen hoisted the signal that they had wounded aboard, and soon a Coast Guard boat pulled alongside to take off the wounded. Irwin asked Jarvis if he wanted to go as well, but Jarvis said he'd like to stay aboard with his shipmates. If he went to a hospital ship, he wasn't sure he'd make it back to the 614.

From their anchorage some three miles out, they could see little of what was happening on the beach. The destroyers dueling with the shore batteries were now well inshore of them, and the battleships *Arkansas* and *Texas* had also moved in to just three thousand yards off the beach to blast defenses in the draws. So much smoke and haze drifted over the beach that they could not see anything happening there, but they were all sure that they were waiting for orders not to land what they had aboard but to go in to take men off. From what they had seen and from the small bits of information they were hearing on the radio, the invasion on Omaha was a bust. They would have to pull off and take the army over to Gold or Utah.

The crew took the opportunity to go below to get what lunch they could. A few were somehow able to grab a short nap, but most of them brought K rations up on deck. They sat with Pillmore, watching the progress of a DUKW amphibious truck that had been swept well to the east by the tide and was now struggling against the current to get to its assigned landing area. Several guns and mortars were shooting at the little craft, and splashes from near misses often hid it completely from view. But it always reappeared and finally found a place to land.

During this time, Captain Wright and Lieutenant Commander Leide were working inshore, trying to find places to get their craft ashore. At about 11:00 a.m., Wright joined Leide off the O-2 beaches aboard LCH 86—an LCI(L) converted into a headquarters ship—to determine the situation. Conditions had not greatly improved from what Leide had found at 9:25 a.m. Some eight LCTs were sunk or stranded on the beach, and LCIs 91 and 92 continued to burn. He saw no vehicles operating on the beach itself, and LCTs offshore milled around between the line of departure and as close as a thousand yards off the beach. The O-1 beaches seemed a bit clearer, so Wright sent LCIs and other troop-carrying craft east and kept the LCTs off O-2.

It was also about this time, 1:30 p.m., that Leide returned to the beach. He considered that the LCT situation was even worse than before. In addition to the still mixed craft from O-1 and O-2, the craft from Assault Group O-3 had been sent in early. Now, unloaded craft mingled with those yet to land, and damaged craft lay unattended among units that did not have a scratch. He directed the ML to sail among these craft so he could sort through them, sending unloaded craft out to the rendezvous area and seeing to the craft that were damaged or had wounded men aboard. After two hours of such work, he returned to the transport area to get permission from Captain Bailey, the assault group commander on the *Carroll*, to reform his LCTs on the line of departure. Bailey refused him permission, telling Leide that the beach was clear now. Leide immediately returned to the beach and found the situation had not greatly improved at all.

A Second Landing

Throughout the afternoon, Leide dispatched LCTs one at a time to the beach, but as soon as these individual craft neared the shore they came under heavy mortar and machine-gun fire. A few of these LCTs had to retract and move to a safer area. Hardly any of the vehicles from these craft got ashore in one piece. However, the reconnaissance provided by these LCTs identified the spots on the beach that were still under direct fire or were relatively safe. By this time, exit D-1 behind the deadly Dog Green sector had been cleared by point-blank fire from the *Texas* and occupied by the Twenty-ninth Division, clearing the big guns covering the western end of Omaha. Also, smoke from the still-burning LCT 703 and LCIs 91 and 92 provided cover for Dog Red and Easy Green.

Leide had determined that almost 60 percent of the LCTs, including the 614, had not yet landed their loads but that many of the craft with vehicles and personnel—even some loaded with ammunition and explosives—were still operating under fire just outside the line of obstacles. Leide was never again able to organize a regular wave of LCTs. The closest he got was sending in twelve craft between 4:30 p.m.

and 6:00 p.m. Most of these LCTs went to the now relatively quiet Dog Green, and all but one retracted safely. By 6:00 p.m., 60 percent of the LCTs had been unloaded.

Apparently, LCT 614 was among those twelve craft sent in during the late afternoon. Returning to Dog Red Beach, the men thought this time the fire had slackened a bit. Irwin knew to aim for a point farther east, but again he had trouble working the 614 in close to the beach. As soon as the craft began winding through the obstacles it again came under fire from small arms, machine guns, and mortars. As soon as Cromer dropped the ramp, a machine gun hidden in the bluffs just beyond the ruined houses of Les Moulins opened up, causing the men to dive for cover and flatten out on the deck. Several men among the troops suffered wounds. Fortunately, the gun soon shifted targets or was taken under fire by troops now operating on the beach, providing some reprieve. Irwin took the opportunity to order off the army personnel. Some of these men were from the 614's original load who had been aboard since Portland, and others were unarmed but unwounded survivors that the 614's crew had pulled from the water earlier that morning. All had to go ashore, as far as Irwin could decide, so that the survivors had at least some chance of getting back to their units.

Irwin was paying attention to what was going on in front of him, but suddenly he noticed a man slicing through the water. With one hand, the soldier held onto a pipe that was sticking up like the periscope of a submarine, and he held his other hand under the water. Irwin watched as the man edged past them and finally pulled up on the beach with his jeep materializing out of the water under him. Irwin glanced aft and saw that an LCT with fully waterproofed vehicles had disembarked its load directly behind them. With the success of that jeep to assure him that he was close enough to the beach, Irwin sent off one of his three remaining jeeps. As it neared the shore, it suddenly dropped from sight into a shell hole and drowned out. The next driver tried to move well around the first to avoid the hole, but he ended up swamping as well.

The last driver, a sergeant, turned off his engine and walked back to the pilothouse. "Sir, if you want I'll walk to the beach, but there's no sense in losing my jeep as well. I'd just as soon you'd keep it aboard until you can get it on dry land." Irwin didn't see how one sergeant and one jeep could jeopardize the war effort, especially since the jeep was likely to drown out anyway. "You can stay aboard if you want, but we won't be back here. We're headed to the British beaches tomorrow." The sergeant decided to stay.

So at the end of D-Day, the 614 had not been able to get a single one of its vehicles ashore. Except for the several wounded men on board and the one jeep driver, all the infantry finally made it off the ship, but the sailors doubted many of them made it much beyond the beach. The crew had done all they could that day.

Interrupted Rest

When they returned to the line of departure, a control craft came alongside to see whether they had wounded aboard and pointed them to a British LST that had a medical unit. Now, with the freedom to stay a few minutes, Jarvis went aboard to get his eye stitched up. Also, Pequigney's scraped leg had become quite painful and had begun bleeding from all the standing he had been doing that day, so he went aboard with Jarvis to get it bandaged up properly.

Once his two crewmen returned aboard, Irwin realized he had no direct orders about what to do next. He knew the general instructions were for the flotilla to head for Gold Beach the next day, but he was unsure if the LCTs were to sail independently or wait to form up as a group. With evening coming on and his crew exhausted, the only real choice was to anchor for the night and head east in the morning.

Most of the other LCTs had anchored in the rendezvous area near the transports. Irwin could also see that none of the escort ships were anchoring with them. Irwin didn't know it at the time, but the destroyers and frigates had moved to sea to protect the anchorage from attack by German small craft deploying from Cherbourg. All he knew was that the LCTs' position between the transports and the beach seemed an exposed, dangerous place to be, so he decided to look for an anchorage with some security.

Three miles offshore, the battleship *Arkansas* lay at anchor. The oldest, smallest, and weakest of the battleships then in the U.S. Navy, she nonetheless looked massive and mighty to Irwin. He sailed over and anchored as close as he could to the *Arkansas*'s 12-inch guns and bristling antiaircraft batteries, allowing for both ships swinging at anchor. Thus tucked in safely for the night, he stationed one man on watch and sent the rest of the crew to bed. D-Day was over, or so he thought.

During the late afternoon, Leide had been trying to marshal his LCTs in the rendezvous area. At that time, Leide found himself near the USS *Ancon*, so he contacted Admiral Hall to ask permission to sail his craft, as scheduled, to the Gold area. Admiral Hall himself spoke to Leide through a megaphone, telling him to carry out his orders but to leave one group of LCTs behind to replace the craft lost during the day. Just as Leide began carrying out those orders, he was told to release the ML 153 so it could take its nighttime station in the escort screen. Leide and his three group commanders had to board LCT 571, and with speed, maneuverability, and communications thus lost he had no end of trouble dispatching his craft toward Gold. Nevertheless, by 7:00 p.m. Leide had contacted several of the LCTs anchored in the rendezvous area and had gotten them started toward Gold. Getting in touch with the senior officers off Gold Beach to tell them the LCTs were on their way proved even more difficult with the minimal communication equipment of the LCT. Finally, about 11:00 p.m., he flagged down a Coast Guard vessel and used its better communication gear to contact the Assault Force G commander and arrange for his LCTs to begin unloading operations the next day.

LCT 614, anchored out with the warships, missed that evening's sortie toward the Gold area, and by the time Leide had contacted the commander of Assault Force G, the crew of the LCT had set the anchor watch and settled in for the evening. The respite didn't last very long. About 11:30 p.m., just after dusk at that latitude, four Junkers Ju 88 bombers attacked the anchorage. Two of these planes targeted the *Arkansas*, silhouetted by fires on the beach. The ships had no time to open fire before the lead plane dropped its five hundred-pound bomb, which landed just thirty-five yards off the battleship's starboard beam. The blast caused only superficial shock damage on the battleship, but the bomb's effects on the little LCT were almost comic. The underwater shock wave hit the LCT as though it were a giant hammer whacking the ship. The little craft shook so violently that Carlson, asleep in one of the top racks, fell to the steel deck on his butt. The men ran topside, and Irwin lost no time ordering them to start the engines and pull up the anchor.

The anchorage was alight with tracer fire. Five minutes or so into the attack, one of the planes dropped in flames a hundred yards to port of the *Arkansas*. All this shooting was too much for Carter, who had been forced to restrain himself all day. As the next couple of planes came in, he pointed his 20mm in the direction everyone else was shooting and fired off several bursts. A few minutes later, two more planes crashed within a mile of the *Arkansas*. Carter doubted he had contributed, but at least he felt better. Irwin ordered Pequigney to steer for the rendezvous area, where many of the other LCTs lay at anchor unbothered by the aircraft. He had finally realized that the LCT's best protection was the fact that it was practically invisible, a worthless target to the pilots who wanted the honor of hitting a battleship or transport.

He also learned that they were not out of the war just yet.

7

FRENZY AND STORM

Something of the violence of the Normandy invasion, and of the direct role of the LCTs in Operation Neptune, can be seen in the raw numbers of craft lost. During World War II, the navy lost seventy-one LCTs in combat, storms, and accidents. Of that number, twenty-five craft—more than a third—went down during Operation Neptune (at least fifteen of these were on D-Day itself and the others over the next few weeks). Of those twenty-five craft, fourteen belonged to Lieutenant Commander Leide's O-2 LCTs, seven belonged to Assault Force U, and four to O-1.

To put those numbers in perspective, LCTs in the Pacific theater suffered twenty-three craft lost, and operations in the Mediterranean cost the navy some nineteen LCTs. Most of those forty-two craft, as well as four others lost in the Atlantic, fell victim to weather. In terms of crucial combat duties during the assault phase of an operation and in terms of subsequent combat losses, the invasion of northern France was certainly the LCTs' climactic moment. But even more would be demanded of these little craft off the Normandy beaches in the weeks and months ahead.

For the crew of the 614, the longest day was followed by the shortest night. By the time they anchored in the transport area, it was well after midnight. About 5 a.m. on June 7, the watch started getting the exhausted, and by now grumpy, crew up and to their underway stations. Already, several LCTs were chugging independently eastward to the British beaches, and the big warships were heading shoreward from their nighttime stations at sea to take up their gunfire support stations. The men were much less tense than the day before, but from their position a couple of miles offshore, they could see sporadic explosions on the beach. The sound of the explosions took several moments to reach them, and the disconnect between the sight of an explosion and its noise added to the surreal scene. But they knew that the battle had not yet passed safely inland. Under the explosions, the men and vehicles on the beach were busy organizing for the push inland or clearing away the horrible clutter left by the violence of the invasion.

Early on June 7, Leide sent two of his group commanders, Lt. M. E. Wierenga and Lt. A. Macaulay, to another LCT to take charge of the craft heading to Gold Beach while he and the other group commander, Lt. D. A. de la Houssaye, remained on LCT 571 to round up individual craft from off Omaha. That task took all day, since the LCTs were scattered throughout the anchorage—some as much as eight miles from the transport area. Around noon, he went in to the beach to determine how many LCTs had been lost, but the situation was still so confused that he could gather no accurate information. The best he could do was gather as many stranded and wounded LCT sailors as he could. At 12:35 p.m., he sailed up to LCH 86—flagship of Captain Wright, who was now in command of Assault Group O-2—to request permission to take his gathered craft onto Gold Beach.

Wright, concerned about the heavier-than-expected losses among the LCTs, hesitated to release Leide and his group. Instead, he ordered Leide to take the survivors to the nearest LST and then stand by for further instructions. By 3:20, Leide was growing impatient, and so he went over Wright's head and contacted Rear Admiral Hall directly. Hall told him to proceed with his assigned duties. Leide requested that the message be forwarded to Wright and headed off to Gold Beach, finally making contact with the commander of Assault Force G at 6:15 p.m. He found that thirty-four of his LCTs had already reported and had settled in to their task of unloading the transports. Another three LCTs had reached Gold Beach under tow or under their own power, but they were too damaged to begin operations without some repair work.

Once in the British area, Leide and the group commanders set up their headquarters aboard LCI(L) 507. This craft had not been modified as an LCH, so Leide and the other Flotilla Twelve staff assisting him had to use standard LCI communication gear, which was minimal but admittedly superior to that carried by LCTs, to direct the American LCTs as best they could. Using the radio call sign "Mary," the flotilla command soon had some semblance of control over its wayward and scattered flock.

Soon the radio airwaves were filled with navy gibberish. Bigger navy ships have four-letter call signs, such as NGMV, that they use instead of their names. In Morse code or semaphore or other forms of signaling, this tends to speed things up, but over voice radio it must be spoken using the phonetic alphabet: November Golf Mike Victor. The numerous small craft operating off the assault beaches had no such call signs or even names, so they were simply referred to by type and number. A radio call to LCT 614 would be spoken as "Charlie Tare Six One Four." The merchant ships were referred to as personnel ships ("Prep Sugar," in the navy's phonetic alphabet of the time) or mechanized transports ("Mike Tare"), and their names had been replaced with numbers. So a voice transmission would sound similar to the following: "Mary to Charlie Tare Six One Four. Proceed Mike Tare Five Three Zero, bearing Zero One Eight. Mary out." There was little need for coded transmissions.

Although he still referred to himself officially as "Commander, Flotilla Twelve," Leide had really assumed a more senior command over all American LCTs operating with Assault Force G, including LCTs from Flotilla Twelve and Flotilla Twenty-six. Lt. A. Macaulay, who commanded LCT Flotilla Twenty-six, became in effect Leide's executive officer. At this time, Lieutenant Rockwell also returned to Flotilla Twelve from his detached service with the DD tanks and resumed his duties as the commander of Group Thirty-five, but because of Leide's expanded duties, Rockwell became the de facto commander of Flotilla Twelve. Other Flotilla Twelve group commanders included Lt. j.g. M. E. Wierenga of Group Thirty-four and Lieutenant de la Houssaye of Group Thirty-six. Flotilla Twenty-six group commanders were Lt. F. C. Wilson of Group Seventy-six, Lt. J. Hintermister of Group Seventy-seven, and Lt. B. J. Burch of Group Seventy-eight. Lt. Cmdr. L. B. Pruitt, in charge of LCT Flotilla Nineteen off Omaha, had been given command of all American LCTs operating on the far shore, dubbed Task Group 123.3, but he might as well have been on the moon as far as Leide was concerned. The American LCTs operating with the British had become an essentially autonomous command. That Leide was able to carry out his task under such conditions speaks volumes about him as a leader and an officer.

At full strength, some seventy American LCTs were assigned to the two flotillas off the British beaches—thirty-four to Flotilla Twelve and thirty-six to Flotilla Twenty-six. That meant Leide, Macaulay, and the six group commanders had to shepherd some 140 ensigns and lieutenant j.g.s (though not all LCTs had their complement of two officers) and some 840 enlisted men. In short, Leide had a very large command for a lieutenant commander. In the "blue water" navy of World War II, a lieutenant commander generally skippered nothing larger than a fleet submarine or destroyer escort, which had crews of only two hundred or so officers and men; a crew of almost a thousand officers and men could easily have taken a heavy cruiser into battle. That such a large command was given to a lieutenant commander gives some indication of the navy's attitude toward the little Charlie Tares.

Settling into Business

Once under way toward Gold Beach early on June 7, Irwin and Pillmore had the men clear away some of the battle damage and litter from the day before and then eat as good a breakfast as they could. They knew that as soon as they got to Gold that they would be busy immediately. In only a few minutes, the men had cleared off the little ship and set normal underway watches. The rest of the men filed into the little galley. The talk quickly shifted from speculation about what awaited them on Gold Beach to a more immediate question: "Where the hell's breakfast?" That was quickly replaced with, "Where the hell's the cook?" One of the men stepped forward to the crew's compartment and found the cook snuggled asleep in his rack. "What are you doing here? C'mon, let's get breakfast going!"

The cook rolled over. "Go to hell. I've been up ever since that plane came over last night."

The crewman shook the cook roughly. "To hell with that. You got duty just like the rest of us, so go cook." But by the time the cook got up and dragged himself into the galley, Gudger and Cromer already had breakfast going.

"It's a good thing I grew up in a big family," Cromer said. "I'm used to fending for myself. But if we had to depend on you, we'd never get anything." Cromer's words, meant to shame the cook into action, had the opposite effect.

"Well, if you guys have everything under control, I'm going back to the sack. I've been up ever since those planes came over last night. I didn't want to be caught in the sack again if they came back."

Despite the cook, the crew finally got their breakfast and were soon up on deck, smoking and looking at the Normandy coast slipping by to starboard. That was their last respite for quite some time. About 7:00 a.m., just as they began to see the ships off Gold Beach, they could hear firing from up ahead. The men gathered near the gun tubs for a better view. Andin, one of the shortest men on the crew, stood on the anchor winch. "Are they starting another assault?" he asked.

Carter shook his head. "No, look. See the bursts up in the air? That's flak. They're having an air raid." As most of the men scanned the sky for German planes, Kleen kept his eye on the ships, looking for messages.

"Oh, jeez, look," Kleen said. "That ship's been hit." Heavy black smoke was rising from one of the larger ships.

Sparky couldn't resist the temptation. He went down to the tank deck, flung open the door to the crew compartment, and yelled, "Air raid! Air raid!" Soon, the cook came running on deck, fumbling with his helmet and life jacket. When the men up on the gun tubs began laughing, the cook gestured obscenely at them and went back inside. None of the men bothered to tell him there really was an air raid.

Irwin was on the verge of sending the men back to general quarters when the firing from the fleet dribbled to a halt. As they approached the British fleet, they realized the large ship that had been hit was HMS *Bulolo*, the Gold force flagship. As the smoke rising from *Bulolo* turned white and thinned, indicating her crew had quickly gotten the fire under control, Irwin warned the men to keep a watch in case the planes turned back and then set a course for *Bulolo*. As they approached, the British flagship's signal lights began flashing. Kleen watched a few moments and then told Irwin that *Bulolo* was directing them to their first customer.

Irwin told Pequigney to shift course, and then he, Pillmore, and Kleen began scanning the hundreds of merchant ships anchored off the beach to find the one with a specific number painted on a small canvas square hanging off the bridge wing. Once they spotted it, Irwin conned the ship toward it while Pillmore got the crew ready for going alongside. Both Irwin and Pillmore were a bit nervous about this first loading from a ship at sea. In fact, their training at Solomons Island had stressed hitting and retracting from a beach, not this kind of intricate seamanship. They took every precaution in the book.

Just as in hitting the beach under fire, getting an LCT alongside a freighter and tying up involved an all-hands evolution. In addition to the regular engine room and navigation crews, three two-man crews handled the three rope fenders that were to prevent the ships' hulls from grating together. One of those crews took up station well forward, another right aft, and the third roamed about amidships to place the fender wherever the need arose. Four other men made up two two-man line-handling teams. One man had a heaving line—a light line with a weighted "monkey's fist" knotted at one end—that he would throw to the men on the freighter's deck. Once that line was across, they tied it to one of the larger mooring lines, which the freighter crew pulled up and wrapped around a bit.

Once the LCT was secured alongside, the freighter crew began lowering trucks and other vehicles loaded with supplies. With the fighting still close to shore, there was no time for loading bulk deck-loads of cargo; the food and ammunition had to be ready to head for the front as soon as it hit the beach. As the crew positioned the last vehicle on deck, the freighter sailors lowered a cargo net over the side, and the drivers for the lorries climbed down to the LCT. An officer called down from the deck of the freighter: "You are to take this load to Jig Green Beach, heading One Six Eight. Report to the beachmaster that this is load Four Seven." With that, the merchant seamen began unceremoniously dropping the 614's mooring lines onto her deck.

Heading to the beach, some of the 614's crew thought they were taking part in another first-day assault. British battleships, cruisers, destroyers, and even an ungainly looking monitor fired over their heads at targets ashore, while the sea offshore was crowded with landing craft of all sizes, from the tiny DUKWs to LSTs. A few artillery rounds exploded on the beach itself, but the explosions were much more sporadic than the day before and did not seem aimed at any particular target. The indirect nature of the German fire was both reassuring and worrisome. It showed the Germans no longer had a direct view of the beach, but it also meant that a shell, like lightning, could just as randomly strike them as any of the other craft.

When the LCT had approached the beach, Kleen signaled its load number to the beachmaster, who directed the crew to their landing spot. It was a textbook landing. The anchor splashed down on command, the ship slid right up onto the beach, the ramp splashed down, and the vehicles rumbled off, one after the other. Finally, the sergeant who had spent the night with them waved and drove off. Watching him go, Irwin said to Pillmore, "I wonder how the hell he's going to meet up with his outfit."

As soon as the sergeant and his jeep had rolled onto the beach, the beachmaster, a Royal Navy lieutenant commander, waded to the front of the ramp and called out through a megaphone which Mike Tare they were to load from next and its heading from the beach. Carlson began reeling in the anchor cable, and the 614 headed off for its second load on D+1.

The cycle repeated throughout the day: load, beach, unload, retract, and load. The crew got relief only briefly during their transits to or from the beach or as they paused at a service barge for fuel and lubricants. The crew grabbed lunch and dinner as they could, with some doing short-order cooking and others opening up boxes of army C and K rations. As the long Normandy day wore on, the 614 made as many as half a dozen landings. Sunset did not come until almost eleven o'clock, and as they unloaded in the dusk the crew were all looking forward to anchoring for the night. But as the last lorry in that load drove off the ramp, the beachmaster directed them not to their anchorage but to another Mike Tare.

Irwin protested that his crew had been at this all day and were exhausted and needed some rest. The beachmaster apologized but explained patiently that there was a war on, that his orders were to send the next available LCT to this ship, and that the 614 was the next available LCT. At this time, Leide wasn't fully set up aboard LCI 507, so Irwin had no higher authority to appeal to. Reluctantly, he had Carlson start winching in the anchor and gave Pequigney the heading for the next freighter.

As it turned out, that freighter was not the last assignment for the night. By the time they had loaded from it, returned to the beach, gotten yet another load assignment, and steamed back to the anchorage, the night had grown very dark. Cromer, on lookout forward, called out that they were approaching a ship, but Irwin had no idea if it was the right ship or, indeed, whether it made a difference if they took a load from any of the ships out there. He dared show no light at all, even a flashlight. He had Kleen hail the ship to identify it, and they played a tense game of blind man's bluff while looking for the ship they were assigned.

Sporadically through the night, German planes appeared overhead in twos and threes. It was a most eerie combat, with bombs exploding sometimes closely, tracer fire arching up from the Mike Tares and warships, and little LCT 614 threading among the totally blacked-out ships, which resembled a fleet of Flying Dutchmen come home at last. Over the radio, they could hear occasional alerts as patrolling British warships spotted German torpedo boats probing the fringes of the invading fleet. And two or three times during the night, a massive explosion marked some poor ship detonating a mine.

That first night, Irwin's nerves were stretched taut. The little bit of training he'd had in ship handling in the dark was long ago and far away in the sheltered waters of the Chesapeake Bay with his instructors by his side or within radio call. Here, he had complete responsibility for a craft that he'd had under way scarcely more than five days total, and he had to take her through unfamiliar, mined, crowded, and unlit waterways while German planes dropped bombs at random among the ships in the anchorage and E-boats prowled around over the horizon, looking for any gap in the defenses. He wasn't exactly in the same position as Sir John Jellicoe, the commander in chief of the British Grand Fleet during the First World War who felt he was the only person on either side who could win or lose the war in an afternoon, but Irwin knew he faced an infinite number of ways to die or screw up royally. The latter, a very real and immediate possibility, worried him most.

His ship-handling capabilities were further hampered during the night by having four men, almost a quarter of his crew, manning the 20mms. During the day, these men assisted with line throwing or handling fenders, but on this first night, when Irwin needed them as fender handlers or as extra lookouts, Carter and Sparky stood at the port gun and Johnson and Jarvis at the starboard one, waiting for a plane to come by close enough for them to shoot. Their duties reduced the number of men available for line handling or relieving the men at underway stations, but with the number of air raids through the night and the fact that the LCT had to keep company with the supply ships that were attracting the planes' attention, Irwin felt he needed to keep them where they were.

The warships, even the smallest patrol craft and mine craft, had several ways to detect, track, and target attacking aircraft. If the ships were well offshore, or the planes came in at altitude, the ships' radars would pick up the aircraft well before they reached firing range. The ships inshore found that the coastal bluffs interfered with their radars until the planes appeared over the anchorage, but even then their radars could track planes that were a few miles off. They even had a number of lookouts with low-power night binoculars that could watch planes closer in. In contrast, the only fire control equipment on the LCT were the young eyes of the two gunners and the two loaders. That may have been enough had they been able to tell where the other ships were shooting, but on that first night, when one ship opened up, all the other ships opened up as well, shooting in all different directions.

Carter soon realized he was not going to get a chance to show off his excellent marksmanship, but he wasn't going to let an opportunity to shoot get past him. He ordered Sparky to change magazines and to put in the one that was loaded with all tracers. He didn't have long to wait. As soon as the nearby ships began firing, Carter pointed the 20mm up to the sky and emptied the magazine in one long burst. A 20mm is loud enough to be heard anywhere topside, even above battle noise. Irwin, already keyed up, failed to appreciate the beauty of Carter's impromptu fireworks. The upshot of the chewing out Carter got was that he would henceforth shoot his gun only under orders or in the direst emergency.

Learning Seamanship

In the days and nights following the invasion, the 614's crew honed their seamanship skills. The continuous trips from beach to anchorage and back gave them plenty of practice in ship handling and navigation. In just a day or so, the crew had little trouble getting alongside a Mike Tare and tying up. The trips to the beach became streamlined as they realized they did not need to drop the stern anchor with each landing. The increased efficiency also allowed the men to get some rest during the cycle of loading, beaching, and returning for another load.

The improved seamanship skills were especially important in the incredibly busy waters off Gold Beach. In fact, two major naval operations were being conducted in the same time and place. Operation Neptune continued with the dozens of LCTs and rhino ferries and other beaching craft plying the waters and getting men and matériel ashore, and with the warships providing gunfire support. The second activity, code-named "Operation Mulberry," began on June 7 with the arrival of materials to construct the artificial ports off Gold and Omaha Beaches.

The plan for the Mulberry harbors consisted of three main sections. An outer breakwater was fashioned from a string of floating concrete structures called "bombardons," and just inside this was a line of old freighters and obsolete or damaged warships, code-named "Gooseberries," which were towed into position and sunk. Within the breakwater was a more elaborate system of concrete caissons called "Phoenixes," which were constructed in England and towed across the channel and sunk into position. Finally, within the Phoenixes were the pontoon causeways called "Whales," which led to the beach from floating pier heads called Lobnitz units. Designed to rise and fall with the tides they allowed LSTs to unload over them despite the set of the tide.

Construction of the Mulberry harbors (the one off Omaha was Mulberry A, and the one off Gold was Mulberry B) was scheduled to take only two weeks, during which time the only way to get men and equipment ashore was directly over the beaches and involved primarily LCTs. So in the days and weeks following the assault, the press of shipping off the invasion beaches, and Omaha and Gold, in particular, was astounding. Battleships, cruisers, and destroyers maintained gunfire support stations as close to shore as possible to reach far inland. Destroyers, frigates, and corvettes maintained guard against German submarines and surface craft. Minesweepers patrolled the anchorages and waterways for moored mines and mines dropped nightly by German bombers. Tugs plodded along, towing Gooseberry hulks, Phoenix caissons, and Whale sections. Merchant ships arrived continuously, bringing fresh divisions and their supplies.

The task of the assault group commanders was to clear the area of shipping as quickly as they could. However, the loss among LCTs and smaller craft had been heavier than expected, making each one of the craft that remained especially valuable. Some of the larger British LCTs had been designated to join the LSTs in the shuttle service between France and England, bringing supplies in and casualties out. In view of the losses suffered by LCTs, though, these craft were reassigned to the assault group commanders. Likewise, the large LSTs were earmarked for rapid turnaround and were not supposed to begin beaching until well into the week following D-Day. However, on the morning of the seventh, no fewer than a hundred LSTs sat off the British beaches, and all available LCTs had been assigned to unload the MTs. Rear Adm. sir Philip Vian, in overall command of the three British beaches, had no choice but to order the LSTs to dry out. Consequently, at high tide the LSTs began beaching so that, once the receding tide left them clear of the water like so many toy boats in a drained bathtub, the equipment and supplies aboard them could be unloaded. The process worked so well that Rear Admiral Kirk, in command of the two American beaches, followed suit. Soon, even small coasters were ordered to beach themselves for unloading.

Through this choked waterway chugged the 614 and her sister LCTs, shuttling men and vehicles and cargo from ship to shore, trying their best not to hit anything or get rammed. Operations under these conditions at night, under total blackout, were indeed tense. Irwin, who despite his baptism by fire was still a wet-behind-the-ears skipper of a mostly landlubber crew, had one of only two possible fates in store for him and his men: either they would become adept at ship handling very quickly and contribute to the war effort, or they would disable the craft in a collision and his career would end with a court-martial.

The First Casualty

The lack of seamanship skills soon led to the 614's first serious casualty. Sometime within that first week after the invasion, the LCT lay with its port side tied up to a merchant ship. Both crews had stopped for dinner, leaving no one on deck. With a fairly heavy sea running, Pillmore began to worry about their small fenders not offering enough protection, so he went topside to check. Indeed, he saw that the fenders kept the ships' hulls from grinding together, but when the ships went into a trough they would roll into one another, and the LCT's anchor winch would bang into the merchant ship's hull. Pillmore saw John Dowling, one of the motor macs, also on deck and called him over to help adjust the fenders. Dowling leaned between the bigger ship's hull and the anchor winch to adjust a fender just as a wave pushed the two ships together again. Dowling was trapped for several seconds, and as soon as the ships rolled apart he fell to the deck.

Pillmore pulled him away, hoping that Dowling just had the wind knocked out of him, but it soon became apparent that he was more seriously injured than that. He was conscious, but he couldn't speak for some moments afterward and continued having trouble breathing and couldn't move. Then he started complaining of tingling and seeing double. Pillmore had Kleen signal for a launch to take Dowling to a hospital ship. In an area choked with shipping, the launch took an agonizingly long time to reach the LCT.

A day or so later, the LCT got a message to send Dowling's belongings to the hospital ship; he was being sent back to England. Some time after that, the crew got word that Dowling was being sent back to the States, but they never learned what happened to him. The 614 had gone through the fighting at Omaha Beach and the sporadic shelling and air raids off Gold, only to lose its first crewman not to enemy action but from poor seamanship.

(It turns out that Dowling's return to the States was only indirectly related to his injury aboard the 614. He was being treated at a hospital in London and was almost ready to be released for duty when he got caught in a buzz bomb attack. He was uninjured by the blast, but the experience so soon after the horrors of Omaha Beach rattled him and he began showing signs of combat fatigue: dizziness, sharp headaches, and again seeing double. He was sent back to the United States for neurologic treatment for what we now know as post-traumatic stress disorder.)

After Dowling's accident, a more cautious crew took its seamanship more seriously. The frequent landings made beaching operations routine. This had become easier once the British beachmaster units surveyed the beaching areas and marked the underwater wrecks and sandbars and deepest shell holes, and engineers bulldozed the obstacles off within the first couple of days. Soon Gold Beach was as easy to land onto and retract from as had been the concrete hard in Portland. The

The only surviving portrait of LCT 614 by Luther Carter. The image apparently portrays the ship headed to France, given the rough water, the other ships in company, the uncovered guns, and the mast still in place. But note too the rusty hull, an understandably lasting impression that Carter would have had of the ship. *Author's collection*

This is perhaps the only official U.S. Navy photograph (80-G-272378) of the LCT 614. It was made from an antisubmarine patrol blimp from squadron ZP-22 in February 1944 as the LST 291 rounded Florida on the way to New York and then England. The photo (apparently the original is out of focus) clearly shows the relative sizes of the LST, LCT, and LCVP. Note the crated equipment on the LCT's deck and an access plate opened on the port bow locker, just forward of the open door, apparently to allow work on or installation of the ramp engine. Both the LST 291 and the LCT 614 have the small black numbers of uncommissioned warships. *Author's collection*

Luther Carter posing at his battle station, the portside 20mm gun. The man and weapon seem an easy fit here, but in combat Carter would be wearing a life jacket, a helmet, and a gas mask bag around his waist, and he would be strapped into the shoulder harness to allow him to aim at higher angles. Note the open ready-ammunition locker at right, the canvas bag to catch empty cartridge cases, and the counter-recoil spring (probably the replacement for the one he lost overboard) and housing over the middle part of the barrel. *Author's collection*

Roy Carlson at the controls of the anchor winch, his battle station on D-Day and his normal beaching station. He is facing aft, with the port 20mm gun just visible behind him. The photo only hints at how exposed he would have been in an assault landing, which is why he spent most of his time during D-Day morning with Carter in the gun tub. *Author's collection*

At twenty-two, Ens. Don Irwin, skipper of the LCT 614, was the oldest man on the ship. The unbuttoned jacket pocket and the hands in the pockets are distinctly nonregulation. *Author's collection*

Ens. George Pillmore, here about twenty years old, served as the second officer of the LCT 614. Note his sleeves are slightly rolled up, indicating he has probably been working alongside the men. Trained as an engineer, Pillmore was instrumental in keeping the LCT 614's equipment operational during its long months operating on the Normandy beachhead. *Author's collection*

Frank Pequigney, the LCT 614's quartermaster, standing in front of the door to the main crews quarters. (Note the high step in; the designers seemed to anticipate a certain amount of water sloshing along the deck.) Directly above him is the ready-ammunition locker for the port 20mm, and the ladder to the gun tub is angled to avoid its being blocked by vehicles crowding the deck. *Author's collection*

Roy Carlson and Francis Kelly served as two of the principal engineers of the LCT 614. They were also two of the oldest guys on the ship, apart from Ensign Irwin. Kelly was essentially the ship's chief engineer, the senior motor machinist's mate. They are facing forward, with the anchor winch housing visible above Kelly's shoulders. *Author's collection*

Woodrow Johnson served as the ship's medic and manned the starboard 20mm at battle stations. He's facing forward, with the crew's quarters to his left, the galley behind that, and the ship's head behind him on the starboard side. Beside his right foot is a void access plug, and behind that is a recessed padeye, which the crew used as makeshift stoves when the galley range conked out while they were in Normandy.
Author's collection

A rather faded photo shows Fred Kleen (with pipe), Frank Pequigney, and Chester Wajda in their worn work uniforms. Kleen transferred to the LCT 614 when the ship's original signalman became sick in Halifax, Nova Scotia. Wajda was a seaman second class whose battle station was supposed to be near the ramp. Note the variety in headgear and work jackets; Pequigney seems to be wearing combat boots.
Author's collection

The causeway in the background and the battered appearance of the bulwark behind the men indicate this picture was made in England, probably late November 1944. Standing from left: Taylor (?), Jarvis, Carlson, and Andin. Squatting: Kelly, Wajda, Stefanowicz, Johnson, Carter, and Kleen. Note the mix of right-arm and left-arm rating badges—deck ratings such as gunner's mate and signalman were considered senior to engineering ratings. *Author's collection*

The men are standing right aft, with the catwalk and open door to the wheel house visible at upper left. From left: Singheim, Pequigney, Jarvis, Kelly, Wajda, Stefanowicz, and Carter (note knife). *Author's collection*

This picture poses an absolute mystery. Carter wrote on the back that this is the crew of the LCT 590 and that all of the men except those arrowed (identified as Hugh Alsworth, Minn.; James Holland, Penn.; and the skipper) were killed on D-Day. The LCT 590 took DD tanks onto the beach on D-Day and was badly hit, suffering three men killed and two wounded, but the names don't match. The picture was obviously made in England just before the invasion: notice the camouflage netting on the LCTs in the background, the boxes of C rations stacked on the deck beside the men, and the ubiquitous airing laundry. The photo also shows to good effect the narrow slits that substitute for windows in the wheel house. The ship in the background is an attack transport, perhaps the USS *Thomas Jefferson* (APA 30). *Author's collection*

A shot looking westward long the seawall at Ver-sur-Mer, France, between Gold and Juno Beaches in the British sector. Barbed wire still hangs from the small posts just behind the seawall, which is broken in a few spots, and to the left are the ruined foundations of a building. The LCT at the right edge of the picture is the 535, which served as Lt. Dean Rockwell's "flagship" during the famous DD-tank episode on D-Day that won Rockwell the Navy Cross. *Author's collection*

A photograph of a Lobnitz pier head in the Mulberry harbor off Arromanches. It was designed to float up and down the legs to provide a constant unloading height for LSTs. This one is packed with German prisoners waiting transport to England. *Author's collection*

The crew gets a short break on the beach off Ver-sur-Mer, to the east of the busy Mulberry port at Arromanches. Standing: Pequigney, Kelly, Cromer. Kneeling: Jarvis, Carlson (with Skippy), and Kleen. *Author's collection*

Carter beside a captured German tank. Although he identifies it as a Tiger, the tread configuration suggests it's a Panther armed with an 88mm gun (the tank's turret is pointed aft). The photo was probably taken at a British vehicle park (note the Bren carrier to right) behind Ver-sur-Mer. *Author's collection*

Irwin, who took art classes in college, drew several cartoons depicting the LCT's activities in France. This one plays on the disconnect between the flotilla staff ("Mary"), comfortably stationed on a large merchant ship anchored in the Mulberry harbor, and the LCT crews battling the weather beyond the Gooseberry or Phoenix breakwaters. Irwin is saying the LCTs sometimes seemed in danger of inadvertently but unavoidably "drying out" on the decks of the mechanized transports ("Mike Tares"). *Courtesy of Don Irwin*

And it is quite frequently that we take time out and have a little chat with the B.B.M. while we are at the causeway

We are greatly alarmed when he threatens not to pull our kedge out the next time we are on the beach.

As the officer in charge of the LCT 614, Irwin had plenty of experience with the sometimes strained relations between the LCT skippers and the British beachmasters (the "B.B.M."). The reference to "kedge" refers to the LCT's dependence on having a good anchor placement astern of them in order to retract after drying out; they sometimes had to ask the British personnel to drag their anchors farther out. *Courtesy of Don Irwin*

The LCT 614's skipper on the ramp at the repair facility near Saltash in England, November 1944. Irwin was about six feet tall, so the photo shows the size of the LCT's ramp and bow lockers. On D-Day, Cromer had to lie atop the locker just above Irwin's head to knock loose the dog holding the ramp. *Author's collection*

Roy Carlson with his right hand on the anchor cable, which gave him and Pillmore some anxious moments on D-Day. Carlson is standing above the galley (the aft port deckhouse), and the hasp of the anchor is just visible to the left. Note the gasoline cans stored on the deck in front of Carlson. *Author's collection*

The only picture of the LCT 614 under way, headed back to England. The picture shows crated gear along the port side of the tank deck, helmets and life jackets on the railing near the starboard gun tub, and another LCT just barely visible ahead of them. The photo was made from the catwalk just outside the wheel house. *Author's collection*

The view of the tank deck from the conning position atop the wheel house. Note the canvas-covered starboard 20mm gun and the glimpse into the gun tub. The ship shows plenty of evidence of its hard service on the Normandy beaches. Puddles of water highlight the wear of the deck, and the ramp looks almost worn smooth. Barely visible along the tank deck center line are the recessed padeyes used officially to tie down vehicles and unofficially as oil stoves. *Author's collection*

This view of the starboard deckhouses of the LCT 614, taken at the repair facility in England in November 1944, features the starboard gun tub, where Jarvis got the tracer through his life jacket on D-Day. Note the missing mast and the railing atop the wheel house knocked inboard at a fairly obvious angle, evidence of contact with various freighter hulls. The door to the officers' quarters has a wooden pallet for a stoop and a sign above it (perhaps the one Irwin put up telling the men to wipe their feet before entering). The equipment on deck in the foreground is the handy billy fire pump and various hoses, apparently associated with cleaning the voids in the hull sections beneath the tank deck. The ship moored aft of them appears to be a minesweeper, which often doubled as antisubmarine escorts. *Author's collection*

The USS LST 1008 visits Shanghai, China, sometime after the war. This LST ferried the LCT 614 on the long voyage from Norfolk to Inchon, Korea. While aboard the 1008, the LCT 614 crew learned of their planned participation in the invasion of Japan, experienced their last combat (air raids at Okinawa), and heard the news that the war had ended. The 1008 was eventually given to the Chinese and in the 1990s was on display at a Chinese naval museum in Qingdao. *Author's collection*

On liberty on June 2, 1945, in Colon, Republic of Panama, the crew of the LCT 614 celebrate their last day on the American continent before what they thought would be the invasion of Japan. Front row (left to right): S 1/c Glenn Dunnegan, S 1/c Paul DiMarzio, and S 1/c Chester Wajda. Middle row: BM 2/c Edward Townsend, S 1/c Lloyd Butler, and EM 2/c Francis Coffas. Back row: QM 3/c Frank Pequigney, MoMM 2/c Francis Kelly, and F 1/c John Jarvis. Not pictured are SC 3/c Gerald George, S 1/c Lucian Conn, and S 1/c Melvin Buchsbaum. Jarvis, Kelly, Pequigney, and Wajda had been with the LCT 614 at Normandy. *Courtesy of Frank Pequigney*

Lieutenant (junior grade) A. J. Banks, from West Virginia, served as the skipper of the LCT 614 during its deployment to the Pacific theater. A high school physical education teacher and boxing coach, Banks saw action as an LST boat officer at Salerno and Anzio before being selected to command the LCT 614. His experience as a boxer and a teacher made him popular among the crew. *Courtesy of Frank Pequigney*

This unsailorly deckhouse provided some additional recreational space for the crew. Lt. (j.g.) Banks looked the other way as the men reassigned some of the construction material on the wharf in Jintsen, Korea, and Paul DiMarzio built the structure as a place to play cards. It appears to be braced between the two after deckhouses (the wheelhouse is visible to the left), and Coffas wired it for lights and heat. The space beneath the house also seems to have attracted quite a bit of garbage (the entrance to the ship's head is under there somewhere). *Courtesy of Frank Pequigney*

A photo of Carter's gun collection taken in 1950. The muzzle and tip of the magazine of the MP 40 show up on the right, beneath a German helmet. The display of cartridges along the shelf features a 20mm round in the center. Carter took the Schmeisser, and perhaps one of the other weapons, to the "Battle of Athens," a voters' riot in August 1946, just before he and Pequigney began classes at Tennessee Wesleyan College. *Author's collection*

On the day following the "Battle of Athens" in August 1946, residents of McMinn County, Tennessee, vented their anger against the thugs of the Crump political machine by overturning cars with out-of-town license plates. In this photo, people in the foreground stand on an overturned car while the crowd seems focused on something going on in the background. The snapshots are stamped on the back with "Horton's Drug Store, Athens, Tennessee." *Author's collection*

The MV *Charlie Bamsu* off Walker's Cay during the Bahamas Aerial Magnetomic Survey, sometime in early 1947. After Carter quickly discovered college life was not for him, he found himself back at sea for a short time. The four craft involved in the expedition were prosaically enough named *Adam*, *Baker*, *Charlie*, and *George Bamsu* (no "Dog" or "Echo"). *Author's collection*

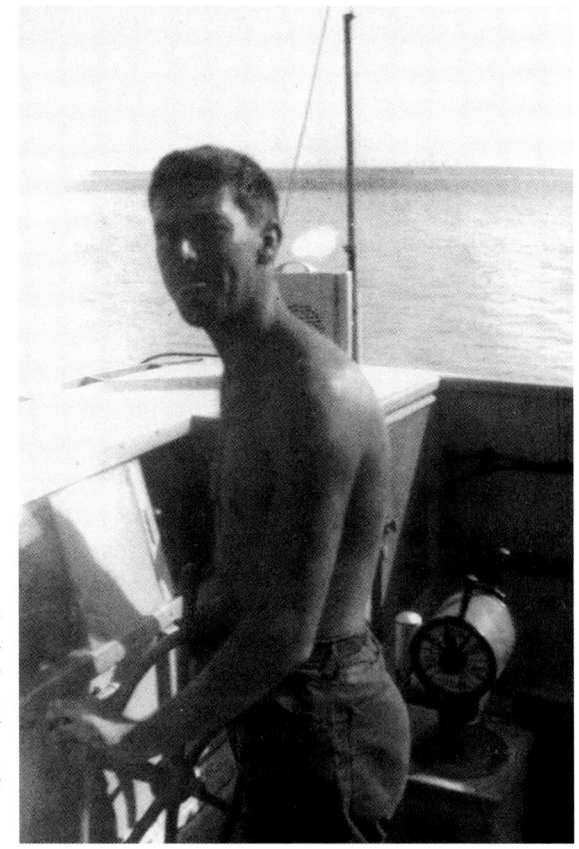

Carter at the wheel of the MV *Charlie Bamsu*, making a characteristic editorial comment to the photographer. In this picture, Carter is still a few months shy of his twentieth birthday. *Author's collection*

crew began dispensing with the anchor unless they had to beach against a heavy cross tide or strong crosswinds, increasing their chances of broaching.

The only evolution that took some time to perfect was going alongside one of the Mike Tares. The freighters could accommodate four, and sometimes even six, LCTs at a time. Especially in these first few days after the invasion, the LCT(6)s had to come alongside port side to the freighter to prevent the LCT's mast from interfering with the freighter's cargo booms. Coming alongside to moor on the Mike Tare's port bow or starboard quarter was obviously the easiest, since it entailed simply circling around behind or ahead of the ship and moving up into position. Mooring to the port quarter or starboard bow required a bit more ship handling in timing the approach, but unless another LCT was already tied up amidships this could be accomplished by a rather shallow, arcing turn. Sometimes the LCT skippers preferred to overshoot the ship and back into position. Coming alongside amidships was always the hardest to accomplish, especially if other LCTs were already alongside forward and aft. This maneuver required the LCT to come in at speed to maintain steerageway and then to back down on all engines while turning the craft to crab it into position.

This tricky task was made even trickier when the weather, relatively nice on the seventh, took a turn for the worse over the next few days and by the fact that the 614 had to operate with only two engines. Like tugboat engines, the LCT's diesels were designed for power rather than speed, since the craft needed quite a bit of energy to pull itself off the beach after grounding at full speed. Therefore, an LCT gained some slow-speed maneuverability by working the engines; by backing one outboard engine at full speed and going full speed ahead on the other outboard engine, an LCT could practically pivot in place. However, LCT 614 had lost much of this ability through the loss of the port outboard screw, and with the great demand for the LCTs' services off the beaches, there was no time to spare to allow her to beach for repairs.

On at least one occasion, while coming into an amidships position, Irwin misjudged the angle and his speed. Just as he started to back his engines, wind caught the LCT's high bow and he rammed the corner of the ramp into the side of the freighter. The British sailors on deck, waiting to catch the LCT's heaving lines, started waving them off, saying they were going to sink the ship. Irwin hoped they were kidding, but as he backed off he noticed they had knocked a hole in the ship large enough to stick his head through. Fortunately, the hole was well above the waterline and would get even farther from the water as the ship unloaded. He expected a bit of trouble from the freighter's captain, but the merchant skipper was a bit too eager to get unloaded and out of the anchorage that was still a target zone for the German bombers.

Early on, the nightly bombing raids caused some concern for the men aboard the 614, but it soon became apparent that the planes were after the big ships. At first, Irwin had the 20mm's manned during alerts, but as the men themselves quickly became used to the raids, the typical navy horseplay soon showed up. One evening, Sparky hid Carter's helmet liner in the ready service locker. When the alert sounded, Carter jumped into the tub and clanked the steel outer helmet onto his head. For the duration of the raid, the helmet slipped all over Carter's head whenever he tried to look up.

The only man on the crew who did not learn to ignore the raids was the ship's cook. The men on watch began to notice that the cook paced the deck with his helmet and life jacket on all night long. As soon as dawn appeared, he would go into the compartment and hit the sack, telling the other men that he was too tired to cook. When they tried to force the issue, the cook would slap something together or purposely undercook or overcook the food. Soon, no one on the crew asked for anything from the cook. He stayed in what little good graces he could by keeping the officers fed, but soon very few of the crew liked him at all.

At first, the men tried to get the cook over his fear in the gentle and loving fashion sailors have shown for their shipmates down through the centuries. They would wait for him to go into the compartment in the morning and give him time to settle down. Then they would pick up hammers and wrenches and anything heavy they could find and begin beating on the bulkheads of the compartment, yelling, "Air raid! Air raid!" As he came scrambling on deck fumbling with his life jacket and helmet, the men had a good laugh at his expense. One evening, Carter was sweeping out the compartment during an air raid. When he came on deck, he noticed the cook standing by the bulwark and looking up. Carter walked quietly up behind him, yelled, "BOOM!" and slapped the dustpan over the cook's helmet. The cook tried to jump overboard, but luckily he got tangled up in the cargo netting hung over the side.

Still a War Zone

Elsewhere, though, the air raids were no laughing matter. During that first week of the invasion, dawn revealed to the men of the 614 some new victim either sunk in the shallow water or burning. Aircraft sank or damaged some seven Allied ships during the first week of the operation, and the mines laid by them sank or damaged another twenty-five. So although the men of the 614 mostly felt no personal danger from the aircraft, the raids were a very real threat to the shipping off the beaches.

The raids also provided a few moments of awed fascination. One evening, Pillmore was up on the conn when a raid started. It was a clear evening, and he distinctly saw what appeared to be a smaller plane attached to the back of a bomber. The two separated, and the bomber began a descent toward the anchorage almost directly at them. It crashed into the water with a tremendous explosion but fortunately caused no damage to them or to any of the shipping nearby. Pillmore had apparently seen one of the few attacks made by a "Mistel" guided bomb. A war-worn Ju 88 would be outfitted with radio control gear and stuffed with as much as eight thousand pounds of explosive, often a massive shaped charge designed to penetrate bunkers or armor. The pilot of a fighter plane mounted on the bomber's back flew the contraption to the target area, released the drone bomber, and then guided it to the target. The Mistels had been used with some success on the eastern front against bridges and power plants, but they proved less effective against the shipping off the French coast.

The constant threat of air raids meant that the shipping area had to be kept blacked out; absolutely no lights were to be visible at night, including smoking on deck. This greatly complicated the task of the LCTs, which were supposed to find their particularly assigned Mike Tare in the middle of a choked anchorage. Despite the danger, Irwin soon fell into the habit of approaching ships on the bearing he had been given and then having Kleen use the blinker light for a few seconds to find the number.

As dangerous as the aircraft were, the German E-boats posed almost an equal threat to ships along the edges of the invasion fleets. These craft, somewhat larger than the American PT boats but similarly armed, accounted for no fewer than eighteen ships that were sunk or damaged during the first week. The first such craft to tangle with the fleet operated out of Cherbourg, but soon other squadrons arrived in Le Havre and began harrying the British forces. One of the most notable of their successes came on the night of June 9, when E-boats hit a convoy of five LSTs escorted by a single British destroyer with a famous name, HMS *Beagle*, namesake of the ship that took Darwin to the Galapagos Islands. They had just entered the Bay of the Seine and were approaching the waters off Normandy when the E-boats attacked. LST 314 sank with half her crew, and LST 376 was so badly damaged by a torpedo that she had to be scuttled.

This nipping at the heels of the invasion fleet worried the task force commanders. If the E-boats had such success on the fringes of the fleets, what would happen if they managed to penetrate the screen and get in among the ships in the anchorage? With Le Havre just over the horizon from the British beaches, the squadrons operating from there posed an immediate threat to the ships supplying the troops ashore; a concentrated, high-speed attack from such a nearby base would give the British patrols little time to react. Admiral Vian did not intend to tolerate such a threat, and in a rare instance of Royal Navy and Royal Air Force cooperation, he asked for and got a massive bomber strike against Le Havre.

Just at dusk on June 14, more than 200 Lancaster bombers flew over the anchorage off Gold Beach, lining up on Le Havre. Among these aircraft were 22 carrying twelve-thousand-pound "Tallboy" bombs intended to destroy the E-boats in their reinforced concrete pens. Two hours later, 119 more Lancasters came over in a follow-up attack on the shipping in the harbor. In all, the German Navy lost three torpedo boats (slightly smaller but faster than an American destroyer escort), thirteen E-boats, and numerous other mine craft and harbor vessels. The next evening, a similar raid farther up the coast at Boulogne sank another thirty German coastal craft. These two air raids removed the effective surface threat to the British fleet.

Not all the action taking place off the beaches was defensive in nature. British battleships and cruisers maintained gunfire support positions off the beaches. Indeed, because of the slow advance of the British troops ashore, the gunfire support ships stayed off the British beaches throughout June. The Royal Navy's famous battleship *Warspite* stayed off the Normandy coast, returning only to reload or to replace worn barrel linings. (The *Warspite* may not have had the glamour of other battleships, like the *Hood* and *King George V*, but she was certainly a veteran, having fought at Jutland in 1916, Narvik and Calabria in 1940, and Cape Matapan in 1941.)

Also among the bombarding ships were the strangely configured battleships *Rodney* and *Nelson*. These ships were designed with three weapons of triple 16-inch gun turrets sited forward of their towering superstructures, an arrangement necessitated by the need to keep the ships, built in the 1930s, within the restrictions of the Washington Naval Treaty. The 16-inch guns on these ships had a much longer range than the older model 15-inch guns of the *Warspite* (although at Calabria, the

Warspite had made a hit on an Italian battleship at more than twenty-six thousand yards—the record at that time for a hit by a battleship on a moving target at sea); therefore, they were in high demand well into the summer. On at least one occasion, the *Rodney* took up station just to seaward of the 614's anchorage and jarred the crew awake with the blast from its guns. Two of the battleships were damaged during this time. When the *Warspite* returned to England to have its guns re-tubed, it struck a mine on the way and was not in action off Normandy again. The *Nelson* also fell afoul of a mine, this time off Normandy, on June 18 and was not repaired in time to return to the beaches. Not only battleships but also cruisers and destroyers and the oddly configured monitors of a variety of ages and descriptions and nationalities gathered off the British beaches to lend their guns to the fighting ashore.

Nor was the artillery around the beaches all outgoing. The narrow beachhead established by the British meant that for several days all the British beaches were subject to indirect artillery fire from the Germans. On Gold and Juno, it took the form of harassment fire, since the Germans were not able to get forward spotters in a position to relay the fall of shells. On Sword, however, the British were a long time securing the far side of the River Orne, and as a consequence that beach remained under observed shelling throughout June. On June 16, one of the stranger experiences of the campaign took place on Sword. That morning, five American LSTs (226, 307, 331, 332, and 350) dried out, and no sooner had they started unloading than they came under artillery fire. LST crews half jokingly referred to their craft as "large slow targets," but these five ships had become the sailor's worst fear—"large stuck targets." Fortunately, the German forward observers were not as good as their Allied counterparts; instead of being shot to pieces, the ships suffered only fifteen hits among them. They lost five men killed and twenty-six wounded, but the ships' crews were able to get their cargoes ashore relatively intact and to get their ships under way with the next high tide.

Establishing a Routine

With all this shooting going on around and over them, the 614 crew had no doubt that they were still very much in the war for those first two weeks after the invasion. But the combat around them became merely the backdrop against which they lived and worked. First and foremost everyone's attention was directed toward learning the seamanship necessary to operate and maintain their LCT. They also had to learn to pace themselves so that they could keep themselves going in the face of the unrelenting task they had been given. At first, they tried to stick with the stations they had been assigned and keep the ship fully manned at all times. This simply wore the men out in a very short time.

Nor did the weather need to be particularly stormy to complicate the LCT's already bad handling characteristics. During the hectic days immediately after the invasion, when every available LCT, LCM, rhino ferry, or any other barge-like craft was pressed into service to get men, vehicles, and supplies ashore, the LCTs paid little attention to how they were getting alongside the Mike Tares. Given a choice, most skippers at first preferred going alongside with the LCT's port side against the freighter. This maneuver kept the LCT(6)'s mast, stepped abaft the pilothouse on the starboard side, away from the larger ship's hull. But even then, an LCT offered the crew very little good working deck space for going alongside. The tank deck was too low, the top of the bow lockers was too tiny, and the tops of the deckhouses were too cluttered with gear.

So the 614 was taking quite a beating. It started with damage to the ship's equipment but soon extended to the ship. The first loss among the gear was the ship's useless little fenders. Pidgeon-Thomas had sent the LCT to war equipped with little rope fenders similar to the kind pleasure craft use when they tie up on a lakeside dock. In the restless waters of the channel, the constant grinding of the 150-ton LCT against the side of a 12,000-ton freighter soon chewed those fenders into pulp. Some of the guys who lived in harbor towns or inland waterways remembered the protection carried by tugboats, and soon the 614 was protected by an armored belt of truck tires lining the sides of the craft.

Heavy use also wore out the mooring lines in short order. With the constant rolling and pitching of the two vessels, the small lines soon broke. Someone came up with the idea of using the wire towing cables. They certainly did not break, but after only one or two instances of the LCT and ship rolling away from one another, or the ship riding up on a wave while the LCT dropped into a trough, the wire cables soon threatened to pull the LCT's bits right out of the deck. The only things left to try were heavy, 3-inch hawsers. These worked fine, being heavy enough not to break, but with enough give in them to not damage the bits. The problem, of course, was that these heavy lines were the devil to work, and the civilian crews on the freighters complained constantly about having to haul them up from the deck of the LCT.

After the 614 lost Dowling, Irwin was reluctant to moor port side to again. Mooring starboard side to, though, brought the LCT's stubby wooden mast into the ship-handling mix. Stepped on the after edge of the pilothouse, the mast served only to carry the American flag and for hoisting flag signals. It wasn't terribly tall, as warship masts tend to be, but it was tall enough. Soon after Dowling's loss, the mast got tangled up in a freighter's loading boom and broke off. Its loss proved no particular handicap to the ship, and soon after the big storm of June 19, Leide ordered all LCTs to remove their masts.

The one result from losing the mast, however, was that it no longer served as a bumper for the pilothouse. With the mast gone, the pilothouse was now clear to crash against a freighter's hull, putting Irwin, Pillmore, and Kleen in pretty much the same danger that Dowling had been. The constant banging of the pilothouse against various hulls had soon hammered the railing around the top to a jaunty fifteen-degree angle. Even the whip radio aerial, mounted "safely" on the forward inboard corner of the pilothouse, was eventually jutting out over the tank deck. But somehow the 614 escaped any disabling damage and kept plying the waters off Arromanches.

As the crew had learned, mooring alongside a freighter and taking on a load of vehicles posed plenty of danger to the men and the LCT, but sometimes getting the vehicles ashore led to plenty of frustration as well. Some of the vehicles had been stored in the freighters with their lights on or their ignition switches not turned completely off, and by the time the vehicles got onto the LCT's deck their batteries had completely drained. When the British Army personnel came aboard to land the vehicles, they were stumped about what to do. Gudger, the North Carolina farmhand, rose to the occasion. Knowing about tractors and other kinds of farm machinery, he would tinker with the engines until he could get them running and drive them off the ship.

After about a week, the critical backlog of supplies had been cleared, and all the LSTs that had been crowding the anchorage had been able to dry out and return to England for additional loads. Up to that time, the LCTs could carry only vehicles or men—loads that could take themselves off the ship in short order and allow the LCT to retract quickly and head out for another load. With the backlog cleared, easing up the desperate need for LCTs, the craft could now be used for crated supplies, the unloading of which required the LCTs to dry out.

Drying out had a few disadvantages. With no seawater to run through the coolant pumps for the engines or the generator, the LCT had no electrical power for the heaters. The lack of seawater also meant they couldn't pump the toilets, so the crew had to walk up the beach to the army's latrines. The oil-burning stove still worked for those who cared to use it. Of course, the greatest advantage of drying out was the opportunity to sleep. The high tides were roughly twelve hours apart, and unloading the supplies generally took only an hour or two, depending on the load and the number of British Army personnel who showed up to carry off the crates. On the beach, only one man needed to be on watch in the pilothouse, primarily to listen for calls over the radio, so the others could rest. Some few lucky ones could even get an unheard-of eight hours.

Drying out also meant a chance to get off the ship, which they had not been able to do since they left England. There was no official liberty, and the town of Arromanches was pretty much off-limits to military personnel, but the men could walk around on land and even had time for a little souvenir hunting. This soon after the invasion, German and British equipment still littered the beaches and inland areas in piles. The men had almost unlimited access to as much of it as they cared to carry. Particularly popular were the standard German-issue sidearm, the Walther P-38, and knives and helmets. On one of those early occasions, Carter was excited to find what he thought would make the perfect souvenir, a German helmet with a large shrapnel hole in the side. When he picked it up, though, his elation turned to horror; the helmet still contained pieces of the wearer's head and brains. He placed it back in the sand and walked away.

The British soldiers bringing back a steady supply of prisoners from the front kept the men on the beaches well supplied with souvenirs, so they soon had a thriving trade going with the men on the merchant ships who wanted some physical proof that they too had been part of the invasion and subsequent battle for Normandy. Pistols, knives, and helmets soon became the coin of the realm, and the men eagerly traded them to the merchant mariners, usually for hot food or freshwater showers.

Some of the odder items, though, puzzled the men and became fodder for idle speculation. Chief among them were the thousands of cartridges they picked up with wooden bullets. The going explanation at the time was that the wooden bullets were meant to wound rather than kill, the theory being that if you kill a man, you take only one enemy soldier out of action, but if you wound a man, you remove not only him but also the two other men it takes to carry him away. Not until much later did a few of the men figure out that the wooden bullets allowed the Germans to conduct "live"-firing exercises without expending real ammunition, which by that time was coming into short supply.

By June 18, the LCTs and their crews had settled into a kind of routine. Occasional dry outs allowed the men some rest periods, and the backlog of shipping had cleared enough that every so often some of the LCTs were allowed to anchor for the night. The men of the 614 were becoming proficient at other tasks to help each other. Carter and Andin were learning ship handling from Pequigney so that he didn't have to stay at the wheel the whole time they were under way. Kelly learned the anchor winch from Carlson so the two of them could swap on and off. Clark, especially after Dowling had been injured, got help in the engine room not only from Jarvis and Kelly, the ranking motor macs, but also from Cromer and Gudger, two of the more mechanically minded of the deckhands. The German air and surface activity had thinned out by this time, and the Mulberry harbor was taking shape, so the men were beginning to feel as if they were operating in a busy but secure backwater. That Sunday, June 18, was a warm, sunny calm day that seemed to promise that the worst of their Normandy experiences were behind them.

The Storm

That night, however, the weather began to deteriorate quickly. By dawn, the winds were gusting to tropical storm strength. The 614 tried to take a load to the beach that morning. They beached successfully, and most of the large military vehicles they carried got ashore with no problem. But among the British soldiers was a chaplain, who held the rank of captain, and his assistant, an enlisted soldier called a "batman." These men had with them a small civilian-type car, and the chaplain and his batman agreed that they would never be able to get their car through the heavy surf that was building. They asked if they could stay aboard until a better opportunity arose for landing.

As the 614 retracted from the beach, Irwin had Kleen call Mary (command) and report they had been unable to land their full load. Mary answered that other craft were beginning to make similar reports and ordered Irwin to take the 614 well out into the channel and anchor until the storm blew over. As they headed to sea, the crew began to batten the ship down for the storm. They were a bit bemused as they watched the chaplain and batman try to lash the car against one of the deckhouses with a small rope they had brought with them, apparently to use as a clothesline. The sailors pitched in to help secure the car with stronger line, not only to help the chaplain, but also to ensure the car didn't break loose and begin careening across the deck. Once the car was secure, the chaplain and his batman flipped a coin to see who would ride out the storm in the car and who would have to fend for himself. The batman won the toss and quickly climbed in the little vehicle to settle in for the night.

Once past the line of Gooseberry breakwater ships and the outer anchorage, the craft could disperse fairly widely. They dropped anchor, payed out twice the normal length of anchor cable, and then braced to ride out the storm. By this point, most of the men were too tired to get seasick. The other LCTs and medium-size craft also spread out and anchored all over the channel. The smaller craft—DUKWs, LCVPs, and the like—took shelter within the line of Gooseberries and Phoenixes that were in place. Rear Admiral Vian, realizing that no ferry craft were available, asked that all convoys that had not already left England be delayed until the weather cleared. There was nothing to do but hope that the storm would leave as quickly as it had come. One of the few things that never changed as ships evolved from oars to sail to steam is the seaman's dread of getting caught in a storm against a lee shore, or exactly the predicament the invasion fleet now found itself facing.

That night, ships that had already left England began to show up off the beaches. Before reaching the shelter of the breakwater, these ships had to thread their way among the anchored and powerless landing craft. At one point, an LCI towing a Phoenix caisson bore down on the 614. It saw the anchored LCT in time to avoid a collision, but the landing craft passed by on one side and the wind pushed the caisson over to the other. Fortunately, the tow cable caught the 614 across the fantail and rode up on deck, but the weight of the LCI and Phoenix threatened to set the whole tangle adrift for shore. Pillmore finally got a megaphone and told the LCI skipper they were going to cut the cable, making clear that it was a statement of intent, not a request. He then set a couple of the men to work, chopping the wire cable with fire axes, and they were soon free of that particular threat. He wondered how the LCI skipper would ever be able to regain his tow or even if such a feat of seamanship were even possible.

The storm, of course, did not blow over that night. In fact, if anything, the storm continued to strengthen during the day on June 20. The northeast wind didn't gain very much power, but the length of time that the wind blew over the water meant that the seas grew larger and larger. By the twentieth they were running almost nine feet high. A nine-foot sea is nothing for ships even as small as destroyers, but it was almost the height of the tops of the LCT's deckhouses. Nor was the LCT designed to ride out a storm at sea. Its stern anchor kept its rectangular hull backward against the motion of the waves instead of facing into them, and the fact that they had an anchor cable instead of a chain meant that they had much less play when waves crashed into their stern. The result was that the low, flat stern would dig into the waves rather than ride up over them. The small collapsible bulwark across the fantail did nothing to keep the water off the ship, so breaking waves washed constantly along the tank deck.

Simply getting to the head under these conditions was incredibly dangerous. When the need arose, the man had to decide between two routes. The quickest way was to go out the after door from the crew's quarters and wait for the stern to start to rise on a wave; the man had to time his dash across the tank deck between the walls of water moving forward. For the men who couldn't run quickly or who had trouble timing waves, they could go out the forward door, swing over to the ladder leading up to the port gun tub, walk in the rain to the catwalk that led across to the pilothouse, and then climb down to the door to the head. Most men chose the mad dash across the deck.

That second night of the storm was much too dangerous to allow the chaplain or the batman to stay in their vehicle, so the crew made room for the batman in their quarters, and the chaplain stayed in the officers' space. That space became a little less crowded when Irwin decided to move to the pilothouse for the rest of the storm—to be on hand if he were needed, he said, but also to obey his Iowa instinct to get as high above the water as he possibly could.

The seas washing over the stern of the LCT began collecting near the ramp, which was not entirely waterproof. Although scuppers ran under the bulwarks along the sides of the tank deck, water was coming aboard much faster than it could drain out, and the wind and oncoming waves prevented the water from pouring off the open stern. Soon the tank deck was under at least a foot of water, which added a tremendous amount of weight to the little craft. With the added weight, the inevitable started to happen, and they began to drag anchor. Irwin had Carlson pay out more and more cable until almost all of it was off the reel, but the cable simply did not have enough play in it, and the anchor was not large enough to bite deeply into the sandy bottom. By this time, Irwin knew enough about the LCT's capabilities that he didn't even think about lighting off the engines and trying to claw his way back out to sea. Their only hope was that the storm would run out before their sea room did.

At dawn on June 21, the men could tell that they were slowly dragging their way toward the line of bombardons and Gooseberries, not toward the soft sand of Gold Beach. Getting dashed on shore would be a bad enough fate, but at least the men would have some chance to reach land. Going against the blockships would be much worse because the LCT would almost certainly sink out from under them, and then their bodies would be thrown against the tangled mess of the sunken ships. Survival under those circumstances would be nothing short of a miracle.

By the time of the dog watches on June 21, the 614 had dragged to within a mile of the Gooseberries, and a mile to a sailor is no distance at all. The most pessimistic of the crew began to plan their last-ditch efforts at survival. The LCT had a dingy and a rubber raft in which the men might conceivably work their way between the sunken ships, or they could don life jackets and put themselves at the mercy of their individual luck or skill. But all that day, the wind had been slackening slowly but perceptibly, even if the waves had not yet begun to weaken. Irwin said nothing to the men about getting ready to abandon ship, and in time the wind and sea slackened to the point that the anchor stopped dragging.

About that time word came over the radio that fourteen LSTs had been able to beach on Juno and retract successfully. The need for food and ammunition for the soldiers had led Rear Admiral Vian to take the first slackening of wind to risk a landing. With that news and the continued dropping of the wind that evening, the 614 was back in operation. The little LCT's luck, which had brought them through practically unscathed on Omaha, had continued to hold.

8

CALM AND OBLIVION

By morning on June 22, the situation off Arromanches had become as critical as if the British forces had been encircled by German armor and naval forces. Although the storm prompted the British beachmasters to ask for a delay in sailings from England, ships already in transit had crowded into the anchorage even though they were unable to unload. These new arrivals clogged not only the anchorage but also the ability of the smaller vessels to transfer their cargoes ashore, creating an immense backlog of supplies sorely needed by the troops.

On land, the storm had been merely a nuisance, and for those three days the army had not stopped its consumption of ammunition, fuel, and food despite the fact that very little cargo had made it across the beach. But by the end of those three days, the units on the front lines began to feel the indirect effects of the storm as their supplies began to run out. These severe shortages held up the British as effectively as a Panzer division, forcing the army to postpone its planned offensive to encircle Caen (Operation Epsom). Also, the Admiralty feared that the growing press of ships in the anchorage could tempt the Germans into a determined air attack. As a result of these pressures, the need for the rapid unloading capabilities of the LCTs led to a working pace as unrelenting as it had been during and immediately after the invasion.

LCT 614 weathered the storm with little structural damage, though the crew found themselves as exhausted and as miserable as ever. On the evening of June 22, even before the wind and waves fully subsided, Rockwell began calling the LCTs of Group Thirty-five back into service. The 614, with the chaplain and his little car still aboard, headed back to the anchorage for the next load, cleaning up the superficial storm damage as they went. As his batman got the car packed and ready for landing, the chaplain said his good-byes to Irwin and Pillmore, giving them each a small cross as a thank-you gift. After they had taken on their new load of lorries, the 614 chugged into the relatively calm waters of the Mulberry harbor, and the crew crowded topside to see what fate they had escaped.

The seaward sides of the concrete Phoenix caissons had been battered by scores of craft ranging from LCVPs to small coasters, many of which lay still wedged or sunk against the breakwater. Farther in, the unfinished Whale jetty looked as if it had fared somewhat better than the caissons had, but still several craft had crashed into it as well. The beach itself was as littered with craft and debris as Omaha had been on the afternoon of D-Day itself. Barges, pontoons from the jetty, LCMs, and LCTs formed a seemingly unbroken barrier to the beach, and in the distance to the west of the Mulberry, the destroyer HMS *Fury* sat completely out of the water under the cliffs. The *Fury* had struck a mine during the height of the storm. The explosion knocked out the ship's power, and her crew had no way to keep her off the rocks. Seeing a ship as large as a destroyer dried out by the storm, the crew realized how lucky they were that the LCI and its tow hadn't dragged them ashore.

Operations in the British sector had taken on renewed vigor because Mulberry A off Omaha had taken a more severe beating. There, the American naval commanders had thought the summer storm would blow over quickly and ordered the landing craft to shelter within the Gooseberries. Consequently, many of these craft were driven ashore or against the Whale jetties, wrecking themselves and the causeways. The jetty itself was so badly damaged that senior officers decided not to repair it. And the dozens of craft driven ashore would require the engineers to spend more than a week dragging them back to sea and repairing their damage. In the meantime, the remaining craft were set back to unloading directly over the beaches, just as they had done on D+1 and after. The British Mulberry B had taken a beating, but it was reparable and would become the only operational Mulberry.

LCT 614 and her sister craft were soon back into their routine, with half the crew getting rest while the craft loaded or unloaded, and the other half getting rest on the trips outside the Mulberry to the anchorage. It was an arduous task, and the only thanks they received was from the occasional freighter skipper or crewman who thanked them for letting the larger ship get out of the target area. Official thanks came in the form of a message from Leide. Apparently, the storm had given him time to examine beachmasters' reports and the many messages from the flotilla's craft. Of the forty or so LCTs that had reported to the Gold area, LCT 614 was one of only ten craft that had been able to operate continuously since the invasion. Of those ten, several—like the 614—had kept up operations still with unrepaired damage suffered during the battle, now almost a month earlier. Leide's letter of commendation provided the crew their only hint that their unrelenting work was not going unnoticed. The more cynical of the crew noted, however, that the thanks came from the flotilla commander, not someone higher up.

A New Enemy Arises

Once the weather cleared, everyone expected the nightly air and naval attacks to resume, but as it turned out the raids let up considerably. As before the storm, most of the attacks occurred in the Sword area, directly across from Le Havre, but no one ignored the enemy E-boats' ability to make an end run and strike at the center of the invasion fleet. News of continued, if random, attacks kept the crews alert and aware of the fact that they were still operating in an active combat area, not safely behind the lines.

Two weeks after the invasion, the German Navy introduced "human torpedoes," or one-man submersibles that carried a single torpedo each. A pilot operated a Neger craft from a modified torpedo, trying to work past the escorting warships to launch the torpedo slung underneath. In two attacks, on the nights of July 5 and 7, these craft sank three minesweepers and damaged the Polish-manned British light cruiser *Dragon* so badly she was scuttled as part of the Gooseberry breakwater. They were also suspected in the sinking of the destroyer HMS *Isis* on July 20.

Also, of course, mines still littered the area, both ashore and off. As late as August 21, the British lost ships to mines. But by the middle of July, the men on the LCTs at Arromanches felt relatively safe in their crowded, well-traversed harbor because all the mines there by then had been either swept or struck, and the attacks by air (which often included dropping mines as well as bombs) and sea had become quite rare. It was almost as if the storm had also washed away German interest in the beaches.

During the days following the storm, the weather was still rough. To make matters worse, though, the reduced threat of attack allowed the irascibility of the merchant captains to resurface. Although the U.S. Navy had been notorious early in the war for letting cargo shipping swing idly at anchor for weeks before unloading, the British had learned through their early experience with shipping shortages to turn around merchant ships as quickly as possible. The backlog and delays off Gold were therefore unheard of by some of the Red Ensign masters, and some of them tended to blame these problems on upstart American LCT skippers. Also, the letup in the attacks simply gave the merchantmen the time to get irritated at the LCTs bashing against the sides of their ships. Before the storm, while the anchorage came under frequent air and surface attacks, the cargo ships paid little attention to the damage; the freighter skippers wanted to unload and get out of the area quickly. Now that the attacks came so infrequently, they regained their sometimes ill-tempered disdain for the navy.

During that period, Irwin had been ordered alongside a fairly large freighter. When they approached, the freighter signaled that the craft should come alongside amidships, between two LCTs already tied up on the bow and stern. Some of the other LCT skippers had told Irwin that getting into the midships position between already moored LCTs was much easier if the ship went in stern first or what they called a "Chinese" landing. After having already knocked a hole in one ship, Irwin decided to try backing in and told Kleen to signal the freighter for permission to do so.

Since the 614 still had only two operable screws, Pequigney and Kelly found their tasks much simplified by backing in. When crabbing in, they constantly received orders to change rudder and throttle settings, sometimes before they had completed the previous set of commands. This time, though, once they got lined up, Kelly left the throttles at full astern, and Pequigney needed only slight rudder adjustments to keep the craft on course. The fact that the LCT's pilothouse had no aft-facing ports was no major problem, except that they could not anticipate Irwin's commands.

Up on the conning position, Irwin and Pillmore watched their approach with keen interest. Irwin realized that in this kind of approach, timing the throttle orders would be much more crucial. If he called for forward thrust too late, the LCT would ram the freighter with its flat, sharp stern. Too soon, and the craft would wallow embarrassingly distant from the larger ship and perhaps drift into one of the other LCTs already alongside. Pillmore was ready to offer assistance, but he was just as glad he got to watch one of these approaches before he had to try one himself.

As it turned out, Irwin timed it just short of correctly. "Both engines astern one half." As the little ship slowed, Pillmore leaned over the lifelines to tell Cromer and Andin to get ready with the fenders. "Both engines astern one third," Irwin ordered. Gudger and Carter stood by with heaving lines, ready to throw them up to the freighter's crew. Irwin continued his commands: "Both engines stop. Both engines ahead one half." A short pause. "Both engines stop." The brief forward thrust took away the craft's aftward momentum, and for a fleeting moment the 614 lay perfectly poised for its stern-first mooring. With shouts of "Heads up!" Gudger and Carter threw over the heaving lines, and Cromer and Andin held their fenders against the LCT's stern. But the forward push of the center and starboard engines had nudged the ship's head slightly to port, and at that moment a wave caught the starboard bow and pushed the LCT aside and astern. With a crunch sickening to any seafarer who heard it, the square port quarter of the LCT drove into the side of the freighter right at the waterline and right at the seam of two hull plates.

As soon as the 614 drifted away from the freighter, Irwin could tell that the collision had started the plates and that the freighter was taking on water, though it was so slight an amount that it would be more a nuisance than a problem. Certainly the ship was in no danger of sinking and did not need to be drydocked; repairs to the plates would be a half day's work at dockside. But as the 614's crew finished mooring their craft to the freighter, the freighter's crew assessed the damage. Shortly, the ship's master leaned over the bridge wing with a bullhorn.

"Skipper! Skipper of the 614! Report to me on the bridge!"

Before Irwin could even curse adequately, a sea ladder unrolled down the ship's side. As Irwin climbed up to the deck, he wondered what kind of royal ass chewing he was going to get from the salty merchant master. The irony of the situation had not escaped him. One moment he had been the officer in charge of an American man-of-war; now he was simply a lowly ensign headed for public humiliation. But when he got to the bridge, the utter contempt of the merchant captain caught him off guard. The ship's master muttered a few words about the lack of seamanship of the U.S. Navy and then told Irwin to write an entry in the ship's log that he was indeed responsible for ramming and damaging the freighter. Once Irwin had written the entry and signed it, he was curtly dismissed. Heading back to the 614, Irwin realized the ass chewing would have been better—at least it would be over and done with—but the log entry was an official document and would likely require an official response. For days later, he wondered when he would hear from Leide or Rockwell about this incident.

The growing tension between the navy and merchant ships manifested itself among the crews as well. Gone were the days that the crew could barter for not only quantity but also specific types of food from the freighters with a few souvenirs nabbed quickly off the beach. Now, the 614's crew was lucky if the merchant sailors treated them like humans. One particular source of irritation for the LCT crews was the failure of the merchant ships to shut off water pressure to their heads while the LCTs were alongside. Ship's heads use seawater from the fire mains for flushing, so raw sewage comes out of vents in the side of the ship with some force. Generally that posed no problem even for ships tied up next to one another, because the flush vents were well below deck level. Unfortunately, the LCT's main deck was only a foot or so above water, and the bulwarks along the sides were about four feet high. Any LCT moored underneath a head vent could easily get the raw sewage on deck or on a crewman.

During the hectic days, unloading a freighter was an all-hands evolution for both the LCT and the merchant ship, so the merchant crews' visits to the head had to wait until the ships had parted company. But when the pace slowed, some of the merchant crewmen found their services were not required full time, and therefore calls of nature could override calls of duty. At first, the LCT crew would yell at the men on the freighter, but yelling at the men on deck did not get the message to the men in the head. They found it did not reach the crew of the next freighter they went alongside either. Soon, standard procedure dictated that men on deck with no specific duties, such as tending fenders or heaving lines, would be armed with potatoes and mallets and use the potatoes to stop the discharge for an hour or so before they softened and dropped out. For one particularly offensive ship, Sparky pounded a wooden damage control plug (designed to stop up a shell hole) into the vent. The men knew the merchant sailors could do nothing about it until they reached port, which they hoped was far away.

Still Under the Gun

Within a week after the storm, the situation had improved. Much of the backlog of shipping and supplies had been cleared, and the Mulberry B artificial harbor became operational. The LCT crews hoped the Mulberry would shoulder much of their work, but essentially all it meant was that the LCTs could be released from quick turnaround loads, such as troops or vehicles, and could be used for cargo. Although loads of crated supplies or ammunition meant harder work for the crew while loading or unloading, they also meant that the craft would dry out to unload— and that, in turn, meant at least a few hours' rest for the whole crew.

One night the cycle of tides seemed to work out perfectly. They had taken on a load during the evening and beached at high tide before midnight. The crew took full advantage of this rare opportunity for nighttime sleep, and at dawn they awakened for a leisurely breakfast before the lorries arrived to take off the cargo. The smell of breakfast cooking attracted the attention of three British sappers who were still in the process of clearing mines from the dunes. Life was idyllic for those few moments on a warm, sunny morning, with a hot breakfast after a relatively luxurious four hours' sleep in the dark and now company to break the monotony of the same dozen faces.

After breakfast, with a hearty thanks and a bright "cheerio," the sappers walked off the ramp, and the crew began to get ready for the lorries. A moment later the calm of the morning's idyll ended with a loud, nearby explosion. No one had heard the screech of an incoming shell or bomb, even though the plume of smoke appeared fewer than a hundred yards up the beach. Someone had stepped on a mine. Almost the entire crew ran off to see if they could help, and they found their three British sapper friends. The man who stepped on the mine died quickly, torn apart by the force of the explosion. One of the other men suffered numerous shrapnel wounds and was in dire need of assistance, and the third seemed intact but clearly dazed by the blast.

Carlson took one look at the carnage and, heedless of the other mines that likely lay in the area, crawled off into the dunes and was violently sick. Irwin ordered Johnson and Kleen back to the ship—Johnson to get the first aid kit and Kleen to radio for assistance. The others helped the two survivors out of the dune area and onto the beach itself. When Johnson returned, Irwin and Pillmore gave them both shots of morphine to keep them comfortable until British Army medics arrived. The war, it seemed, was still very much with them.

And the war was still all around them. The German attacks did not completely stop after the storm. All through July and into early August, German submarines probed at the edges of the convoy routes, and coastal forces continued to harass the shipping off the beaches. The occasional air raids included the dropping of mines into the anchorage with some random successes. One of these included Admiral Vian's flagship, the antiaircraft cruiser *Scylla*, which was so heavily damaged on June 23 that it saw no further service in the war.

After the big air raids on Le Havre, the threat of direct attacks from E-boats diminished, but the Germans devised other methods of long-range attack. In addition to the human torpedoes mentioned earlier, the German Navy deployed Linsen radio-controlled motorboats packed with explosives. These weapons had their greatest success in the sinking of the destroyer escort HMS *Quorn* as late as August 3.

These threats certainly had no chance of defeating the invasion fleet, but they certainly proved worrisome and all too deadly. They also constantly reminded the crew of LCT 614 that even into August, the Normandy beaches were still not far enough behind the front lines.

Time on the Beach

Toward the end of June, two events raised the hopes of the LCT crews that their work may be drawing to a close. On June 26, the major port of Cherbourg fell to the Allies after heavy bombardment by Rear Adm. Morton Deyo's battleships and cruisers on June 25. However, the Germans had carried out extensive demolition and mining operations before the port fell, and engineers would need more than a month to get the facility operational. Still, it was something to hope for among men who were beginning to feel abandoned.

Of more immediate interest to the crew of LCT 614, on June 29 British engineers finally got the Whale jetty in operation. The large LSTs could now lower their ramps onto one of the Lobnitz pier heads and unload without drying out or even landing. The little LCTs also used it occasionally, but their thin hulls posed a problem. Skippers who were used to shoving their craft against the smooth sides of a freighter found that such careless seamanship did not go unpunished against the protruding steel beams of the causeway. In as many days after Mulberry B became operational, four craft had impaled themselves on the jetty and flooded their engine rooms. With no major repair facilities available, a flooded engine room meant an incapacitated LCT. Other forms of lax seamanship and discipline were also taking their toll on the availability of craft, on their maintenance, and on relations between the U.S. Navy and the Royal Navy.

Leide's growing irritation with his flotilla and the circumstances they were forced to operate under are evident in his task unit orders dated July 5:

ABOARD USS LCI(L) 507
From: Commander, U.S. LCTs, Gold Area
To: Officers-in-Charge, All U.S. LCTs, Gold Area
Subject: Task Unit Orders

1. The following task unit orders are to be obeyed implicitly:
    (a) Use of Item Causeway pontoons No. 1 and No. 2. The causeways are numbered from west to east. From seaward in, No. 1 on the starboard hand, No. 2 on the port hand. You shall always enter Gooseberries

from the east gate. Do not enter between the concrete blocks and the shore. Upon entering Gooseberries, the beach master shall be contacted immediately for instructions. Have your signalman ready! Be alert! Know your load! Pass this information to shore so that unloading will be expedited. If vehicles are not waterproofed, report this. Steel or cast iron wheeled vehicles, rock crushers, and cranes shall not, REPEAT, not be unloaded on pontoons. The beach master will direct unloading or disgorging of such equipment. Obey him implicitly! U.S. Navy personnel shall not drive vehicles to shore. In the absence of drivers, the crew may drive vehicles to pontoon and return to craft at once. Anchors shall be used at all times. No exceptions! If necessary, the Rhino barge shall also be used. This is discretionary. Four craft have been totally disabled by flooded engine rooms. Regardless of circumstances, loss of craft for unloading purposes aids the enemy. Flooded engine rooms, resulting in total loss of all engines, is a major calamity. Do not expose yourself unnecessarily. Set proper watches in engine room when beaching. Failure to carry this out will result in stringent disciplinary action.

(b) All Officers-in-Charge of LCTs shall remove masts from their craft.

(c) All Officers-in-Charge of LCTs shall not expose anchor engine to side of MT [mechanized transport] when unloading. "Chinese" landings are permissible when necessary. No anchor engine replacements are available. Do not carelessly immobilize your craft.

(d) Loads of petrol or water should not be taken from MTs unless specifically directed by "MARY."

(e) Stores or personnel can be unloaded on King Red Beach, King Red Hard, or King pontoons as directed by the beach master. His word is law! Vehicles are to be unloaded only on Item and Jig beaches and Item pontoons.

(f) Fresh stores can be obtained from any U.S. LST in the area. Report refusals to this command. The number of the LST is essential. Do not beg! Do not humble yourself! Merely make a respectful request. You are to go no further. Keep "topped off" with water, fuel, and lubricants from barges in the area.

(g) No LCT enlisted personnel are allowed on shore on liberty. Enlisted men accompanied by an officer, and all properly in uniform, are per-

mitted ashore for sightseeing purposes. This privilege is not to be abused and is not in any way to restrict the operating efficiency of the craft.
- (h) A radio watch is to be maintained from 0600 to 2300. The radio transmitter is to be secured at all times except when transmitting. The radio receiver with amplifier turned on is to be opened from 0600 until 2300. "MARY" keeps a 24-hour receiver watch. You may contact "MARY" at any time for emergencies.
2. These orders are to be read carefully! They are to be kept available for inspection at all times! They are to be obeyed!

Irwin and Pillmore understood that the exclamation marks told much about Leide's frustration with his skippers as well as the deterioration of the flotilla's fortunes during the month following the invasion. They understood that the 614 had escaped most of Leide's gripes only by the slimmest fortune. The collision that injured Dowling could have, just as easily, knocked out the 614's anchor engine, and their latest collision could have punctured the 614's hull.

Essentially, the LCT skippers—ninety-day wonders who were mostly fresh out of college—had been given command of a naval vessel and then put in an area far away from any senior U.S. Navy officers. Even when coupled with the combat experience the men had gained on Omaha Beach, youth and autonomy are not part of the recipe for discipline. As a result, the attrition rate of the limited number of LCTs had become increasingly high, and Leide hoped to get the skippers to realize that an LCT immobilized by lax seamanship was as much a German victory as a craft blasted by direct enemy action.

But as the weeks trudged on into months, the independence of the LCT skippers and crews became increasingly important to carrying out their mission, even if it did cause headaches to Leide and the group commanders. As Leide's message indicated, within a month of the invasion the LCTs found themselves loaded to capacity with supplies headed for the beach but were getting very little for themselves. No doubt some of the food—especially canned goods like fruit—loaded onto the craft never made it ashore, but the crews understood the even graver situation of the combat troops in the field and limited their pilfering to a few items.

American ships, particularly the LSTs shuttling directly between the beaches and England, were duty bound to share supplies with the little craft, but by this time they had all made enough trips that their crews were well supplied with souvenirs, and American cigarettes were obviously useless bartering currency. Consequently, the LSTs became increasingly difficult to deal with. They were generous enough with canned goods, army C and K rations, medical supplies, coffee, and especially English mutton (almost universally disliked throughout the U.S. Navy; the 614 crew developed the standard operating procedure of immediately scuttling all mutton that came aboard), but the LSTs tended to be stingy with the true galley treasures of the more perishable items, such as eggs, milk, and other fresh meat.

Fortunately, British ships could still be bribed with American cigarettes. They were often quite free with butter and eggs and various meats (especially mutton). And when delays at the anchorage became unavoidable, the British crews also tended to be hospitable, allowing the Americans on board for hot meals and hot freshwater showers. This was a welcome change from the grudging hospitality many of the soldiers said they had experienced in England while waiting for the invasion, and it made the LCT men wonder if the American merchant sailors had some deep-rooted animosity toward navy seamen.

Tensions also grew between the American and British LCT crews. The British LCTs were larger than the American craft but had a much smaller anchor. Consequently, in any wind the British LCTs almost invariably dragged anchor and sometimes drifted dangerously close to other vessels. Generally, shouting or using the blinker light or blasting a police whistle drew the British crew's attention to the situation, but Irwin strictly forbade the man on watch from firing a warning shot with the .45.

The British crews were also occasionally careless in their use of the anchor while beaching. Sometimes they would drop anchor while running parallel to the beach, go behind the landed 614, and then beach on the other side. The 614 would then be stranded until the British craft retracted and sometimes even until the next high tide. On one such occasion, the English ship's anchor cable snagged across the stern of the 614, and the crew attacked it with fire axes.

To make matters worse, the 614's cook was becoming increasingly intransigent. The air raids and surface actions had let up, but his relationship with the rest of the crew had already become a total loss. And since most of the crew had taken to fending for themselves in the galley, he had made little effort to regain their good graces. His primary duty had become checking the supplies that they did receive, overseeing storage, and bringing up supplies from the voids into the galley. He continued to cook for the officers, but he prepared nothing more complicated than short-order type meals for the crew.

One day the 614 and the other LCTs got word that an official meat ration had arrived. The procedure here was for the LCT with the supplies to anchor, and the other LCTs would slowly steam by. Sailors on the supply LCT would then throw over a gunnysack, too often filled with mutton but sometimes holding a variety of pork and beef. The meat, of course, had been refrigerated but not frozen, so when the gunnysack hit the steel deck of the LCT, it made a rather distinctive splat. With the crew looking on, mouths watering, the cook tore open the gunnysack and looked, a bit dismayed, at the red, glistening beef. Thinking, no doubt, not about the taste but about the amount of work that would be involved in storing, preparing, and serving it, he stood up and declared, "This meat is spoiled." Without giving the others time to react, the cook chucked the gunnysack over the side. His shipmates stood dumbstruck until Carlson and Kelly—acting simultaneously as if on telepathic orders—picked the cook up and tossed him overboard.

The supply situation eventually became so chronic that some members of the crew began to suspect that rations and matériel meant for Flotilla Twelve was being siphoned off and sold on the French black market. As the rumors circulated and grew, Leide and the group commanders came under heavy suspicion. But likely the woes of Flotilla Twelve were the result of the most common of military snafus—that is, they had become someone else's problem. The U.S. Navy assigned the flotilla to the British area, thinking the Royal Navy would take care of them, but, in turn, the Royal Navy considered these little American ships to be an American responsibility.

As if lacking adequate supplies weren't bad enough on morale, the crew was also not getting any time off. A week or so after the storm, the LCTs stopped running loads at night and began to carry more frequent loads that required them to dry out, so the crew was able to catch up on sleep occasionally or to get their feet on land for a short time for a quick look about or to pick up a few souvenirs. But none of those short respites could replace even a few hours of liberty when they could forget the navy and enjoy a few beers.

The best recreation the crew had was still what they could grab by driving the British vehicles onto the beach. Leide's orders stipulated that the crew could drive vehicles onto the pontoon—and, by inference, the beach—but should return immediately to the ship. The orders did not stipulate how far they could drive, and sailors are particularly adept at exploiting ambiguity. When heading ashore with a load of lorries, the crew would pick out the vehicle they wanted to drive, and as soon as the ramp was down they were off, ostensibly looking for the nearest British vehicle dump. Sometimes they would not find their way back to the ship for hours.

This is when Pequigney learned to drive. As a teen in New York with ample public transportation, he had never had the need. Gudger, who by the time he was eight could use a clutch as well as other boys could use a fork, found Pequigney's lapse particularly amusing, but he took the big Yankee in tow. Despite the odd British vehicles—right-hand-drive lorries and Bren carriers—and the occasional American jeeps, soon Pequigney was picking out his vehicles with the rest of the crew and driving off into the villages.

The only other sizable American unit operating in the area was a maintenance unit tasked with the salvage and repair of the landing craft and other service vessels. Soon after the push to relieve the clogged shipping created by the storm, LCT 614 received orders to report to the maintenance unit for repairs. Although the men welcomed this respite from the constant work, they soon learned they had not been given a liberty call. The salvage crews had almost as little supply support as the LCTs, and they depended mostly on cannibalizing immobile LCTs for spare parts. In fact, cannibalization had become such a part of life on the invasion beaches that the repair crews had painted signs on the sides of wrecked LCTs that read "Hands Off!" or "All looters will be shot." LCT 614 dried out among the rusting craft, among which was LCT 612—the craft that went into Omaha Beach alongside the 614 and was so damaged that it had to be towed off. For the next day or two, the shipfitters repaired the broken screw, patched up bullet holes in the bow, and strengthened spots on the hull damaged from the numerous landings and bumps against freighter hulls.

A Cumshaw Mission

While the shipfitters worked, the 614's crew was able to catch up on maintenance of their own. Working constantly, the crew had not been able to do any of the small chores necessary for the upkeep of a ship. Soon the little craft was enshrouded by drying signal flags and airing mattresses, littered with removed hatch coverings and pulled machinery, and surrounded by the smell of fresh primer coat and spilled lubricants. The disorder made the 614 so indistinguishable from the wrecked craft around it that Irwin kept up the armed watches not so much for military discipline as to prevent their not-so-obviously operational LCT from being cannibalized along with the wrecks.

Carter used the time to strip down the 20mms, which had scarcely been touched since the invasion. Pillmore took an interest in the weapons, so Carter spent some time explaining their workings and maintenance needs. With Sparky off making electrical repairs and Johnson assigned to inventory and resupply, Cromer became Carter's real partner in stripping down the weapons. To release tension on the counter-recoil spring—the massive spring around the barrel that brought the weapon back into firing position after a round was fired—Carter pulled back and held the bolt open while Cromer slipped a wrench over the barrel and loosened the nut that capped the spring. Because of the strength of the spring, safety precautions prescribed pointing the weapon away from the ship while loosening the spring. The precaution proved fortunate this time. The bolt slipped out of Carter's hand just as Cromer finished loosening the nut, and the spring sailed forty or fifty yards out into the channel.

Cromer sat by while Pillmore chewed Carter out. No spring meant no weapon, and no spares meant no repairs. The ship had effectively lost 50 percent of its firepower. When Pillmore went below to see what could be done through official channels, Cromer stood up. "Come on, Carter. I know how to fix this," Cromer said, picking up the wrench and a scrap of paper. Cromer brushed off his uniform as well as he could, straightened his hat, and walked purposely toward the ramp. As Carter followed Cromer to the closest wrecked LCT, Cromer explained to Carter the niceties of one of the oldest of navy traditions, cumshaw.

Going through official supply channels, sometimes even (or maybe especially) in wartime, meant a lot of paperwork and wasted time. Usually, when on a cumshaw mission, a sailor took various goods from his ship to a neighboring vessel and traded them for the things he needed. The men of the 614 had been cumshawing souvenirs for food and showers almost since they had arrived in France, but this cumshaw mission was truly in the spirit of the tradition. The 20mm needed to be fixed immediately, going through supply would take time and require explanation, and Rockwell was certain to get wind of it and chew out everybody aboard. But as the LCTs had little anyone else wanted, this mission sought to obtain the needed counter-recoil spring in exchange for a little audacity.

Cromer and Carter boarded the wrecked craft, climbed up to one of its 20mms, and made sure it was intact. Cromer then made a show of looking at the scrap of paper and examining the gun. "Yes, it's this one," he said loudly, handing Carter the wrench. "Take the spring from this one." They soon had the part they needed and walked back to the ship completely unmolested by the salvage personnel. Carter had learned the number one rule of navy acquisition: "Look like you know what you're doing and no one will bother you. Sneaking around only attracts attention."

The short stay with the maintenance unit had an unexpected bonus for the crew. The cook ran into an old friend (whether an old shipmate or someone from home, the crew didn't care) and shortly asked to be transferred to the maintenance unit. No one objected, and the cook became the first member of the original crew to transfer off the ship. His replacement caused a few moments of doubt. LeRoy Singsheim, from Schenectady, New York, was an older guy, a bit stocky, and by all appearances rather serious. Pequigney got him talking, finally, and discovered that Singsheim had quite a story to tell.

He was originally on an LCT that went in on the first wave. It was hit several times and knocked out, with many of its men killed. The survivors made it ashore, and no longer having a navy unit to report to, Singsheim picked up a rifle and joined the soldiers huddled under the seawall. When the soldiers went inland, Singsheim stayed with them for quite some time, perhaps weeks. When he finally rejoined the navy, he was not commended for his initiative and bravery, but he was given a general court-martial for desertion and awarded a bad conduct discharge. The punishment in an odd way rewarded his actions; he could have been shot. In further recognition of his actions, the discharge was suspended, and he ended up as the new cook on the 614. The food aboard immediately improved.

The War Moves Inland

During the rest of that long French summer, the operations of the LCTs ebbed and flowed in relation to the series of offenses by the British and Canadian armies. Late in June, delayed by the storm, Field Marshal Bernard Montgomery launched Operation Epsom, a failed attempt to encircle Caen to the southwest. This operation involved heavy support from the Royal Navy, including the battleship *Rodney* with its nine 16-inch guns, the monitor *Roberts* with two 15-inch guns, the light cruiser *Belfast* with twelve 6-inch guns, and the antiaircraft cruisers *Argonaut* and *Diadem*, armed with ten and eight 5.25-inch guns, respectively. The bombardment from this concentrated task force was as heavy as anything the 614's crew had seen since D-Day and the week or so immediately afterward. The men were also a bit amused to see the *Rodney* being maneuvered by tugs so that her massive screws wouldn't touch off any pressure mines on the shallow channel bottom.

In early July, Operation Charnwood launched the final British attack on Caen, which they captured on July 10. Later that month, British forces pushed toward Aunay-sur-Odon in Operation Bluecoat. And in two big offensives in the first half of August, Operations Totalize and Tractable, the First Canadian Army advanced toward Falaise. The four-day battle in the Falaise Gap, between August 18 and 21, ended organized German resistance in Normandy. The Allies pushed on quickly after that, liberating Paris on August 25.

Each of those offensives required less and less cooperation of the big warships as the British Army pressed inland, but each one brought renewed and unrelenting demands for the services of the LCTs both to support the buildup before the operation and to supply the forces during the advance. Only after an advance halted did the LCT crews have a slight respite. These ebb periods were relative, with more frequent dry outs and no operations at night but days as busy as ever. During those times, the rumors began to take hold: the causeways were fully operational and could handle all the cargo, or Cherbourg had been cleaned up and all the shipping would be diverted there. But just as the crew began to convince themselves that their work was drawing to a close and they would soon return to England, another big push would require renewed activity.

Those ebb periods did allow some additional rest beginning in July. With the beaches no longer under artillery fire and most of the minefields cleared, the British navy had designated a stretch of beach off La Rivière and Ver-sur-Mer as an off-duty area (it would be an exaggeration to call it a rest and recreation area). Situated in a quiet place between Gold and Juno Beaches, the steep beach allowed the LCTs to land at high tide with their ramps almost against the seawall. Atop the seawall, a promenade road ran the length of the villages, offering a few pubs and cafés that were not off-limits to military personnel. On rare warm, sunny days, the crew could take a swim call.

On one of those warm afternoons, Carter and some of the other men were sitting at one of the cafés, sipping beer. The sound of heavy diesel engines heralded the approach of a tank, but when it hove into view they saw what they took to be a German Tiger. Its appearance caused a few tense moments before they learned it was captured and being driven by a British crew. They then took turns posing for photos with the armored monster.

On another occasion, the rare liberty afternoon turned into a late evening. Carter and his buddies were tardy returning to the ship and decided to take a short cut through the dunes, singing and laughing and momentarily carefree. Suddenly, someone yelled at them, "You stupid blokes. You're in the middle of a bloody minefield!" At that point, it was just as dangerous to turn back as to walk on, so they pushed ahead in single file. They did stop singing.

Irwin and Pillmore were also able to relax a time or two. One chilly evening, the British beachmaster, an army officer, invited the 614's two officers to his quarters on a wrecked British LCT high on the beach. The beachmaster promptly handed the two Americans large tumblers, which he filled with rum. At first the amount of rum didn't bother them—they were both game American college lads—but with the first sip of the fiery brew they both knew they could not possibly finish those drinks. They had no wish to insult their host by refusing the drinks, nor did they want to seem less stalwart than the Briton by not being able to handle the booze. Irwin waited until the beachmaster had Pillmore deep in conversation, then he sneaked out on deck and dumped most of his rum onto the sand, saving a little to nurse the rest of their visit.

On the way back to the 614, Irwin told Pillmore, "Now I know why the beachmaster always seems to have that ruddy glow. That stuff was like a red-hot poker all the way down. I had to slip out and toss my drink overboard."

Pillmore laughed. "You know, I did the same thing," he said. "When you were talking to the beachmaster, I slipped out the hatch and poured most of mine out, too." Irwin hadn't noticed Pillmore's absence, and he hoped for the sake of British-American relations that the beachmaster hadn't, either.

Irwin and Pillmore had at least one other outing with an Allied officer. They became acquainted with some Canadian pilots who flew from a temporary strip just behind the beaches. The pilots invited Irwin and Pillmore to lunch, and they heartily accepted. After lunch, one of the pilots invited them to take a short hop in one of the observation planes to view the front. This time the American officers' acceptance wasn't quite as hearty, but they finally decided they couldn't pass up the opportunity.

The Canadian normally flew Typhoons, a big fighter-bomber much like the American P-47 Thunderbolt, but here they were flying a slow observation plane. Once they neared the front, the pilot kept close to the treetops, explaining that they could easily escape any patrolling German fighters by ducking down below the trees. Soon they flew over an area where the ground was plowed up with tank tracks and shell holes, signs of a recent tank battle, and a little farther on they saw a line of foxholes on the front. Irwin found himself wondering why in the world he was there. The LCT duty was risky enough, and if he got shot down and killed on a completely unauthorized joyride, he doubted the navy would pay his life insurance to his new wife.

Eventually they made it back to the airstrip, where they faced a new adventure. The pilot came zooming in for a landing but could not get the little observation plane onto the ground. As he pulled up, he explained that he was used to coming in with the fighter at full throttle, but at speed the little plane built up too much ground effect and wouldn't settle down. The pilot needed two more attempts to get his little craft and his passengers safely back on the ground.

Discipline Deteriorates

As the operational demands on the LCTs began to ease slightly as the summer went on, the men of the 614 began taking any opportunity they could to blow off the steam that had been building over months of danger, constant work, little liberty, and no support from the U.S. Navy. Their boisterousness grew once the men realized that they were not under the direct scrutiny of any senior American naval officers. Lieutenant Rockwell, perhaps sensing that such an attitude was permeating the little fleet, decided that the LCT sailors under his command were not going to totally abandon naval discipline. Every Saturday morning he would visit a couple of his LCTs for a matériel and personnel inspection.

The 614 rarely met with his full approval. At first, he simply made suggestions for how things could improve. Of course, given his background as a wrestling coach, Rockwell put an emphasis on physical fitness, encouraging Irwin to lead the crew in calisthenics. The suggestion was ludicrous to everyone, and even after repeated instructions to spend time in physical training it became merely a running joke. One day, Carter had the 4:00 a.m.–8:00 a.m. watch, and instead of sounding reveille he hit the general quarters alarm. As the men came running out on deck with helmets and life jackets, Carter boomed down at them from the pilothouse door: "OK, men. Line up down there and let's see some push-ups. One-two, one-two." His shipmates looked at him in disgust a few seconds.

"Oh, go to hell, Carter," they replied as they shuffled back to their racks.

Irwin tried to explain to Rockwell that they didn't have time for spit and polish, because they were too busy just getting the job done. Rockwell would have none of it, and eventually he chewed Irwin out after an inspection. "Listen, Irwin," he said once. "If you're having trouble with one of your men, take your bars off your shirt and take him on deck and show him who's boss." Irwin thought Rockwell, a former wrestling coach, could pull that off, but at 150 pounds Irwin didn't think he could take very many of the men in his crew himself.

As it was, though, Irwin had very little trouble from the men. To be sure, they were not terribly disciplined young fellows, and they had a habit of going off on their own—sometimes in the British vehicles, sometimes on unauthorized cumshaw missions, and sometimes just wandering. Irwin tried to be understanding, but he was also growing very frustrated at the casual attitudes rampant among the crew. The frustration and pressures from Rockwell were beginning to take their toll on the young ensign, and he was beginning to have trouble sleeping.

Pequigney, meanwhile, was having no trouble at all sleeping. Always a sound sleeper, he was hard to awaken in the morning, and he was especially difficult to get out of his rack to go on watch in the middle of the night. One morning, Pequigney was being very difficult to get up, and Irwin finally decided he'd had enough. Irwin held an impromptu captain's mast, found him guilty of sleeping on duty, and awarded Pequigney a deck court-martial. The lowest of the three levels of courts-martial, a deck court could be convened by one officer who had the authority to award a more severe penalty than a skipper could at captain's mast. However, a deck court could not discharge a man from the service (which takes a summary court-martial) or sentence him to death (which takes a general court-martial). Pequigney found himself in front of the dreaded Rockwell, who busted him from petty officer back to seaman and sentenced him to a few days of confinement. Pequigney soon found himself locked up in a makeshift brig set up in the superstructure of one of the sunken Gooseberry blockships.

After Falaise and the liberation of Paris, the Allied armies pushed steadily and quickly eastward, and the LCT crews settled into a long and unrelenting tedium. With the constant practice, going alongside a Mike Tare or beaching had gone from being an adventure to being a chore. The supply situation continued to deteriorate, and the crew found themselves, despite their new skilled cook, depending more and more on army C and K rations for their meals. Eventually even those gave way to British army field rations. The crew found them much inferior to American field rations, with one exception: their cans of soup were fitted with a fuse. A person could open the can, light the fuse, and in a few minutes would have a hot meal. Unfortunately, the soup came in only two varieties—chicken and celery. Soon the LCT was littered with cans of celery soup.

The crew soon found a use for the celery soup. Always the curious one, Carter decided to find out what happened if he lit the fuse without opening the can. He placed the can on the fantail outside the after bulkhead, lit the fuse, and stepped away. After a surprisingly short time, the can exploded with a satisfyingly loud pop. Soon the pilothouse was filled with these soup "grenades," which the man on watch used to catch the attention of drifting British LCTs. The can made a startling clatter to begin with when it hit the steel deck, but when it exploded while the British watch investigated the noise, it definitely caught attention. The cans, of course, did not solve the problem of drifting British LCTs, but they did allow the men of the 614 to feel as if they were getting their message to the Brits through a bit better medium than shouting.

By August, avoiding collision became even more important. By then, the LCT had been so heavily worked that it really could stand no more damage. The bottom under the bow was worn thin, and the hull was dented and even pierced in places. Sounding the bilges and pumping were bothersome tasks that reached a critical stage when one of the voids holding fresh water began to leak and became contaminated with seawater. The equipment and machinery were also beginning to break down. Fortunately, time spent drying out could be put to use for maintaining the engines and the generators, so they gave very little trouble. The only piece of important equipment to break down was the oil-burning galley stove. After a few weeks of nothing but field rations, and as hopes of getting the stove fixed evaporated, Carter and the other former Boy Scouts in the crew began pouring oil into the recessed pad eyes, used to secure vehicles to the deck, and camp cooking over them.

Irwin Gets a Break

The real wear and tear, though, was on the crewmen themselves. The enforced swim call made by the cook was as close to a fight as the crew came among themselves, probably because they were too exhausted for tempers to rise that far. And Pequigney's woes in confinement aboard the Gooseberry was as close as any of them got to any real trouble. Irwin was the first to suffer physical effects of the exhaustion. Although the crew numbered only a dozen or so men, few of them were needed at any one time to operate the craft. They eventually learned everyone else's job so that no one was more idle than anyone else. Irwin and Pillmore were the only officers, though, and while Pillmore could and did command the ship competently and efficiently, he did not feel the constant pressures of responsibility that Irwin did. Eventually, Irwin became so fatigued that he was no longer able to eat or sleep. Once Rockwell learned the full extent of Irwin's trouble, he sent the young ensign off to recover.

Unfortunately, the best facility available was the SS *George W. Woodward*, a Liberty ship the army operated as a troop transport and hospital ship. Since this ship had been assigned to sit off the Gold area, Leide and his staff abandoned the LCI they had been using as flagship and set up shop aboard the *Woodward*. Irwin spent some ten days on the ship, mostly sleeping but also eating galley-cooked meals and taking regular, hot, freshwater showers for a change. The days passed all too quickly, interrupted only by visits by Rockwell or Leide. At night, his sleep was occasionally disturbed by the sound of underwater explosions—depth charges, he was told, being dropped by escorting warships to ward off German human torpedoes.

When Irwin was discharged from the *Woodward*, Leide granted him an unofficial week's leave. Leide explained that he really didn't have the authority to grant a leave, but Irwin and several other of the LCT skippers needed it. So he had leave papers drawn up so that Irwin and the others could travel in France, and soon the young officers were on their way to Paris.

The only way to get to Paris was to hitch a ride on the Red Ball Express. Operation Red Ball started up in the fall of 1944 after the Allies had broken out of Normandy. After the liberation of Paris on August 25, the Allied offensive gathered unprecedented momentum and threatened to outstrip their supply lines (General Patton had to be ordered to stop on several occasions). To keep the supplies reaching the men on the rapidly advancing front, the Americans began a round-the-clock nonstop truck conveyor belt that ran from Omaha Beach through Paris and on to the front. The Red Ball Express was a heroic supply effort on the army's part that made a World War II icon out of the deuce-and-a-half trucks and their mostly African American drivers.

Irwin and the other officers climbed into the back of one of the trucks. Some French civilians were already huddled atop the truck's load of five-gallon cans of gasoline apparently on their way to Patton's tanks. En route, Irwin was awed by the amount of destruction; whole villages were nothing more than rubble. So many buildings had been leveled in the fighting that the driver had no landmarks to guide him, and he made several wrong turns. But once he found his way back onto the Paris road, he worked his hardest to fulfill his orders to get there as quickly as he could. He drove as fast as possible and stopped for nothing. When he had to relieve himself, he wedged the gas pedal and stepped out onto the running board, steering with one hand. His passengers had to fend as best they could.

In Paris, Irwin and the others checked into a hotel that was being set up as the naval headquarters for the city. On the elevator, a senior officer scoped out Irwin and the other young but well-worn ensigns with him. Turning to a companion, he said, "Boy, this staff is certainly growing. I hardly know any of the officers anymore." A bit timidly, they admitted that they were but lowly LCT skippers in from the Normandy beaches, but the officer welcomed them to the hotel.

Newly liberated Paris offered a once-in-a-lifetime mix of danger, mystery, and allure for Irwin. An occasional rifle shot punctuated the night. The visitors were told that German snipers still holed up in the city, and occasionally German sympathizers, such as the women they left behind, would take potshots at the liberators. The young officers encountered a man handing out business cards that turned out to be tickets for a tour of one of the more upscale brothels. Irwin and a couple of the others went in and found it a classy place. They stayed long enough to have a glass of champagne with some of the working girls, but after that they claimed they had to have dinner with their commanding officer and would return later that evening. During the day, Irwin and the others walked around seeing the sights of a city that had largely escaped the ravages of war. On his way back to Normandy, Irwin kept humming that old World War I song: "How you gonna keep 'em down on the farm after they've seen Pa-ree?"

While Irwin was resting and recuperating, Pillmore carried on the duties assigned to the 614. Fortunately, they were operating only during daytime now, and to relieve crowding in the anchorage, they moored in a nest with two or three other LCTs at night. After a day's work and then getting the ship secured in the nest, he could grab an almost full night's sleep of five or six hours. One of his more interesting duties at this time was helping members of the crew cast their absentee ballots for the 1944 elections. Several members of the crew had gotten their ballots and in the evening asked Pillmore, since it was their first time voting, to go over the instructions for them to make sure they were filling out the forms correctly. The men kept prodding him: "Who are you voting for, Skipper?" Pillmore finally came up with the politic answer that he thought their decision was a personal matter that he didn't want to influence. He didn't want to admit that, although he could skipper an LCT, he was too young to vote.

Another Casualty

On the night of August 21, the ship suffered its last major injury among the crew and, after more than three months of combat duty, its first gunshot victim. The ship was moored inside the nest, with LCTs tied up on both sides. At midnight, Carter showed up in the wheelhouse to relieve Andin for the midwatch. Andin handed over the holstered .45 and went below, but fortunately he went to the head, immediately below the pilothouse, rather than to the crew quarters on the other side of the ship. Carter put on the holstered .45, and a few moments later the weapon fired. The bullet entered Carter's foot just below and behind the ankle and exited at the heel.

Andin, in the compartment below, heard the shot and ran up to the pilothouse to see what had happened. Finding Carter writhing in pain, he said he was going for help. A moment later, he burst into the officers' quarters and woke up Pillmore. "Skipper! Carter shot himself!" he shouted and then disappeared through the curtain to wake up Pequigney and Singsheim (who had taken over the duties of medic from Johnson).

With no more information than that, Pillmore hurried up to the pilothouse, dreading what he was going to find. He was almost relieved to find that Carter's wound was to the foot rather than to the head. As he examined Carter, other men began to arrive. Although his main attention was to Carter's foot, he noted that the weapon had clearly fired inside the holster; the bottom of the holster was blown out, and the fired casing was still in the pistol. Carter was in extreme pain, so Pillmore had some of the men carry him to the galley while Kleen radioed Mary for help and Singsheim retrieved the first aid kit. For some reason, Mary would not order the other LCTs to break up the nest so the 614 could take Carter to the hospital ship. Pillmore was told to administer morphine and wait for morning.

The morphine helped ease the pain some, but Carter was conscious and hurting for the rest of the night. They kept him on the galley table, giving him shots of morphine when the pain became intolerable. By the time the nest broke up and the 614 could get him to the *Woodward*, some ten hours had passed. Lt. Simon V. Ward, a navy doctor, treated Carter aboard the *Woodward*. He found that the bullet had passed through cleanly, hitting no bones or tendons, but had caused some nerve damage that left two of Carter's toes numb. The wound was so clean that Ward did not have to perform any surgery; he treated the wound with sulfa powder and bandaged it. The wound was severe enough, though, that Carter spent twenty-three days on the *Woodward*, returning to the 614 on September 14—just two weeks before his seventeenth birthday.

How the ship's gunner's mate was the one who shot himself remains a bit of a mystery. The official version of the story is that Carter put on the holstered but loaded .45 and then brushed against a bulkhead, which fired the weapon. However, in June 1945, Carter was in the Norfolk Naval Hospital in Virginia being examined for a fainting episode. Carter told the doctor then that he had experienced a similar event on the LCT and that when he fainted he fell against the bulkhead. Either way, it's hard to see how hitting a bulkhead could cause an M1911A1 Colt .45 automatic to go off, since it is designed with a grip safety that is supposed to prevent accidental firings. So the "official" version of the incident is clearly fictional.

One clue to the mystery may be provided by another incident some fifteen years later. In the late 1950s, Carter was showing off his "quick draw" to his three sons with a single-action Colt .45 six-shooter. He cocked the pistol and holstered it, but when he tried to draw the pistol, it fired. He stood still a moment, not daring to look. Again the bullet blew out the bottom of the holster, but this time it made a black streak down his trouser leg before hitting the ground right beside his foot. His sons now wonder if his thoughts in that moment of stillness were, "I've done it again."

Autumn for Mulberry

Carter returned to the 614 as the Mulberry B artificial harbor was being shut down. Le Havre was finally captured on September 8, by which time Cherbourg (which had become nominally operational on July 16) was pretty much a fully going concern. Now with two major ports in Allied hands and with other troops pushing north from the beachheads on the Mediterranean coast of France, the need for moving men and supplies over the Normandy beaches had almost evaporated. With the race of Allied armies to the German border during the late summer and early fall of 1944, Normandy's usefulness as a port of supply dwindled as the front moved farther and farther north and east.

Because the Normandy operations were no longer critical to the supply of the army, the navy began tapping the LCT crews to fill positions elsewhere. Cromer got orders in late August, just after Carter shot himself, to report to an LCI, and apparently Clark and Johnson left at about this time as well. Dowling had never been replaced, and the cook's position (as well as Johnson's medic duties) had been filled by Singsheim. And soon after Irwin returned from his leave in Paris, Pillmore was given official command of his own craft, LCT 601. The crew had thus dwindled to ten or so men from its peak strength of fifteen men on and just after D-Day. This number was more the planned size of an LCT crew, but it was fewer than the men of the 614 had been used to operating with. So although the operations of the LCTs had eased a bit, each individual crew member carried increased responsibility.

The usefulness of the artificial ports also dwindled as the channel weather deteriorated with the onset of fall. By November, the weather had turned too rough and cold for safe LCT operations. Unloading the Mike Tares in the outer anchorage became impossible even for the seaworthy LCTs (the crews had begun only half joking about drying out on the decks of the Mike Tares), and so all operations moved inside the shelter of the Phoenixes and Gooseberries. But even that shelter was only relative, and the notoriously bad North Sea weather, which would certainly not blow over as "The Great Storm" had, would soon settle in on top of them.

The combination of factors finally led to the Allied decision to close Mulberry B on November 19. So for the week or so leading up to that date, the LCTs stopped unloading operations, and their crews began packing up their gear and getting ready for the return trip across the channel. They had operated on the coast of France for five full months with very little respite and almost no support from the navy. Certainly they looked forward to their return to England, but in a way they dreaded their return to the "real" navy.

9

RETURN TO NEAR SHORE

The crew's trip back to England was about as opposite to the trip from England as it could have gotten. On the first trip, the deck had been crowded with vehicles, and more than eighty men had vied for elbow room. This time, only a few crates of Flotilla Twelve's equipment was secured to the deck, and with the reduced crew, scarcely a dozen people occupied the little ship. And whereas the weather on the trip to France had been bad, the weather on the return was absolutely horrible. Everyone except Carlson and Pequigney got so seasick they had to stick to their racks. Carlson spent most of the trip in the pilothouse with Pequigney. He would run down to the engine room occasionally to check on things, but the motion at the bottom of the ship, coupled with the heat and smell of the diesels, made the place unbearable. Carlson was also able to spell Pequigney on the wheel for short periods. Their "meals" consisted of crackers, marmalade, and coffee.

Fortunately, the trip took only two days, and soon the fleet of LCTs chugged up the Dart River to a repair base near Dartmouth. Soon the river was almost as clogged with a logjam of LCTs, LCIs, and other amphibious craft as it had been before the invasion. But now, instead of the shiny new ships filled with equipment, a motley fleet of tired and battered craft moored together in nests of two or three vessels along the river. On occasion, a craft would pull out of the nest and move to a rickety-looking pier where heavier equipment was available for the bigger repair jobs. Their duty here was relatively straightforward: get the LCT ready for transport back to the United States.

Over the next few weeks, the crew of the 614 immersed themselves in the most dreaded but ubiquitous task in all of seafaring—taking every square inch of the ship down to bare metal and repainting it. The crew used a variety of chipping hammers, scrapers, chisels, and sandpaper to make an area on the deck or bulkhead shine with untarnished steel, and then they would cover up their day's work with a fresh coat of red lead or zinc chromate primer. That area would then be painted a cheerful hue of navy haze gray.

Along with the painting went a thorough cleaning of the ship, especially in the engine rooms, machinery spaces, and even in the bilges. During the past five months, the crew had been able to do only patchwork repairs and the most basic cleaning and maintenance. Now they had nothing else to do but clean out all the accumulated grease and oil from every odd corner and hidey-hole in the cramped belowdecks area. The crew quarters, head, galley, bow lockers, and every void underneath the tank deck got the same treatment and were cleaned, chipped, polished, and repainted.

And, of course, the backdrop to all of this tedium was rain. In true English fashion, the late autumn weather was rarely anything but a steady gray drizzle. Soon the tank deck, warped and dented from its constant use, was little more than a series of small puddles, and the damp shoes and clothes of the men meant that not a warm, dry place existed anywhere on the craft. The constant damp made the always tedious work of chipping and painting an inhumanly impossible, torturous task worthy of Sisyphus (who, in Greek mythology, was condemned to an eternity of rolling a heavy stone uphill; whenever he reached the top, the stone rolled back to the bottom and his task started anew). And the penetrating wet meant that the men, despite woolen jerseys and other foul weather gear, were always chilled and sniffling.

And, to an extent, they were still cooped up on the LCT, especially if they were nested out in the river. The base personnel ran boats on a fairly regular basis, but on occasion the crew needed to get ashore on their own, either to pick up supplies or run some other errand. The LCT had come equipped with a seven-foot wooden dinghy, but rowing it against the current of the River Dart was more work than they wanted to do. Finally, someone figured out that they could use a handy-billy firefighting pump (powered by a gasoline engine about the size of a lawn mower engine) to propel their little craft. They would lash the intake hose over the side and then hold the output hose under the stern. The pump generated a hundred pounds of pressure, which could push the boat at a fair clip. They could also use the hose to steer, but unfortunately the rig had very little throttle control. It also had the advantage of offering a chance at some horseplay. Carter was using the boat one day, and on his return he saw several of the crew standing on the back of the LCT, waiting for his return. Instead of turning off the handy-billy and coasting up to the craft, Carter puttered past the craft, lifted the hose out of the water, and doused his shipmates. It was neither the first nor the last time Carter's practical jokes earned him wishes of damnation from his friends.

The in-port work is the kind of situation that almost all sailors find themselves in eventually, and generally a crew in this situation finds itself with absolutely no morale. (The running bitter joke at such times is, "Liberty has been canceled until morale improves.") But the men of the 614 had faced lower morale during the weeks of unrelenting work and horrible food back in August and September. Here, the men knew the food would be fresh, that sleep awaited them at night, and that certainly within the month they would be headed home.

True Liberty and Leave

Even better, once they were back in England, Leide had authorized the LCT skippers to grant the maximum amount of liberty and leave possible. For the 614, this meant that half the crew were given a full week's leave to go to London or wherever they wanted, and the other half, except for the two or three men necessary to maintain security watches at night, could have liberty in the nearby town of Torquay.

Torquay, a suburb of the city Torbay, is a resort on the southern coast of England complete with palm trees and landscaped promenades. And as a resort, it offered plenty of top-notch restaurants and pubs. It was the best liberty they'd had since leaving the States, and after the rubble of the shot-up coast of France, it must have seemed like the height of civilization. To reflect that mood, Carter, Gudger, and Pequigney bought top hats to wear while touring the little city. Apparently the Shore Patrol wasn't much of a presence in the town, since they were able to wear the hats long enough for a newspaper photographer to snap their picture and get it in the paper.

Carter was also taken with the little thatch-covered village of Cockington, just west of Torbay. The main "industry" of the village was a forge, which in its small way reminded him of the familiar railroad yards where his dad worked back in his hometown of Etowah. Once the illusion of home started, just about everything became a reminder of home. The thatch and the narrow dirt streets took on the semblance of some of the kudzu-choked towns in southeast Tennessee, and the villagers with their chickens and cows living near the houses could easily have been his grandparents or neighbors. The rural setting definitely gave him a taste of home that he'd not had since leaving Etowah more than a year ago. (His last visit home had been after he graduated from gunnery school in Bainbridge and before he reported to the Amphibious Training Base in Solomons.) He made friends with one of the local families and was able to get a few home-cooked meals while on liberty.

Of course, the main attraction for the men during this time was the seven or ten days' leave they each got. Most of the men headed for London and the amenities of a big city. Carter and some of the others actually took time for some sightseeing. Carter bought a postcard that featured a photograph of the high altar at Westminster Cathedral and jotted off a note to his mom: "Here's a joint we visited."

Although the Blitz was long over, London was still a city very much involved in the war. Occasionally one of the little "doodlebug" V-1 rockets would sputter overhead, or a larger V-2 rocket would crash unheralded on one of the city's streets. So the city was still completely blacked out. The men were used to blackout conditions, but they did feel the contrast in this vibrant major city, especially now that darkness was setting in so early. Finding the pubs, though, proved no great difficulty. The two easiest ways were to either follow a group of British sailors who apparently knew where they were going or simply wander the streets until a woman would come up from behind them, slip her arm around theirs, and offer to lead them to where they wanted to go. More often than not, the woman's offer included the price of her profession, but the men grew savvy enough to allow her to lead them to a nearby pub but not make any other commitment until they had seen her in a lighted place.

Once in the door and past the blackout curtains, the men found the pubs to be bright, cheerful, even raucous places. Now that most of the U.S. Army had transferred to the continent, the English populace had lost much of the resentment that had built up during the year or more before the invasion. However, some members of the British military still felt embittered toward the Americans who had occupied "their" territory. One evening a group of British tars tried to pick a fight with Carter and Carlson. Carlson, especially after a few beers, was never one to shy away from a fight, but Carter still had quite a bit of the Boy Scout in him. A fan of the cowboy matinees, Carter broke a beer bottle against the table and stood up to face the oncoming Brits, hoping they wouldn't recognize his action as a Hollywood cliché. Apparently they didn't, for they backed off without pressing the issue.

In the second week of December, with the LCT 614 freshly painted and now in some semblance of being shipshape, the crew made a day trip westward along the coast back to Plymouth and the Flotilla Twelve headquarters in Saltash. Along the way, Irwin allowed the men to break out the ship's small arms, firing off as much of the .45 ammo as they wanted through the Thompsons and the pistols. Carter wanted to pitch in with the 20mms, but Irwin thought they were too close to shore for that. Once they arrived in Saltash, most of the remaining members of the crew received their orders stateside. Carlson went back on the *Queen Mary*; Gudger, Kleen, and the others found themselves headed to various transports and troopships for the trip home.

Working Back to the States

Carter transferred out of Flotilla Twelve on December 10. Two days later he reported aboard the navy transport USS *LeJeune* (AP 74) at Southampton. His dreams of having a relaxing trip home as a mere passenger evaporated, though, when he learned that as a gunner's mate he would be considered a part of the ship's company and have to stand watch in one of the *LeJeune*'s antiaircraft mounts (she carried a 5-inch and four 3-inch guns, plus an assortment of 20mms). But it may have been his status as an auxiliary to the Armed Guard that allowed him to get some of his souvenirs from the beach past the authorities. In addition to the obligatory German helmet, gun collector Carter had bypassed the standard loot of Lugars and P-38s and was bringing home a flare pistol and an MP-40 Schmeisser submachine gun. Somehow it worked out that someone had disabled the flare pistol by whacking its chamber with a hammer so that a flare would no longer fit in it, but he took the MP-40 all the way back to Tennessee in perfect firing condition.

The *LeJeune* headed to sea just before midnight on December 16 in a gale, and the next day joined up with its convoy. The trip to the States was particularly miserable and cold, especially for those four hours that Carter was supposed to be standing watch on the mount; it was even wetter and colder than the watches he had done on the LST. One night the officer of the deck looked down from the bridge wing and didn't see Carter at his station. He had the bridge watch call down to the mount on the sound-powered phones: "Where are you?"

"I'm here under the gun," Carter replied, suddenly (and belatedly) worried that discipline on the transport would be stricter than it had been on the LCT.

But soon the bridge watch replied. "OK," he said, "as long as you're on station and haven't fallen overboard."

After that, Carter spent those watches huddled up in his foul weather gear as far underneath the gun mount as he could wiggle. This convoy was much faster than the trip outward had been, and on December 27 the ship pulled in to New York Harbor. The next day, Carter reported to the naval facility at Lido Beach, Long Island, and from there he began his thirty-day homecoming leave.

The 614 Heads Home

Back in the Plymouth suburb of Saltash, Irwin found his crew whittled down to just six men. The crew was further reduced very early on when the other crew members learned one man had brought a venereal disease back with him from London. Irwin had the man transferred to the local naval hospital and thought he'd seen the last of him. Irwin was now the skipper of an LCT crewed only by Pequigney, Kelly, Jarvis, Wajda, and Singsheim.

Now that they were headed home, Pequigney wanted to be reinstated as a petty officer after Rockwell had busted him back in Normandy. One afternoon, he went over to Flotilla Twelve headquarters, where the staff was busy loading up boxes for their own trip back to the States. Pequigney told the yeoman on duty that he wanted to take the test for quartermaster third class.

"You been up for rate before?" the yeoman asked.

"Yeah, I was a third class but got busted over on the beaches."

"Listen, Mac, you don't need to take the test."

Pequigney started to get a bit angry. "I know I don't need to take the test, but I want to go back up for rate. I've served enough time."

"Don't worry about it. Just forget it."

Pequigney wasn't about to just forget it, and he started shoving the yeoman around. "It's my right to go back up for rate, and I intend to do just that right now."

The yeoman could tell that Pequigney was getting ready to do more than just shove. "Listen to me. You got busted over in France, right? So you don't have to take the test to go back up for rate."

Pequigney finally understood what the yeoman was trying to tell him and stepped back. The enlisted men on the flotilla staff had no desire to cart around boxes of useless files; therefore, they had either trashed most of their records in France or burned them in England. Among the "lost" records were items of a temporary nature, such as disciplinary records. Pequigney made sure that his petty officer's pay would be reinstated and then went back to the LCT and immediately began sewing rating badges back onto his uniforms.

Flotilla Twelve changed as well. Lieutenant Commander Leide received orders keeping him attached to the naval forces in England. He ended up being one of the few Flotilla Twelve people to see combat again. In March 1945, he was selected to command a group of small landing craft (twenty-four craft in all, mostly LCVPs supported by a few LCMs) that ferried Patton's Third Army across the Rhine. The craft were carried to the river aboard large flatbed trucks. In some towns, houses had to be demolished to allow the big rigs through.

On March 23, Leide's boats hit the water and began carrying assault troops across to the German side of the Rhine at Oppenheim. The craft were under direct fire for part of the day and under heavy Luftwaffe attack for the next few days, but Leide was able to keep the men and armor flowing across the river. By March 26, army engineers had spanned the river with two pontoon bridges, but Leide's craft continued in operation, making other assaults at Boppard on the night of March 25 through 26, at Oberwesel on the afternoon of March 26, and, in the most heavily resisted crossing, at Mainz on March 28. For his actions here, Leide was awarded the Legion of Merit with the Combat "V."

On December 18, Irwin and the five stragglers reported aboard LST 540, and early that evening the 614 was hoisted aboard. They sat around Plymouth for several more days. Rumor had it that they were being held in case the German counteroffensive, which had been launched on December 16, would require the navy to mount another massive cross-channel resupply effort. But by December 19, the Allied armies had stopped the German advance, and a few days after that the Allies began regaining the ground they had lost. With the Battle of the Bulge now clearly destined to be another Allied victory, the navy crewmen relaxed and started loading for home.

On December 23, LST 540 moved to Turnchapel Hard to load a large crawler crane through the bow doors, and then they moved across the river to Cattedown Wharf to load cargo. While there, the seaman whom Irwin had transferred to the hospital because of his venereal disease tried to rejoin his shipmates. Irwin explained to the man that his orders included only the five men and that the seaman would have to return to Flotilla Twelve headquarters for further assignment. The next morning, Irwin made arrangements for his transfer, and soon after lunch he went ashore. They spent Christmas there, moored to the same wharf where the 614 had been launched from the LST 291 on May 4. The mood this time was much lighter, and the LST crew tried to celebrate Christmas with special chow and a few other impromptu merrymaking endeavors. They steamed out of Plymouth on December 27, the same day that Carter arrived in New York aboard the *LeJeune*.

The convoy back to the States was an all-navy collection of amphibious craft—mostly LSTs but also some LCI(L)s and APs. The North Atlantic winter weather was a constant factor in the voyage, but this time the U-boats left them alone and they had a fairly relaxed cruise home. As with Carter's return trip aboard the *LeJeune*, this was a direct voyage back to the States, and the convoy reached Norfolk on January 13, 1945.

Eager Homecomings

The crew still had a few days of work before their leaves started. The 614 was not hoisted off the 540's deck until just before 2:00 a.m. on January 16. That day, they took the craft over to Imperial Docks in Berkley, Virginia, for a complete, professional refurbishment. Once they handed the LCT over to the dockyard, the crew found themselves in a confusion of command about as bad as during their stay in France. Irwin wasted no time getting started on his thirty-day leave to reunite with his new bride, and in his haste he forgot to sign leave papers for his crew. Pequigney, as the ship's de facto yeoman, decided that their leaves were granted, just not signed. Beacuse he had no idea whether any of the Flotilla Twelve command structure had made it to the States or whether they were now under the shipyard command or even which of the two should sign the papers, he decided to assume the responsibility himself and signed the papers "for the commanding officer," whoever that may be. Then they all took off.

The navy took some time to figure out that the 614's crew was missing. A couple of FBI agents showed up at Pequigney's house just after he left to head back to Norfolk. His mother was very frightened about what was going on until she was able to get back in touch with him. He and Wajda returned to the amphibious base at Little Creek about the same time. They were given prisoner at large status and restricted to the base. A few days later Jarvis showed up, and Pequigney—still a PAL—had to go to the gate and sign him in. Jarvis had the more harrowing tale. He had spent his leave at Singsheim's home in upstate New York. One afternoon they were sitting at the kitchen table, essentially passed out drunk, and the Shore

Patrol showed up and carried Singsheim off, leaving Jarvis alone and stupefied at the table. Apparently Singsheim's general court-martial had not been "lost" the way Pequigney's deck court-martial had been, and he ended up going straight to jail. Jarvis sobered up enough to find his way back to Norfolk, and when he told the others what had happened to Singsheim, they packed all his belongings so they could be shipped once the Shore Patrol told them where to send them. It was the last they ever heard of Singsheim.

For a second time, Pequigney found himself in front of Rockwell at a deck court-martial. Rockwell looked at Pequigney and then leafed through his service record. "Pequigney, haven't you been in front of me before? I think I remember you from the beaches, but there's nothing here in your service record about a previous court-martial." The second line saved him.

"I don't know anything about that, sir," Pequigney said, ignoring the first question. "I don't have any control about what goes in my service record."

Rockwell smiled slightly at the correct answer; he knew that the record keeping for Flotilla Twelve hadn't been as complete as it should have been. But nonetheless, Pequigney soon found himself in the brig at Portsmouth Navy Yard, where he spent Easter Sunday.

Meanwhile, a small LCT 614 reunion took place in Georgia. Although fairly close with his family, Carter still did not want to spend his entire leave in Etowah. Somehow he hooked up with Cromer in Thomaston, Georgia, who had with him a buddy from the LCI he had been assigned to. The three of them planned a fairly energetic trip to Lake Brashear along the Flint River near Albany. They spent several days camped out in a small wooden shack, and to an extent the outing was similar to the Boy Scout camping trips Carter had enjoyed a little more than two years earlier but in a completely different lifetime. The men boated and fished a bit; one day, Cromer caught fourteen pounds of catfish, which made a sizable feast for the guys. But unlike the Boy Scout trips, this time the guys spent a large portion of the time drinking and partying with some of the local women. The party soon broke up, though, and Carter stopped back in Etowah briefly on his way back to Norfolk.

614 Battered Again

On February 12, the Old Dominion Marine Railway yard in Berkley finished its three-week overhaul of the LCT 614. It charged the navy $6,028.93 to replace the engines, take out all the dents, step a new mast, rework the wiring and plumbing, patch a hole in the ramp, and repaint the ship in its new Pacific Fleet colors. The navy issued orders that the refitted 614 was to be ready for sea again by March 23, a bit more than a month away. To help get the LCT ready for its next trip to sea on the deck of an LST, shipyard workers welded a series of angle iron brackets along the hull of the craft. These brackets, some four or five along each side, jutted out from the ship about six inches so that once the LCT was placed once more on the deck of an LST, shoring could be wedged under the brackets to help secure the LCT in place. When the LCT was launched from the LST, the crew simply would knock the brackets off with a heavy mallet.

The next Saturday, February 17, the 614 lay quietly moored outboard of the LCT 404 at Pier O at Lambert's Point, Norfolk. Only about five men of the new crew had reported aboard; the five veteran crewmen were still on leave (or AWOL or incarcerated), and the rest of the replacements were yet to arrive. The few men aboard the vessel were observing a typical in-port Saturday routine. Once the men had completed their duties of sweeping the compartments and shining the brightwork, the men who did not have liberty hit their bunks to sleep or read. One of the new men, a seaman deuce named William Murphy, went up to the pilothouse to stand watch.

Almost all navy watches are four hours long. That doesn't mean they all seem the same length. If the ship is under way, the watches seem fairly equitable because the life of the ship continues apace around the clock and the men generally have plenty to do. In-port watches, however, are a different matter altogether. The various day watches through the week have enough activity to them that the men on watch have enough to do to keep the boredom at bay, and the morning and evening watches slip by as the watch keepers perform the rituals of rousing the ship to life or putting it to sleep at night. The dreaded in-port midwatch, from midnight to 4:00 a.m., contains some entertainment as the men on liberty return to the ship (or are returned to the ship by the Shore Patrol), and the stillness of the hour leads to long and frank conversations among the watch standers.

The weekend day watches, however, are absolutely endless—a total vacuum of activity that is often downright painful to endure. The worst is the Sunday noon to 4:00 p.m. watch, which seems to last all day long. Second to it is the Saturday forenoon watch, 8:00 a.m. to noon, which starts with a bit of activity as the duty sections change, but the latter portion of it drags on. By 9:30 a.m. on that particular Saturday forenoon watch, Murphy was essentially alone on a dead ship. And tied up in the yards, there wasn't even much water traffic for him to watch. The only thing left to do that morning was to call up a couple of the men to set out fenders and handle lines when a tug showed up with another LCT that was to tie up on the port side of the 614. The men on deck felt the ship sway beneath them as the tug jammed the two LCTs together, but as soon as the other LCT's lines were aboard, the other men went below again, leaving Murphy once more alone at his watch.

As the morning wore on, Murphy stepped outside the pilothouse and saw that the port quarter of the 614 was under water. He ran down to the galley and opened the engine room hatch, discovering that the engine room was completely flooded. The watertight doors between the main engine compartment and the generator rooms on each side were both open, allowing water into all three of the principal engineering spaces. Fortunately, the ship was getting power from the shore, so Murphy was able to start the pumps, but the damage was already done.

The next day, repair personnel came over to survey the damage. Structural injury to the 614 was surprisingly slight. A three-inch-long and half-inch-wide slash in the hull apparently was caused when the tug jammed the craft together and one of the shoring brackets on the other LCT pierced the 614's hull. It would be an afternoon's work to dress up the gash and weld plates over it. The flooding of all three engineering spaces caused the real damage. The three engines and both generators would have to be replaced, and all electrical equipment and wiring in the compartments would have to be repaired. On February 20, the crippled little craft was towed to the Frontier Base in Little Creek for repairs.

Irwin returned from leave to find a situation far different from what he expected. Instead of an LCT 614 getting ready for sea, he found his craft back in the yards for a major refit and a good portion of his crew in the brig. He soon learned, though, that getting the craft and crew back together would not be his problem. In short order, he got a promotion to lieutenant junior grade and orders to report as gunnery officer aboard LST 637. As a division officer, he had command of as many or more men as he had as skipper of the LCT but without the ultimate responsibility for the ship itself. In that regard, Irwin felt that his life had indeed improved.

A New Skipper and Crew

Replacing Irwin was a very experienced young officer, Lt. j.g. Andrew J. "Jack" Banks from Seth, West Virginia. Banks had already graduated from college before he signed up for the navy; he had been on the college's boxing team and after graduation taught high school physical education. After Pearl Harbor, Banks began talking with the navy recruiters, and he was told that if he signed on for the navy's V-7 program that he could go straight on to midshipmen's school. He did so and was sent on to Chicago, but once there he learned that the next class would not form for another three weeks. Consequently, for the next three weeks Banks had nothing to do but enjoy his stay in Chicago.

After graduation and his commission, Banks was assigned as the boat officer of LST 174. As boat officer, he was in charge of the six LCVPs the ship carried, making sure they were maintained and keeping tabs on them during assaults. On the way to Europe, a chief boatswain's mate learned that Banks thought he was a pretty good boxer, so the crusty old salt challenged the wet-behind-the-ears ensign to a boxing match, thinking it would be a good way to finally beat the snot out of one of these ninety-day wonders. The skipper approved the match, and the two finally squared off in a makeshift ring set up on the LST's upper deck. Banks made short work of the "Boats." Fifty years later, Banks said simply, "I beat the poop out of him."

LST 174 saw plenty of action in the Mediterranean theater, participating in the assaults at Salerno and Anzio. During these landings, Banks went inshore with the LCVPs to oversee their activities and to be on hand in case one of them got into trouble. His experience under fire drew the attention of his skipper, who appointed him to take special training for the demolition crews being put together for the invasion of southern France. Before that invasion, though, Banks was sent back to the States, where he ended up being fingered as LCT 614's new skipper.

His experience as an officer and as a teacher helped make him quite popular with the crew. He knew just how much of the regulation navy to take seriously, he knew how to communicate his intentions to the crew, and he knew how to relieve their tedium as much as was in his power. He relied heavily on his petty officers, especially Kelly, and once he returned from the brig in April, Pequigney, for those two men knew the 614 better than anyone else on board.

In addition to Pequigney and Kelly, only two others of the European theater crew remained—Wajda and Jarvis, neither of whom had yet been promoted (of course, it was by the grace of God and the yeoman on the Flotilla Twelve staff that Pequigney was again, or still, a petty officer). Some of the new men who came aboard were quite experienced themselves. Francis G. Coffas came aboard as an electrician's mate second class, another "Sparky." He had served on LCT 625, which was part of the O-1 Assault Group at Omaha Beach. On D-Day, Coffas took a few shots at Wing Commander Josef Priller during the German aviator's famous dash along the invasion beaches. On the LCT's port gun, Coffas fired at Priller as the Luftwaffe pilot and his wingman passed astern of the ship. When he swung around to starboard, the muzzle blast of the 20mm rattled the 625's skipper up on the conning tower. Later, the 625 helped rescue men from the stricken and sinking transport *Susan B. Anthony* after she hit a mine off Omaha.

The only other petty officer to come aboard with the new men was Edward G. Townsend, a coxwain (third-class boatswain's mate). He was from Salisbury, on Maryland's Eastern Shore, and came to the 614 with plenty of sea duty behind him. Unlike the men of the 614's original crew, he was highly adept in deck and marlinspike seamanship, skills that served the little ship well in the coming months. He gladly instructed the other deck sailors in their duties, especially in rope work.

Other men came from brief assignments aboard other ships but had not seen any action. Paul DiMarzio's first sea duty was aboard the battleship *New York*. A sister ship of the *Texas*, the *New York* had seen some action off North Africa in 1942, but she had missed the Normandy invasion. As the ship was working up for a Pacific deployment, DiMarzio found himself after only a month aboard headed for amphibious training at Solomons Island. After the battleship, the little Gators looked incredibly puny, and DiMarzio wasn't sure that he, as a deck seaman, had anything to offer. So he volunteered to be trained as the ship's cook, and off again he went to be trained as a baker. Once aboard the 614, DiMarzio showed a variety of skills, from carpentry to marlinspike seamanship (learned largely from Townsend).

And, of course, several of the new men were raw "boots." Glenn Dunnegan was a seaman deuce from DeWitt, Iowa, who had never seen a ship before. He was a bit of a duck hunter, though, and tended to gravitate toward the guns. So although he never went to gunner's mate school, he inherited Carter's billet on the ship. Pequigney and the others kidded him about not shooting himself in the foot, a joke he thought was merely an insult until he heard the story about Carter.

The crew was rounded out by unrated seamen Melvin Buchsbaum, Lloyd Butler, Lucian Conn, and Gerald George. Perhaps because of the experience gained off the Normandy beaches, the balance of this crew was quite different from the 614's original bunch. In 1944, the men had been pretty much evenly split between deck sailors and engineers; in this crew, Kelly and Jarvis were the only motor macs, and "Sparky" Coffas was the only other engineer. That may have been an idiosyncrasy of this particular crew, or it may have reflected the navy's realization that basic deck seamanship was more valuable on an LCT than technical proficiency was.

On April 1, 1945 (the Easter Sunday Pequigney spent in the brig), American marines went ashore on Okinawa. As the 614's new crew fitted the LCT out for its next deployment, they followed the war news closely. As April turned into May, the war in Europe ended and sparked quite a bit of celebration stateside. But for the sailors of the 614, waiting to head to the Pacific, they knew that the last months of the fighting would be horrible, considering the pounding that the kamikazes were giving the navy off Okinawa. By the middle of May, when the 614 was at last ready for sea, the battle for Okinawa still raged, yet everyone knew the issue was a matter of when the island would be captured, not if. Logically, only one invasion remained for this war—Japan.

10

SLOGGING ACROSS THE PACIFIC

LCT 614's transport into the Pacific war was LST 1008 (which the crew called the "Ten Oh Eight"), commanded by Lt. R. M. Laden. Unlike LST 291, which had taken the 614 to Europe while fresh from its post-commissioning shakedown cruise, the 1008 had been operational for more than a year and was a fairly efficient fleet unit. During the weeks just before the 614's crew reported aboard, the 1008 had loaded up with more than twelve thousand rounds of 40mm and almost twenty-six thousand rounds of 20mm ammunition, and they were at sea conducting a structural firing test off Point Lookout, Maryland, when the news came that Germany had surrendered. They had all known for some time that the war in Europe was winding down, and their attention had already shifted to the Pacific. In fact, very soon after the crew had settled down from their East Coast V-E Day celebrations, the ship headed up to Davisville, Rhode Island, where the crew spent a week at the Advance Construction Battalion Supply Depot loading pontoon causeway sections and cargo for the Seabees' use in the Pacific war. From there, they headed back to Norfolk to make final preparations for going to Japan.

On the morning of May 24, 1945, the 1008 lay moored to the crane dock at Norfolk Navy Yard in Portsmouth, Virginia. At 9:00 a.m., Lt. j.g. Jack Banks and the twelve men of the 614's crew reported aboard. They were Electrician's Mate Second Class Francis G. Coffas, Motor Machinist's Mate Second Class Francis J. Kelly, Quartermaster Third Class Frank Pequigney, Coxswain Edward G. Townsend, Fireman First Class John G. Jarvis, Seaman First Class Chester J. Wajda, Seaman First Class Melvin Buchsbaum, Seaman First Class Gerald E. George, Seaman Second Class Lloyd E. Butler, Seaman Second Class Lucian E. Conn, Seaman

Second Class Paul F. DiMarzio, and Seaman Second Class Glenn Dunnegan. Within an hour LCT 614 itself had been hoisted aboard and secured to the deck. With the 614's crew came the commanding officer of LCT Flotilla Forty-three, Lt. Arthur M. Rose, and his staff of four officers and eight enlisted men. For Pequigney and the other veterans of the Normandy beaches, this many LCT officers in such proximity made them a bit uncomfortable, but the men so quickly became absorbed into the crew and routine of the 1008 that the officers stayed pretty much invisible.

The 1008 sailed the next evening, steaming independently for the Panama Canal. In a way, the week at sea was the first time the 614's new crew really had time to get to know one another. During the few months they had spent in Norfolk, they had been busy getting the LCT ready for sea, stocking supplies, training, and, of course, taking as much liberty as possible because they had no idea when or whether they would see the United States again. Consequently, a few of them spent a few liberty hours together, and they had worked a bit together as a crew, but they really hadn't had a chance to simply chat with one another. The voyage down the East Coast provided an opportunity to do that.

With the war in Europe now over, the only threat they faced in that leg of their voyage was the remote chance that a stray U-boat whose captain didn't know, or didn't care, that the war was over would take a potshot at them. That possibility was so remote, almost a month after Germany's surrender, that the 1008 neither had an escort nor set dawn or dusk general quarters. The first day out they held drills, and the crew stood Condition 3 watches, which meant no smoking on deck after sunset. But apart from that, they were in a very real sense sailing under peacetime conditions.

In fact, during the eight-day transit to the Panama Canal, the ship held general quarters drills only three times. During their first full day at sea, the general quarters and emergency drills lasted a little more than an hour, but on the other days the exercise took only about thirty minutes. The major part of a general quarters drill is to see how quickly the men can get to their stations and button up the ship. Only during the last exercise, on May 31, did the gun crews get a chance to shoot. Almost as common as general quarters drills were engine breakdowns. On the evening of May 26, the port engine had to be stopped for an hour for repairs. The engine started acting up again during the midwatch of May 31; the engineers slowed the engine to make repairs to the line providing coolant water to the engine. Some fifteen minutes later the engineers brought the engine back up to full speed, but no more than twenty minutes after that the coolant line still wasn't working properly. The engine had to be stopped completely for more than an hour and a half before it was fixed.

The engineering problems went by unnoticed by most of the 614's crew, and the general quarters drills served only as almost welcome diversions from the underway routine. As the ship headed south into the springtime gulf, the men took advantage of the routine to relax on deck or to play the ubiquitous game of cards, both of which provided opportunity for them to chat about themselves and speculate about what they would find once they got to the western Pacific. The big LST even had room for the men to move about and find a little space for themselves, since the 1008 was carrying only a small amount of cargo and very few passengers—mostly the 614's crew, who really weren't being treated as passengers, and the flotilla staff, who were. As a result, the tank deck and upper deck were both free for the men to roam. Someone even set up a basketball hoop on the tank deck. It was as close to a pleasure cruise as one could get without women or booze aboard.

By the time the ship reached the Panama Canal Zone, LCT 614 once again had a fairly unified crew—unified enough, at least, to go on liberty together. The ship pulled into the Canal Zone during the midwatch of June 2 and anchored in the harbor, but soon after sunrise it moved to the docks at the Coco Solo Naval Station. It was a Saturday morning, and the ship wasn't scheduled to start through the canal until Sunday morning; in short, they had time for a rousing, one-night liberty call. As some of them had done in Boston on St. Patrick's Day 1944 (their last night in the States before going to Europe), many of the crew chose this liberty call to have photos of themselves made. The Canal Zone wasn't exactly the States, but it was American territory, was on the continent, and had the important distinction of not being Norfolk.

The next day, the 1008 got under way at 9:00 a.m. to move to an anchorage at the mouth of the canal. They spent about forty-five minutes at anchor—not time enough to break sea detail but plenty of time for the crew to breakfast and have a few cups of coffee amid the in-port Sunday routine before having to settle in permanently to their sea detail stations for the transit. It was, all in all, a pleasant Sunday afternoon passing through the locks of the canal, watching the monkeys, and taking in the peaceful tropical scenery that lined the placid inland waterway. Except for Pequigney, who spent much of the time at his sea detail station on the bridge, most of the 614's crew had little to do until the ship entered the locks and they had to man lines and fenders. Even then, the work wasn't terribly taxing for an LST crew, since the locks could handle even the new Iowa-class battleships and Essex-class carriers. The much smaller LST could warp in and out of the lock gates fairly handily (as handily as an LST could navigate anything), so by 6:00 p.m., the 1008 had cleared the last of the locks. Just after 7:00 p.m., the ship cleared the canal and gained the open sea. They were on their way to Pearl Harbor.

Pearl Harbor

Unlike the Atlantic, the Pacific was still a war zone. However, Japanese submarines had not ventured east of the Hawaiian Islands since 1942, when a few of the large fleet submarines had operated off the U.S. West Coast. Even in those early months of the war when the U.S. Pacific Fleet was badly crippled, submarine attacks on shipping between Hawaii and the West Coast were rare (although reports of attacks were plentiful), and in February 1942 one Japanese submarine cruiser shelled an oil refinery in Ellwood, California. Now, in mid-1945, the eastern Pacific was an American backwater, and again the 1008 sailed along independently and unescorted. As they had in the Atlantic, the crew stood Condition 3 watches, but they did not stand routine dawn and dusk general quarters.

Here in the Pacific, the pleasure cruise feel of their voyage began to fade. In the European theater, subsurface weapons (mines and torpedoes from both submarines and E-boats) accounted for twelve of the sixteen LSTs lost in combat. In the Pacific, aircraft were the ships' particular nemesis, having accounted for eight of the ten LSTs lost in combat in that theater. Consequently, during the eighteen-day voyage to Pearl Harbor, Lieutenant Laden exercised the gun crews at antiaircraft shooting on more afternoons than not. Usually the drills consisted of the skipper calling the crews of the ready guns—the 40mm mounts already manned under Condition 3 watches—into action and seeing how many rounds the men could get off in just three or four minutes while shooting a few rounds at some imaginary target on a given bearing and angle. Since the whole ship would not go into general quarters for these drills, the shooting provided some of the rare bits of entertainment the men had. The live-firing exercises cu minated on June 17, a Sunday afternoon, in an extravaganza of firing off flares and having the gun crews aim at them while the ship practiced evasive maneuvers. In the twenty-minute exercise that afternoon, the men at the 40mm guns fired off almost eighty rounds.

Also on this leg of the cruise, the engines gave only a little trouble. The freshwater coolant line on the port engine gave out again, forcing the engineers to shut the engine down for an hour and a half. Three days later, the lube oil line on the starboard engine acted up, but the engineers fixed that problem within half an hour of shutting down the engine. The engine problems were relatively slight, and since the 1008 was operating independently, the two slowdowns weren't an embarrassment to anyone but the engineers.

On June 20, the 1008 entered Hawaiian waters, a shipping choke point that still held the remote chance of a Japanese submarine lurking about. That morning, the ship began a standard zigzag pattern, an LST's only defense against submarines. That afternoon the crew drilled at general quarters, and the next morning, well after dawn, the captain set general quarters again as the ship approached the island and entered the swept channels off Pearl Harbor. By this stage of the war, the ship faced a greater chance of striking a mine that had broken loose from its moorings than of encountering a submarine, but buttoning up the ship to contain any possible damage and to improve watertight integrity under such conditions had become a wartime ritual.

The 1008 sailed into Pearl Harbor and headed to her assigned berth in the West Loch, well away from Ford Island and the central part of the harbor, which suffered the brunt of the attack now some three and a half years earlier. Little of the damage from that historic event remained; only the *Arizona* and the *Utah* were not raised (and both are still there). Otherwise, the place was a thriving seaport, totally inundated with sailors and soldiers and almost as crowded as Portland, England, had been just before the Normandy invasion. As it was, the crew had only two nights of liberty in Pearl. It was twice as long as in Panama, but with the larger number of American military people around it seemed less satisfying. The men understood, though, that it was going to be their last, best liberty until probably after the war. So they took advantage of what they had.

Under the circumstances, it's incredible that only one man of the 1008's crew got into trouble. A second-class steward's mate, assigned to serve the officers in the wardroom, sneaked into the ship's service officer's stateroom and took $318. He was caught on the quarterdeck with almost all of that cash stuffed in his shoe. He was clamped immediately in the brig under armed guard, and just a little more than an hour later, Laden held a captain's mast. On the evidence of a bill with a hole in it that the ship's service officer was able to identify, Laden awarded the hapless sailor a general court-martial and transferred him off the ship to the authorities ashore.

Only one LCT 614 sailor ran afoul of navy regulations. Sparky Coffas, the electrician and one of the senior petty officers on the crew, wandered back onto the LST some four hours after his liberty expired. Normally, sailors guilty of such a crime would be given extra duty and perhaps a short confinement, but Coffas was not officially a member of the 1008's crew. He was handed over to Banks, who devised an appropriate unofficial punishment.

The stop at Pearl was not just a liberty call. The crew had plenty of work to do during the two days in port. The first day, the LST took on some stores, including eighteen thousand gallons of water and forty-nine thousand gallons of fuel oil, and then disembarked the staff of LCT Flotilla Forty-three. The next day, they took on some additional cargo and their main load of more than a hundred men destined for the forward base on Guam. These men were mostly members of several construction battalion (Seabee) units, but among them was a small contingent of army personnel: a second lieutenant and ten men, mostly sergeants, of the Twenty-first Radio Security Section. With all these passengers aboard, the amount of free deck space was sharply reduced, and the tank deck basketball games were over. But of more importance to the crew of the 614, they got their second officer, Ensign R. E. Carlson.

Voyage to Tedium

That evening, the 1008 sailed from Pearl Harbor. This time, the ship sailed as part of a small convoy, Task Unit 13-11.44, made up of five other LSTs and a landing ship, medium (LSM). That night the 1008 kept station some thirteen miles from the task unit flagship, LST 997, but after sunrise the ships formed into their normal sailing disposition. LST 997 led the right column, followed by LSTs 846 and 859 and LSM 344. The 1008 took station as the rear ship of the left column, led by LST 871, with LST 732 in the middle. The ships settled into their cruising speed of ten knots and headed toward Eniwetok.

Three days into this twelve-day voyage, the 1008 had finally gotten close enough to the Pacific war that the crew began manning battle stations at dawn. In the Atlantic while aboard the 291, the crew had gone to general quarters at both dawn and dusk, but here they buttoned up the ship only at dawn. At that time of year and at that latitude, these dawn general quarters were being set between 5:00

a.m. and 5:30 a.m. and lasted half an hour or more. The timing was such that the men who got off watch at midnight didn't lose too much sleep, but the guys who stood the midwatch got only a little more than an hour's sleep when they went off at 4:00 a.m. Sailors are notoriously good at snatching what sleep they can when they can, but even healthy young men need stretches of unbroken sleep to stave off the effects of sleep deprivation. Under these conditions, even without an immediate threat of being shot at, moods tend to deteriorate quickly.

Had the sunrise alerts been the only change in their at-sea routine, the crew would have felt more of an urgency in this period. But any residual feeling of "pleasure cruise" evaporated with the constant maneuvers the officer in tactical command (OTC) of the task unit (the captain of the LST 997) ordered the ships into from time to time. None of them came in the dead of night, though on June 28 the OTC used the time of dawn general quarters to put the ships through a few drills. Some in the crew thought the maneuvering was a waste of time, that perhaps the OTC had confused the ungainly formation of LSTs for a squadron of destroyers, but the officers and more meditative crewmen understood that if the task unit did come under air or submarine attack, the formation would need to know how to maneuver together. For everyone on board, the tactical drills made the war seem all that much closer.

On the morning of June 29, the ships conducted their only live-fire exercise of this leg of the cruise. In a little less than twenty minutes, the 1008 fired off 236 rounds of 40mm ammunition, almost twice as much as during the several live-firing exercises the ship had conducted while steaming from the Canal Zone to Pearl Harbor. This time the 20mm guns joined in, firing 557 rounds at imaginary targets. The noise and tracer fireworks served as a hemispheric farewell, for that evening the little fleet crossed the international date line. At 6:00 p.m., what had been the afternoon of June 29 became the evening of June 30.

The task unit reached Eniwetok on the morning of July 5. This atoll had been captured in February 1944, and already it was a major backwater. The principal forward staging area was now in Ulithi at the western edge of the Caroline Islands, although Eniwetok was well placed as a fueling stop for short-legged ships such as destroyers and LSMs on their way from Pearl Harbor to either the central or south Pacific.

The task unit stayed at Eniwetok only one night while the ships topped off fuel tanks (the 1008 took on a bit less than twenty-five thousand gallons, or about half of what she had taken on at Pearl). It was certainly no liberty port, although a few men made it ashore on ship's business or to stock up on personal items (toiletries, uniforms, etc.) not available in quantity on the LST. Early the next afternoon, the task unit was again at sea, continuing to Guam.

Leaving Eniwetok, however, the ships were able to conduct an extensive and useful gunnery exercise. Before, the gunners had no real targets to shoot at, but this time an aircraft from Eniwetok towed a target sleeve past the ships that had formed up in column. All the guns participated, with the port battery getting first crack as the plane made three passes with the sleeve, and then the starboard battery got its three passes. In all, the exercise lasted more than an hour, and the 1008 shot up 617 rounds of 40mm and 1,720 rounds of 20mm.

The five-day voyage to Guam continued the at-sea routine the task unit had established after leaving Pearl Harbor. Farther west, the ships now had to set dawn general quarters stations as early as 4:30 a.m. Apart from that, this at-sea period offered even fewer distractions than had the leg from Pearl to Eniwetok; the task unit commander drilled the ships on tactical maneuvers only once. Life aboard the LST had become tediously dull and monotonous, and now that the ship had more than a hundred Seabees and army personnel aboard, the tank deck below and the main deck above offered little space to wander about or to be alone.

Added to that inconvenience was the fact that by now the ship was on severe freshwater conservation. The men were allowed a strict water ration for their personal cleanliness, and it meant that most of the time, the men had to take marine showers. At those times, a man would be stationed at the showers to keep track of how long the men ran the water. On the way to Guam, one man in the LST's crew was given a captain's mast for wasting water; as punishment, his freshwater ration was reduced to only two-thirds of a bucket of fresh water a day for seven days.

On July 11, the task unit sailed into Port Apra, Guam. The LSTs moored in a nest out in the harbor anchorage, and the 1008 had some slight fortune in being the outboard ship on the port side of the nest with her task unit mates LSTs 732, 871, and 859. Being outboard, the ship got what little breeze stirred across the harbor and offered the men a bit of a view.

Early the next morning, boats came alongside to take off the construction battalion personnel and the army men from the radio security section who had come aboard at Pearl Harbor. As soon as they were gone, about 10:00 a.m., the 1008 cast off and headed ashore for its first operational landing. She nosed in at the Minecraft Landing in Apra Harbor, trailing three hundred feet of stern anchor cable. At Normandy, LSTs could be landed, dried out, unloaded, and ready to be refloated on the next tide, but here the men felt no particular hurry. The 1008 spent six full days beached as the crates and machinery were taken from the tank deck and delivered ashore.

During this boring and backbreaking week, the men of the 614 crew got a glimpse of what may lay in store for them. On July 16, LCT 1186 came alongside the LST to deliver ten thousand gallons of fresh water. Even in the later weeks at Normandy, the 614 and other LCTs had done the job they were designed to do—land equipment and supplies and men onto a beach—but here was a much newer LCT being used in the inglorious role of a harbor barge. The 614's crewmen felt an odd mixture of envy and relief. They knew they were on their way to the fighting front, most likely the invasion of Japan, and so they felt some relief that they would not be left behind in some backwater port to do the work of a tug and tow. And yet, they felt some envy that with such boring and thankless work, the men of the 1186 knew that they would survive the war and one day go home.

War's Last Gasp

But if the road home for the 614's men led through Japan, its first stop had to be Okinawa. Although organized resistance had stopped by June 21 and the island had been declared "secured" on July 3 (to them, just two weeks earlier), the fighting there continued. Japanese soldiers, individually or in small groups, harassed U.S. troops ashore, and Japanese aircraft, likewise individually or in small groups, attacked the fleet offshore. But already the island was being readied as the forward staging area for the invasion of Japan. Planning for Operation Olympic, the invasion of the Japanese home island of Kyushu in October 1945, was well under way, and the men of the 614 and the 1008 were now part of those preparations.

On July 18, the 1008 finally retracted from the beach and moored alongside LST 732 at pilings in the north harbor. That afternoon, their new complement of passengers came aboard: eight officers and 181 men of the already famous First Marine Division. These men, many of them seasoned combat veterans, were slated to be among the assault troops for the invasion of Japan. The 1008 was assigned to take the men to Okinawa, joining a convoy that would form up in Saipan.

Within two hours of the marines' reporting aboard, the 1008 got under way with LSTs 554 and 830 for the overnight trip to Saipan, dropping the hook in twenty-two fathoms of water in the outer anchorage at 8:18 a.m. The stay in Saipan started with some excitement—the first real taste of the war in the Pacific. A little after 9:30 p.m., the ship went to general quarters in response to a sub scare. The forward fleet anchorages lay well within range of Japanese subs, and these open lagoons were much harder to keep secure than was a fully enclosed harbor like Pearl. Ulithi Atoll was especially prone to such infiltrations, and a sub there had succeeded in sinking the fleet oiler *Mississinewa* in November 1944. In these very waters, a Japanese plane had torpedoed the battleship *Maryland* during the gunfire support phase of the battle to take Saipan almost exactly a year earlier. The scare lasted only ten minutes, and the men topside saw some frantic maneuvering by destroyers and destroyer escorts (DEs) searching for the possible intruder. But soon even that distraction ended, and the men settled down to ten excruciatingly boring days of swinging around the hook.

On July 23, they moved to the inner harbor, where worsening weather on July 29 provided some traditional seamanship as the LST crew rolled out additional chain to the bow anchor to prevent them from dragging in the increased wind. But the ship had no real business in Saipan except to form up with a convoy to Okinawa. While at anchor, the men were beginning to be told something about their assignments for the invasion of Japan. They examined photographs of the Japanese beaches that they would assault, and they attended briefings about the coastal and air defenses the fleet had encountered recently at Okinawa. The officers assumed that defenses on the Japanese home islands would be similar but more intense. The kamikaze attacks, especially, would certainly be even more determined and deadlier than they had been off Okinawa.

During all that time, the men had no liberty. To break the boredom as best they could, Laden would allow the bow ramp to be lowered so the men could take a swim call. And every few days a small number of the men were allowed to go ashore. They were issued two beers apiece, and the only entertainment they could scrape together was perhaps a few hours of sitting under a tree or bargaining for the beers of the men who did not drink or maybe collecting enough men for a makeshift game of baseball. With the LST's tank deck now crowded with marines and their gear, the men aboard ship could do nothing to while away the hours except play cribbage or acey-deucey.

The boredom had become so oppressive that Sparky Coffas began to worry seriously about his mental health. Since he didn't play cards and wasn't a reader, he really had absolutely nothing to do inside the cramped LST. Finally, he asked to go to one of the transports in the anchorage and see if it had a psychiatrist. They didn't, but he was allowed a chat with one of the doctors. Coffas explained how he was getting terribly cranky and short with all the other fellows and then asked whether he was cracking up. "Son," the doctor said, "you're no different from anybody else. Hell, we're all going crazy down here." On his way back to the 1008, Coffas wondered whether he was supposed to take comfort from the doctor's words.

Finally, on August 1, LST 1008 left Saipan for Okinawa in company with convoy SOK 24. The convoy was made up of amphibious ships of various sizes—mostly LSTs, LSMs, and LCIs—with the senior officer in LST 554. The 1008's initial position in the convoy was as lead ship in the second column. The week-long voyage was a no-nonsense combat zone convoy, with the ships standing general quarters at dawn each morning (usually between 5:00 a.m. and 6:00 a.m.). The only incident came on the morning of August 4 when the convoy flagship broke down, and—a bit ironically, given the ship's engineering history—the 1008 was assigned to tow LST 554. The 1008 and tow soon regained the protection of the convoy, moving into position as the second (and third) ship in the second column. The tow lasted a little more than twenty-four hours before the 554 repaired its engines and the crew cast off the tow. Apart from that, the ships would occasionally maneuver alongside one another to highline spare parts, guard mail, or movies.

On the evening of August 6, the convoy reached Okinawan waters. Of course, they knew nothing at the time about the atomic bomb that had been dropped earlier that day on Hiroshima. On the midwatch that night, about 2:30 a.m., the ships went to general quarters as radar picked up planes heading toward them. Within thirty minutes, though, it was clear that the planes were targeting shipping at anchor. The crew stood down, only to go back to general quarters two hours later as part of the dawn routine.

Later that morning (August 7), the skipper of the 1008 became OTC of a sixteen-ship detachment from the convoy heading for Hagushi anchorage. The little fleet consisted of two LSTs, a destroyer transport, eight LSMs, an LCI, and four smaller craft. Laden's career as a fleet commander was short lived, however; little more than two hours after detaching from the convoy, the ships began anchoring off Hagushi, Okinawa. This large, open bay on the west coast of Okinawa had been just a few months earlier the scene of the principal assault landings for the marines who were to capture the island's main airfields.

The 1008 had reached Okinawa just in time to experience some of the last air raids of the war. The first evening there provided no rest for any of the crew as the 1008 set general quarters three times during the night in response to approaching enemy planes. The first was a thirty-minute alert just at sunset. The other two—one just before midnight and the other about 2:30 a.m.—lasted more than an hour each. Fortunately, no ships were hit that night, but for Pequigney and the others who had experienced air raids in England and France, the raids served as an unwelcome reintroduction to the war. As it turned out, that night was the 1008's only brush with the enemy and the 614's only combat experience in the Pacific, and the only casualty was the night's sleep the men had looked forward to in port.

The short stay at Okinawa was a busy time for the men. The morning of August 8, the marines went ashore, and soon afterward the 1008 left the anchorage and beached for several hours. Just before sunset, though, the LST retracted from the beach and headed back to the protection of the anchorage. The next day, August 9, the ship again beached early in the morning, spent the day ashore, retracted, and anchored out for the night.

The men were also busy with training and briefings concerning the upcoming invasion of Japan. Planning for the invasion was far enough along now that they were being told which beaches they would assault, and they were getting information from the analysis of the defenses on Okinawa and what this told the intelligence officers about how the Japanese would defend their home islands. For the navy, Okinawa had been the bloodiest campaign since Guadalcanal; the invasion of Japan itself would be much worse. As a landing craft quartermaster, Pequigney spent quite a bit of time looking at photographs of the beaches and examining charts of the nearby reefs.

Easing into Peace

On August 10, the LST had no business ashore and spent the entire day at anchor. The nearness of the war came home to the men as they learned that a Japanese submarine had torpedoed the freighter *Jack Singer* off Naha, Okinawa—a port city just to the south of them. The *Singer* didn't sink, but the damage led the ship's owners to write it off as a total loss. The anchorage itself seemed safe enough, and that evening the men off watch gathered as usual on the tank deck to watch a movie. Just as people had settled in, though, the movie stopped and the lights came on. In the sudden silence, the men could hear other ships in the harbor firing their guns.

The men braced themselves for the sound of the general quarters alarm, but instead Laden came on the loudspeaker and addressed his men. Apparently the United States had dropped two "super bombs" on Japan, and in response the Japanese had announced that they would discuss surrender terms. The captain's warning that the war was not over just yet was lost in the men's wild cheering and their rush to fire off the 20mm guns in impromptu fireworks celebrations. Somehow, they never turned the movie back on.

Over the next couple of days, the 1008 lay at anchor in Hagushi as the top commanders converted the plans for the invasion of Japan into plans for the occupation of Japan. Many of the same troops and units would be used, but the process of getting them ashore, and their duties once in Japan, would be quite a pleasant change.

On August 13, the 1008 got under way with convoy OKS 20 to return to Saipan and pick up more occupation troops. The ships left Okinawa just in time to maintain the illusion that the war was really over. That night, a Japanese torpedo bomber got past defenses in Buckner Bay (on the other side of the island from Hagushi) and put its torpedo in the stern of the battleship *Pennsylvania*. The hit killed twenty men and caused progressive flooding that almost sank the Pearl Harbor veteran. (The ship was never fully repaired and was used in the atomic bomb tests after the war. It also had the distinction of being the only U.S. battleship to have serious combat damage at both the beginning and end of the war.) The next night, the last successful kamikaze attack of the war resulted in two planes crashing the transport USS *LaGrange* (APA 124) in Buckner Bay. The attack killed twenty-one men and wounded eighty-nine others, but the ship was able to return to the United States under its own power. The *LaGrange* was the last U.S. Navy ship damaged by direct enemy action during the war.

The men on the 1008 knew nothing of these attacks, though. Significantly, on the dawn following their first night out from Okinawa, the captain decided not to send the men to general quarters. More than rumors and celebrations, for these sailors that marked the true end of the war. On the morning of August 15, during the 8:00 a.m. muster, Laden told his men that President Harry Truman had announced the official end of hostilities against Japan. Laden tried to impress upon his men that they still had much work to do in the Pacific, and they would not be going home any time soon.

The official announcement of the end of the war made this six-day voyage to Saipan more memorable than any of the other legs of LST 1008's wanderings about the Pacific. But it had other moments. The engine trouble that had plagued the ship early in the cruise resurfaced just after noon on the first day of peace. Sailing at the head of the fifth column in the convoy, the 1008 suffered an air hose casualty that forced the crew to shut down the port engine. The officer of the deck ordered the starboard engine ahead flank so the ship wouldn't lose too much way, but still the signalman had to hoist the breakdown flag so that the following ships wouldn't try to maintain station on the 1008 as it dropped out of line. Fortunately, the engineers repaired the engine quickly, and the 1008 was able to resume position in the convoy within fifteen minutes of the breakdown.

A New Mission

After that, the cruise went along normally, and just after dawn on August 19 the convoy steamed into Saipan's inner harbor. The 1008 was safely anchored by the time the men went to their 8:00 a.m. quarters for muster. After lunch the following day (August 20), the 1008 moved to the outer anchorage, and there she sat for a full week. During that time, the ship began its transition into the peacetime navy. Twice that week, Laden held one of the most irritating of naval evolutions—the captain's material inspection of the ship to ensure that all the spaces on the ship were thoroughly cleaned and the gear properly stowed. The crew tended to despise inspections because they interfered with the ship's work routine. Sailors have a hard time understanding why it's important to stop doing maintenance on a piece of machinery in order to clean under it or give it a fresh coat of paint. At any rate, the inspections soon became a weekly reality for the men and gave them their first taste of peacetime routine.

On August 27, the 1008 finally was able to move into the inner harbor to take on its load. Just before noon, it moored to the Liberty ship SS *James K. Kelly*, and only two hours later it took on some two dozen men of a construction battalion pontoon crew. These men were to prepare the ship for the work ahead, and they stayed aboard for two days. Their work apparently took longer than planned, for they left the ship only about an hour before it got under way at 1:30 p.m. on August 29.

Convoy SOK 32 took six days to get to Okinawa. Along the way, the 1008 suffered another engine breakdown. The starboard sump tank had become flooded with lubricating oil and had to be fixed. Repairs took only about twenty minutes. The ships were under way on September 2 when they received word that the surrender had been signed in Tokyo Bay. The 1008's deck log marks the moment with the simple entry: "Tested whistle, test was satisfactory."

The convoy formed up into a harbor entry disposition in the predawn gloom of September 4 (including more than half an hour with the engines at full stop—a novelty for men who had experienced nothing but wartime steaming), and around noon the ships steamed into Hagushi anchorage at a stately five knots. (The first time here, the ships had hurried into the protection of the bay at nine knots, with "hurried" being a relative term for LSTs.) That evening, the crew spent seven minutes at general quarters, basically just to remind the men that they were still aboard a warship. Just because the war had ended, the LST had not become the *Queen Mary*.

Over the next couple of days, the 1008's crew and the 614's crew learned their assignments in the occupation operations. They would not go to Japan; instead, the 1008 would ferry the 614 to Jinsen (later known as Inchon), Korea, where the little craft would finally join its unit (LCT Group 115). The 1008 would continue to operate with the LST forces in the western Pacific, and the 614 would help land the marines in northern China and then support operations there. For the 614, at least, the future held at least one more amphibious operation.

On September 6, the 1008 moved south to the anchorage off Naha, where the *Jack Singer* had been torpedoed less than a month earlier. Not until September 8, however, did a spot clear to allow the 1008 to enter the harbor and nose into the LST loading ramp. That evening, more than two hundred passengers trooped aboard the LST: thirty-two men of Company A of the 51st Military Police (MP) Battalion, twelve doctors and seventy-three men from the 86th Field Hospital, one officer and fifty-five men from the 448th Engineer Depot Company, five men from the 3063rd Quartermaster Company, three men from the 66th Portable Surgical Hospital, and one officer and twenty-six men from the 13th Engineer Battalion. For the short trip to Korea, LST 1008 would be a very crowded little ship.

The 1008 returned to Hagushi on September 9 and anchored. For a couple of days, the Normandy veterans were reminded of Portland, being all loaded up and waiting. The ship weighed anchor two days later and joined up with Task Unit 78.1.3 bound for Korea. The unit was made up primarily of LSTs, with the OTC in LST 1126. The voyage to Jinsen had its share of tension. The inland waters of the Yellow Sea had been heavily mined by both U.S. and Japanese forces, and given the propensity of mines to drift away from their moorings, no one could guarantee where the mines were now. After four days of gingerly edging north, the ships began entering the long channel to Jinsen just after first light on September 15. The 1008 was once again lazily swinging around its anchor well before noon.

Another two days passed before the 1008 could begin unloading passengers. Among the first to go were the MPs and the engineers, and soon after them the ship launched the side-mounted pontoons. The next morning, September 18, the LST launched LCT 614 from its deck and detached Banks, Carlson, and the twelve men of the crew. The LCT(6) 614 was once again an independent operating unit.

LCT 614's crew spent a couple of days stowing gear and getting the machinery back in working order. A couple of days after launching, the little craft returned to the side of the 1008 for provisions and ammunition, but after that the two ships parted company for the last time.

LST 1008 had not been assigned to participate in the landings in China. Instead, on September 23, the ship sailed to return to Okinawa. On that trip, although the commander of the task unit was the commander of the USS *Cronin* (DE 704), Laden was again assigned as OTC of TU 78.12.11, made up of fourteen LSTs. The 1008 spent the next several weeks ferrying men and supplies between Okinawa and Korea. It stayed in Asian waters for some time after the war. A March 1946 photograph shows it leaving Hong Kong after delivering winter gear for the new First Chinese Army. (Some time afterward, the navy transferred the ship to the Chinese Navy. At least until just after the turn of the twenty-first century, LST 1008 survived as a museum ship in Qingdao, China.)

As for LCT 614, the time in Korea was relatively short. In England, she'd had less than a month to work up and prepare for the Normandy invasion. Here she had less than two weeks before the landings in northern China.

11

THE FAR EAST

The occupation of northern China—Operation Campus-Beleager—was to be a full-scale amphibious landing on a two-division front. The plan incorporated the hard-won knowledge of three years of amphibious assaults, and yet everyone hoped no force would be necessary. Even the designation of the initial landing time had been changed from the wartime D-Day to the less ominous M-day (Mike-day). The First Marine Division and the First Marine Air Wing would land at Taku, on the western end of the Gulf of Pohai (now known as Bohai), on September 30; these troops were to move inland to secure Tientsin, a fairly large industrial city of some 1.5 million people. Ten days later, the Sixth Marine Division would land at Chefoo (now known as Yantai), on the southeastern end of the gulf across from historic Port Arthur, and also much farther south at Tsingtao. These troops, elements of the III Amphibious Corps under Maj. Gen. K. E. Rockey of the U.S. Marine Corps, were to be transported, landed, and supported by a sizable fleet (Task Force 78) commanded by Vice Adm. D. E. Barbey.

Altogether, Barbey had a fleet of about 225 ships. Most of these (about 190) were assigned to the Taku-Tientsin operation. This task group (78.1) was built around thirty-four transports and attack cargo ships lifting the First Marine Division and First Marine Air Wing from Okinawa. Joining them would be some 130 amphibious craft (LSTs, LSMs, and LCIs) staging from Jinsen, including as many LCTs that could be rounded up in Korean waters. Another two dozen ships, ranging from control craft to destroyer escorts, rounded out the task group. Barbey would sail aboard the command ship USS *Catoctin* (AGC 5). The much smaller Chefoo group (TG 78.6) contained some seventeen transports and cargo ships, accompanied by eleven LSTs. These ships, however, would be augmented by some of the vessels from the Taku group after their first lift to Chinese waters.

Although the landings would take place almost a month after the formal surrender, no one knew whether the Japanese garrison in the area, numbering about fifty thousand troops, would stage a last-ditch stand or even if the Chinese Communist troops, already clashing with the New Chinese Army, would oppose the landings. So although the landings would not be a combat assault, the marines would be backed by a fast carrier task force built around the fleet carriers *Intrepid* and *Antietam* and the light carrier *Cabot*. These ships had been assigned not to simply stand by in case the marines needed air support, but at dawn on the landing day, they were to launch a show of force to discourage any resistance. Each landing force would also have a gunfire support group standing by. The Taku-Tientsin group would be covered by the veteran heavy cruisers *San Francisco*, *New Orleans*, *Minneapolis*, and *Tuscaloosa*, accompanied by four destroyers. The Tsingtao-Chefoo group would be covered by the new battlecruisers *Alaska* and *Guam*, which would also have four destroyers along.

The real threat to the shipping would be the mines sown throughout the Yellow Sea by both American and Japanese forces. The Americans knew where their mines had been placed and how many and what type were there, and following the surrender the Japanese had tried their best, given the mangled communications and command structure that afflicted them, to provide information regarding where their minefields lay. Of course, some minesweeping operations had been under way even before the war ended, but these had concentrated on the heavier shipping routes around Japan and Allied-held areas. The Yellow Sea had, before now, been a rather out-of-the-way place. Also, mines have a terrible habit of breaking loose from their moorings and floating along with the currents and eddies. Mines could be anywhere and everywhere.

In fact, mines had already bedeviled the transport force before it even left Okinawa. Loading at Hagushi, the ships took to sea on September 16 to avoid an approaching typhoon. Just after first light the next morning, the transport USS *Colbert* (APA 145) radioed that lookouts had spotted a mine. Just as the other ships in the convoy received that transmission, their lookouts reported seeing an explosion on the *Colbert*'s port side. The mine hit dead amidships, flooding the Victory ship's engine room and knocking out all power. As dangerous as the hit would have been under normal conditions, the men aboard the ship in the heavy seas on the outskirts of the typhoon faced the very real possibility that the rolling and pitching of the ship would work loose bulkheads weakened by the explosion. The transports *Leon* and *Butte* clawed around to assist, but three and a half hours passed before the *Butte* could get into position to tow the stricken *Colbert*. A fleet tug arrived the next morning to take the *Colbert* in tow, and the rest of the convoy returned to Okinawa to resume loading operations. The *Colbert* didn't make it back into port until September 20, but she was quickly repaired and sailed with the rest of the fleet when they sortied on September 26.

While the transports and cargo ships loaded up at Okinawa, the amphibious ships readied themselves at Jinsen. This group consisted principally of some forty-nine LSTs, forty LSMs, and forty-two LCIs. An initial group of ten or more LCTs were to be towed across to serve as lighters for these ships, and they were to be joined later by other LCTs whose duties with various commands in the western Pacific had ended or eased. The newly arrived LCT 614 was ordered to join the initial group of LCTs that were to be towed across to Taku. Although the ships were scheduled to sail only ten days after the LCT was launched from the 1008's deck, Banks and his men needed to worry only about getting their craft ready for sea, because they would not be ferrying a load on the way across. Working the ship up would take much less time than it had in Plymouth, when the ship was launched from the LST 291 in an essentially incomplete state and had to have much of its equipment installed. Here in Korea, the LCT needed only to take on fuel, provisions, ammunition, other supplies, and the men needed to get everything operational after its almost four months of being deck cargo on the LST.

The men also used this time to settle into their duties. The men who had been with the 614 since Normandy—Pequigney, Kelly, Wajda, and Jarvis—simply picked up where they had left off. Pequigney, of course, had spent the last few months steering the big LST, so he needed a little time to refresh the experience he'd gained in Normandy. Sparky Coffas was a second-class electrician's mate, but he had experience with the anchor winch on his former LCT at Omaha Beach. Although they anticipated few classic beachings here, he would stand in whenever they needed the anchor. After Carter left, no rated gunner's mate had been assigned to the ship; however, Glenn Dunnegan, a young seaman second from the Mississippi "coast" of Iowa, had taken an interest in the 20mm guns on the LST and agreed to play gunner for the crew. And Paul DiMarzio, after his few months as the LST's baker, had to shift into cooking everything for everybody and in a much tinier kitchen.

Gerald George, who was a rated cook, was content to let DiMarzio do the cooking while he acted as the ship's pharmacist's mate and helped Dunnegan with the guns or generally did what needed to be done out on deck.

Oddly enough, although half the LCT 614's Pacific crew had made petty officer, fewer men held specific rates than the Normandy crew had. The Pacific crew had no rated gunner, no rated signalman, and only two rated motor macs (as opposed to five in the Atlantic crew). In fact, the engine room crew was drastically reduced. The changes in the makeup of the ship's crew reflected several things. First, by this time the navy had more than two years' experience operating LCTs for protracted periods; therefore, it had a better idea of what kind of crew was really needed—namely, more seamen, fewer engineers. Second, Camp Bradford and Solomons Island had shifted their training so that everyone on the LCT knew how to do everything, so that once the craft reached its operating area the men could settle into routines as needed (as was happening now on the 614). Third, at this late stage of the war, the extensive training commands ashore, the growing number of forward supply bases, and the huge fast carrier task forces all soaked up sizable percentages of the new recruits, leaving the amphibious forces—themselves now a considerable chunk of the navy—to work with what it could get. That's not to say that the Gator Navy got the dregs of the manpower pool but simply that the navy's priorities had placed them a little further down on the list than those other commands.

Landing the Marines

LCT 614, its crew members now settled into their own routines, soon met up with its new mother LST for the tow across to China. The amphibious force left Jinsen on September 28 and threaded its way through the minefields. A minesweeping squadron led them across the Yellow Sea and cleared a channel through the Gulf of Pohai, but floating mines continued to be a problem. Although no ships were hit, the escorts spotted and destroyed several mines; the occasional explosions made it hard for the men to remember that the war had been over almost a month. They arrived off Taku late on the evening of September 29. The plan was to anchor off the harbor that night with all navigation lights at full illumination to communicate to the people ashore that they had come as a peaceful occupation force, not as invaders. Once the transports arrived the next morning, the marines would go ashore to determine what kind of reception the local Chinese or the remaining Japanese forces had in store for them. Then, the marines would secure the landing areas and the port facilities so that unloading could begin.

The weather forced a bit of a change. Although the LCMs were safely nestled in the well deck of the USS *Ashland* (a landing ship, deck [LSD]), high winds and rough seas in the unprotected anchorage risked damage to the LCTs tied alongside the LSTs. The commander of the amphibious force, Capt. Francis J. Mee, decided to cast off the LCTs and have them seek shelter within the breakwater. They were ordered to anchor as well away from shore as possible and to keep the 20mm guns manned in the case of any resistance.

In the event, however, the people of Taku were very ready to welcome the American newcomers. After all, the Americans would not only bring food and supplies to help rebuild the area, but they would also take away the Japanese military personnel who remained in the vicinity. In addition, the local people hoped the Americans would provide some protection from the Chinese Communist forces massing to the south and who occasionally raided the area. So although the LCT sailors did not meet armed resistance, they did have to fend off a rather enthusiastic welcome.

Also on the night of September 29, the transport force tiptoed its way through the minefields. Despite being preceded by the minesweeping force and the amphibious ships, the transports still encountered almost a dozen mines, some floating between the columns of the convoy. These ships anchored just after dawn on September 30, and because the LCTs had already determined the people ashore were friendly, unloading began immediately. The first marine rifle companies ashore faced a duty they had not anticipated: instead of neutralizing defenses or securing landing areas for follow-up troops, the marines' first task was to be the guests of honor of a celebratory parade, complete with fireworks, put on by the people of Taku. Even the show of air strength launched from the carriers seemed fitting for the celebration, not the anticipated violence. So the dawn of September 30 found the situation at Taku to be a confusion of contradictions. Seaward this had all the makings of a full amphibious assault. Dozens of naval attack transports and cargo vessels lay at anchor, ready to send ashore a reinforced marine division, while just behind them a strong cruiser and destroyer force lay in full view of the people ashore to communicate that the marines would land and would protect them. In the air, planes from the three carriers out at sea flew overhead in another demonstration of force and determination and to scout out possible resistance. Landward, however, the town had all the appearance of a fleet holiday. The townspeople turned out in force not to resist but to welcome the marines and sailors with parades and fireworks, and the bumboats and street merchants were already displaying their various wares to cater to the Americans.

After that, things progressed rather quickly, but the operation was not without its glitches. Because it was not a combat operation, the transports had not been combat loaded. In a combat-loaded ship, the equipment that is likely to be needed first is loaded last so that it is readily available, and the ships are not fully laden to leave enough space in the holds to work the cargo quickly and efficiently. In contrast, these ships had been loaded to capacity, which meant that they simply had to be unloaded in the order of whatever happened to be on top.

Another major glitch was the speed with which events unfolded. Despite no one considered this a combat operation, apparently the planners anticipated the movement inland toward Tientsin to take place at a combat pace. The first marines ashore took along assault gear—heavy on weapons and ammunition but with only one day's rations. As it turned out, the marines, finding the railway open and accessible, went into Tientsin on M-day; however, their heavy equipment and supplies had to travel the thirty-six miles up the Hei Ho River in LCTs and LSMs, which would never win any race with a locomotive. To make matters worse, they found that the port facilities at Tientsin were not yet repaired enough to allow these vessels to unload heavy vehicles, nor were the river banks—steep, muddy, and swept by the swift current—suitable for a classic LCT across-the-ramp landing. So the landing craft had to return downstream to use the better port facilities at Taku.

The marines, therefore, faced a ration shortage by the second day of the operation, and with their rapid forward deployment they needed trucks ashore quickly to deliver the food and supplies. The trucks, however, were originally considered a low-priority item, and they had to be pulled out of the bowels of the ships. Then, of course, the trucks required supplies of gasoline—also originally a low-priority item—that had to be found and dragged out. Unloading the transports, then, quickly became a confused and rushed affair.

The marines did in fact clash with some elements of the Communist army. When advance elements of the Seventh Marine Regiment reached Chinwangtao, north of Taku, on October 1, they found fighting taking place between the Communist forces and the puppet government forces established by the Japanese. The battalion commander stopped the fighting and quickly replaced the puppet governors all along their perimeter. A few nights later, on the third and fourth of October, a full company of Chinese Communist troops raided an ammunition dump at Hsin Ho. They managed to get away with several cases of ammunition, but pursuing Marines eventually regained most of it. And on October 6, the marines fought their first pitched battle with Communist troops as engineers, covered by a rifle platoon, tried to clear roadblocks between Tientsin and Peiping (now Beijing) that a company of Chinese Communist regulars guarded. The next day, backed by armor and carrier air cover, the engineers cleared the roads, allowing the marines to reach Peiping.

As a result of these clashes, in which several marines died, the landings at Communist-held Chefoo were canceled, and the Sixth Marine Division landed instead at Tsingtao. With marines north of them at Taku-Tientsin and south of them at Tsingtao, the Communist forces soon withdrew from Chefoo. The northern edge of the marines' occupation zone, stretching from Chinwangtao to Peiping, continued to be the scene of armed clashes on into January, when a tenuous cease-fire was finally agreed upon among the U.S., Chinese Nationalist, and Chinese Communist forces.

LCTs Prove Their Worth

During the initial landings, the buildup, and the supply of the marines ashore, the LCTs quickly proved their worth. A sandbar at the mouth of the Hei Ho River kept the larger ships out of the ports, and although the LSMs could transit the hastily dredged channel at high tides, they were blocked out for a four-hour window centered on low tide. Also, the pontoon causeways that the LSTs had brought across were essentially useless in the fast-running river. The CBs eventually set up a few of them parallel to the riverbank and connected them to the shore with a Bailey bridge. The small LCMs and LCVPs could skim across the sandbar at any set of the tide, but their light loads barely helped matters, and their small engines had trouble coping with the strong river currents. The LCMs were soon relegated to unloading the LSMs in ramp-to-ramp operations. They also proved useful as river tugboats, keeping the LSMs perpendicular to the shore when they could land or piloting the ships through the channels. The LCMs were also useful as rescue boats, trying to pull grounded LSMs and LCTs out of the mud, but they simply didn't have the power. Once grounded, a craft could only wait for high tide or for the LCM to help it kedge its anchor.

Only the LCTs could carry significant loads straight from ship to shore regardless of tide and current. Plus, they had the operating radius to reach Tientsin. As the commander of the transport squadron, Capt. James K. Davis, later recorded in his action report, "Although the low speed of LCTs handicapped their turn around time while operating in the Hei Ho River, the landing qualities afforded by their shallow draft more than compensated for their turtle-like pace. . . . These craft were also independent of the tide in making passage to and from Tientsin. Consequently, their turn around time for a complete river trip was considerably under that of an LSM."

Under these circumstances, the men of LCT 614 were as busy here as they had been at Normandy. The strong river currents challenged Pequigney's now-considerable experience at the helm of the 614, and taking the LCT alongside the transports and cargo ships in the cold, open waters of the Yellow Sea was every bit as tricky as it had been in the stormy channel. Taking loads into Taku took only a few hours, and they could make two or three such trips a day. But moving a load up the river to Tientsin was a two-day proposition even for the shallow-draft LCTs, especially going upstream against the current that could sometimes reach half of the LCT's top speed. Coming down the river, though, the LCT could sometimes reach the exhilarating speed of ten knots.

And although no one shot at the crews or dropped bombs around them, the place was not without its threats. From time to time they could see armed men on horseback watching them. These marauding bandits were actually, they soon learned, elements of the Communist army, and the LCT sailors were told that they were itching to nab some of the arms and supplies going to the marines. They soon learned of the marines' clashes with the Communists, and that knowledge emphasized how real the threat was to themselves. As a precaution, the men kept the 20mm guns ready whenever they were in transit, and the men on deck carried .45s or kept rifles or submachine guns handy.

The worries about the bandits led to a few run-ins with the locals. The narrow, winding Hei Ho River gave the LCT very little room to maneuver, and the currents degraded the little maneuverability the craft had. In addition, the river's silty bottom and sticky mud banks ensured that any craft that ran aground, especially near high tide, would be stranded until a Chinese tug or another craft could come up. The American commanders in the area warned the landing craft crew to be wary of the bandits trying to board their craft or trying to drive it aground; an LCT—or even an LSM—could easily be pillaged by a group of bandits before another vessel could provide assistance.

Banks's orders in this matter were short and direct: "Don't get taken." If they had to take a load upriver, they would take on the cargo early in the morning and leave in time to make Tientsin before nightfall. The next morning, they would leave to go back downriver in plenty of time to regain Taku in daylight. But under no circumstances were they to operate in the river at night. During those trips, the local river traffic kept the channel crowded with fishing boats, bumboats, market boats, and, for all they knew, even a pleasure craft or two. They would steer around as many of the craft as they could, and for the first few days of the operation, the ship's horn was constantly in use, blasting out warnings, and the men on the ramp yelled and tried to wave them out of the way. But many of the craft were sail, and despite the international rules of the road, the LCT simply could not dodge all of them. On occasion a few of the craft appeared to be purposely bearing down on the ship.

Under those circumstances, collisions were inevitable, and the small wooden boats of the Chinese always fared the worse. Most were glancing blows, and a few sent the sampans scurrying to shore before they sank. The times that the sampans seemed to be intentionally bearing down on the 614, Banks had no choice but to order Pequigney to swerve the LCT to knock the Chinese craft out of the way. Once or twice, these solid smacks against the blunt ramp of the LCT forced the Chinese people to swim to the bank. No word reached the crew that anyone had died as a result of these collisions.

Almost as soon as the marines went ashore, the navy Seabees began constructing temporary artificial beaches on each side of an old stone pier in Taku. Several hundred truckloads of stone and rubble had to be sunk into the mud before the foundation was firm enough to support the landing of trucks across it. Once the initial push, which took about a week, to get the men and their gear ashore had ended, the place made a reasonably good operating base for the LCTs. They could wait in fairly protected waters just inside the mouth of the river and deploy out to the cargo ships whenever necessary. If they picked up a load of vehicles, they could land them on the hard and then move aside and moor. If they had to ferry a load of men or bulk cargo up river to Tientsin, they could be back in a couple of days and ready for another job.

Of course, it was not a base in the true sense of the word. The men still had to live aboard the cramped little craft, and they still had to rely on the generosity of the crews of the cargo ships for hot, freshwater showers. The silty, polluted waters of the river were barely fit for flushing the LCT's toilets; the men had no temptation to shower in it. All told, the operating pace here was a bit more sane than it had been at Normandy, but still it was a difficult time. The cold weather meant that they had to keep the generators running constantly to operate the heaters. The constant running of the generators and the diesels, in turn, meant that the muddy, polluted Hei Ho water constantly ran through the cooling systems. With only two rated motor macs on the crew, keeping the engines and machinery working soon became an all-hands evolution. In effect, every man on the LCT crew became a motor mac. Even Pequigney, who came aboard the 614 not even knowing how to drive a car, found himself down in the bilges and tinkering with the machinery along with everyone else.

Within only about six weeks, operating in the Hei Ho River became almost impossible. With the days getting shorter as autumn progressed, the LCTs soon ran out of sufficient daylight to make the run between Taku and Tientsin. Also, the icy winds from Manchuria kept the men frozen and threatened to finish off the already touchy machinery. At times during their trips along the river, Kelly would report the diesel motors overheating. They would have to stop the LCT in the middle of the river and dismantle the coolant intake lines, which would be filled with shaved ice. To get the engines back up, the men poured boiling water into the intake lines until the ice had melted and the muddy river water would begin to flow in again.

Between landing missions, the men found their encounters with the local Chinese people to be enlightening. One evening after supper, Coffas was helping DiMarzio clean up in the galley. Coffas had a pan full of table scraps—pork chop bones and canned vegetables—that he was going to take aft and dump into the river. As he stepped back onto the fantail, however, a Chinese woman in a boat tied up on the bank next to them started yelling at him and waving a wooden bowl she had. Coffas understood that the woman wanted the scraps for her family, so he waved her over to give them to her. But before he put the scraps in the bowl, she bent down and rinsed the bowl out in the muddy river water. The incident had a profound effect on Coffas and his thankfulness for what he had (although years later, he said, his children soon grew tired of hearing the story).

The 614 and the other LCTs operated in the Hei Ho River for no more than two months. With the marines established ashore, keeping them supplied took only a few ships a week, a pace easily maintained by Chinese civilian tugs and barges. Also, by this time, the larger and more ice-free port of Tsingtao was in full operation, as were marine airfields ashore. So as the weather worsened and the supply situation eased, the operations of the LCTs slowed, allowing some of the men to go on leave up to Peiping. Language barriers were much more of a problem here than they had been in Europe, but the place did have its advantages over Tientsin, plus the men could take tours on up to the Great Wall. Pequigney was scheduled to go ashore with the second group a week later, but just as the first group returned the Communists raided the railway and cut the line between Tientsin and Peiping. By the time the railway was repaired, the 614 was ready to be loaded into the well deck of an LSD (possibly the *Oak Hill* or the *Ashland*) and carried across the Yellow Sea back to Korea.

The Worst Duty of All

The crew hoped that getting pulled back from the forward area off northern China would improve their situation. Life in Jinsen quickly became miserable. The weather was incredibly cold, taxing the tiny heaters in the compartments, and the 614's work quickly devolved into basic yard work—doing some lighterage from ships to the wharves or carrying out water tanks for the ships anchored out. As a result, the men spent a lot of time sitting around aboard the LCT, playing cards, reading, or simply griping about doing nothing. Of course, an LCT was not designed with living comforts in mind. The designers had apparently assumed that the crews would live aboard them for short periods and would mostly enjoy the luxury of the accommodations of an LST or LSD or perhaps even barracks in port. The working navy seemingly decided it had more important tasks to accomplish than worry about the creature comforts of its LCT sailors. They had racks and a galley so let them therewith be content.

One major problem was that the tiny galley table—basically a picnic table—could seat only about six or eight men comfortably, and the decks of the berthing compartments were almost always damp from condensation. So when there was no work to do, the men not only had very few choices about what to do but also no choice about where to go. In a ship some 120 feet long, the fourteen officers and men on the crew were squeezed into three nine-by-twenty-foot boxes.

Finally DiMarzio came up with a plan to relieve the overcrowding and approached Banks with his idea. He had noticed that the wharf areas were filled with construction equipment destined for U.S. forces in Korea and that apparently the high command had forgotten that the LCT sailors were, in fact, U.S. forces in Korea. Therefore, if they took some of those supplies, they wouldn't actually be stealing. DiMarzio had pretty good woodworking and shop skills, and he was sure he could build a shack or shelter of some kind. Banks knew the project itself would give the men an outlet for their energy, and if the thing did take shape it would provide additional space. But where could it go? Banks wanted it off the tank deck so that it wouldn't interfere with their cargo-carrying ability, and it needed to be well away from any of the equipment topside. DiMarzio had a ready answer—install it behind the catwalk over the after tank deck.

The catwalk itself was a rather flimsy, collapsible structure that was meant to hold the weight of only two or three men. But with a framework of shoring material anchored to the deckhouses, the foundation supported what soon became a miniature house. It had a door on each side and a Quonset hut window in the front, and DiMarzio was even able to fashion a card table for it. Coffas wired the place for lights and heat to make it livable. The fact that it was off the deck meant that the cold winds whipping over, around, and under it made it difficult to warm up, but at least the wooden walls didn't sweat as badly as the steel bulkheads of the berthing compartments did. Soon DiMarzio had even furnished the place with a sofa cushioned with thin navy mattresses, and a phonograph with several records showed up that Banks was content to assume the men had bought from the marines. The little house may not have been home, but it helped.

About a month after returning to Jinsen, the crew began to break up as the men's points came up and they were sent back to the States for discharge. This time, however, instead of reducing down to a skeleton crew for transportation back to the States, the navy had no intention of maintaining the 614 as an operational unit. Frank Pequigney was one of the first to get transferred. In early December, orders came along to several of the LCTs for the men about to be shipped home to report to the flotilla headquarters. Pequigney showed up in his working uniform and his seabag, and he and the other men were put on a boat and taken out to the USS *Bremerton*, a brand-new heavy cruiser less than a year old.

Everything on the cruiser was spit and polish. All the brasswork was shined twice a day, the decks swept and holystoned, and the men wore new, freshly laundered uniforms. When Pequigney and the other LCT sailors showed up in well-worn dungaree uniforms—stained, tattered, no rank insignia, and trousers held up with rope—no one on the cruiser knew what to make of them. Were they shipwreck survivors or perhaps even newly discovered prisoners of war who had just been freed? When the officers learned that these men were simply LCT sailors being carried over to Tsingtao for shipment home, they ordered them to go below and not show themselves topside until they left the ship. The officers didn't want the lax discipline and shoddy appearance that was standard on the LCTs to catch hold on the cruiser.

Just before the *Bremerton* reached Tsingtao, a leg infection that Pequigney had picked up in Jinsen finally took hold, so he had to go over to a transport equipped with a hospital. He stayed there a few days, missing the first few transports home. But finally his turn came, and he found himself back in the States and a civilian before the end of January 1946.

Francis Coffas was one of the last of the original Pacific crew to leave the 614. In early 1946, his father died. Instead of granting him emergency leave, the navy decided to go ahead and discharge him. By the time he left the ship, it was already clear that the navy had no intention of keeping it. As people left, no replacements came aboard, and the crew had dwindled to a bare minimum. Just two or three months after Coffas left, the men were all on their way back home.

In April 1946, the navy loaned LCT 614 to the army. The army put a Korean crew aboard, intending ultimately to transfer the ship to the Korean military. But after only one more season of service, the machinery—so abused in the Hei Ho River—simply wasn't worth repairing. In October, the army general in charge of the base in Jinsen sent a message to the Seventh Fleet that simply said the vessel was no longer fit for service and would not be transferred to the Koreans as planned. He asked what he should do with the ship. The navy responded that it had no further interest in the little ship; the army could take whatever equipment it wanted off the craft and then sink or destroy the hulk. The navy waited a discreet time before finally striking the ship from the Naval Register's list on April 4, 1947. However, another year passed before the army, in August 1948, reported to the navy that LCT 614 was in the process of "disposal by salvage." The army never reported what happened after that—whether it towed the 614 out into the harbor and sank it, perhaps as part of a breakwater, or if it just pushed the hulk aside and let it rust and melt into the mud. The Omaha Beach veteran had basically died of neglect.

12

ODYSSEUS IN TENNESSEE

As LCT 614 began her long, wasting death in Korea, the men who had given her life began their new lives as civilians. For most of the men, this actually was fairly easy. Stephen Ambrose, in *Citizen Soldiers*, writes about the disorientation that some of the men from front-line infantry units felt when they found themselves home only a few months after being in combat the last time. For these navy men, however, their last duty stations tended to give them plenty of separation from their combat experience, and on the return trips the spit-and-polish routines of the peacetime navy gave them all plenty of incentive to leave.

True, some of the men had easier times than others had. Some simply went home and picked up where they left off some three years earlier. Others had a difficult time getting their experiences—and the changes to themselves that resulted from those experiences—to mesh with the normal lives they thought awaited them.

Irwin

Don Irwin, the 614's Atlantic skipper, at war's end was a gunnery officer aboard LST 637. He arrived in the Pacific theater too late to participate in any combat assaults, but the 637 did make it to the western Pacific in time to operate in a combat zone before the surrender. Like the men of the 614 and LST 1008, the crew of LST 637 had begun to mull over their role in the upcoming invasion of Japan when they got word that Japan would sue for peace. Before that, the 637 had made supply runs to marine and army units making some of the last roundup episodes in the Philippines, qualifying Irwin for the Philippine Liberation medal.

In late 1945, LST 637 was ordered back to the States. Just before it arrived at Pearl Harbor, some radio messages came in with Irwin's name on them, but he couldn't tell whether they indicated good or bad news. At Pearl, they received several bags of mail that had been waiting for them, but everyone was so busy getting the ship ready for sea duty that no one had time to open the bags and sort through them until they were under way for San Diego. Of course, Irwin opened the letters from his wife before turning to the official navy mail, so not until LST 637 was well out at sea did Irwin discover that he had been ordered to leave Hawaii and relieve a lieutenant aboard an LST operating in the China Sea. Naturally, the orders threw Irwin into a bit of a quandary. He worried whether he would be in trouble for not responding while the ship was at Pearl, and he was highly disappointed because the orders meant another six months of sea duty. But then, Irwin wondered whether this lieutenant was the commanding officer of that other LST or just one of the division officers who had been promoted out of his billet.

He never learned the answer. Upon the ship's arrival at San Diego, Irwin took his orders to the nearest headquarters. The officers there examined them, contacted the Bureau of Personnel, and then told Irwin to forget it. Instead, he was to be sent to Great Lakes Naval Station for discharge. Irwin found himself a civilian again on January 17, 1946. After a short while, Irwin returned to college—this time at the University of Iowa—working toward a master's degree in advertising and journalism. Upon completion of the degree, Irwin had a long, successful career in advertising and settled in Cedar Falls, Iowa.

Pillmore

George Pillmore, like Irwin, found himself the gunnery officer aboard an LST at the end of the war. When he left the 614 in France, he had been given command of his own LCT, the 601. By that time, though, operations in France were winding down, and Pillmore's duty as skipper was basically to get the craft to Dartmouth. Like the 614, the 601 and its crew were both in need of major maintenance before either could be shipped home, so while the 601 lay moored in a nest of LCTs near the repair base, the crew started their rotations of a week's leave in England. One afternoon while many of the crew were away on leave, the 601 was the outboard ship in a nest of some three or four LCTs; the ship on the opposite side of the nest was moored to a buoy in the Dart River. The inboard LCT needed to get under way, and without warning it cast off its lines to the 601, setting her adrift toward an anchorage filled with civilian pleasure craft. Before the men could get the ship powered up, the swift current carried them into the side of a big sailing yacht. Pillmore spent some time after that writing letters of apology to the yacht's owner and letters of explanation to Flotilla Twelve. Soon afterward, the 601 was scheduled to be taken back to the States aboard a cargo ship rather than atop an LST. Pillmore and the rest of the crew were taken off the ship and sent back to the States aboard troop transports. Pillmore never saw any of his 601 crew again.

Pillmore was on leave in Colorado when he learned that Germany had surrendered. Soon afterward, he reported to Camp Bradford for training on LSTs. There he ran into an old Flotilla Twelve friend, Bill Nordstrom, and upon completion of their training the two men were able to get orders to the same ship, the LST 603. The 603 moved down to a shipyard in New Orleans to work up for its deployment to the Pacific, but as it turned out, the war ended before the shipyard work had been completed. Pillmore never made it to the Pacific theater. In October 1945, LST 603 was sent up the Mississippi River to Memphis to help that city celebrate Navy Day. The ship docked for a few days, giving tours and allowing the sailors to enjoy maximum liberty in town. One afternoon a gentleman came aboard and asked around for people who had served on LCTs. Pillmore and Nordstrom both went down to the quarterdeck to chat with the man. One of the first questions he asked was which LCTs the officers had served on, and as it turned out both of Pillmore's craft—the 614 and 601—had been built there in Memphis by the Pidgeon-Thomas Iron Company. The gentleman, in fact, turned out to be none other than Mr. Frank Pidgeon himself. He took Pillmore and Nordstrom in tow, taking them out to dinner and to a high school football game. He seemed delighted in the men's stories of the exploits of the ships his firm had built.

LST 603 made one foreign cruise while Pillmore was still aboard, sailing around the Caribbean to Cuba, Trinidad, and Puerto Rico before going back to Little Creek. In the months following the war, the married officers were the first to be discharged, and so with each departure of a shipmate, Pillmore found himself moving up in the ship's billet—from gunnery officer to navigator and eventually up to executive officer. Once he had the points to get out, Pillmore decided not to take a discharge but to stay in the reserves. He finally made it home in May 1946.

That fall, Pillmore went back to the University of Colorado to finish his engineering degree. Afterward, he took a job with General Electric in Schenectady, New York, and ended up having a long career with that company. As a reserve officer, he made full lieutenant in 1949, and he expected orders for active service when the Korean War started, but those orders never came. He married in 1951, and the young family stayed in Schenectady until 1953, when they moved to Illinois and, two years later, to Milwaukee. During all that moving around and business travel, Pillmore was not able to keep up his navy reserve duties. He was up for promotion for lieutenant commander but simply couldn't get the paperwork in, and several years after that the navy told him to resign or go on the inactive retired list. He chose the latter option, even though it involved no retirement stipend. Pillmore put up with traveling in the harsh Wisconsin winters only about five years before bidding for another transfer, this time to Arizona. He retired in 1982 and stayed in Arizona.

Cromer

William Cromer was one of the few men on the crew who stayed in the navy for a time after the war. He stayed on LCIs after he left the 614, and after the war he gained a command of his own, a tugboat in the Jacksonville shipyards. Putting Cromer, the master of cumshaw, at work in a shipyard was rather like hiring a pyromaniac to guard a fireworks stand, but his tugboat never lacked any kind of gear or needed part. As far as I know, Cromer was the only one of the 614 crew to be recalled to duty during the Korean War, and he served on LST 758. When Cromer and the navy parted company, he stayed on in the shipyards and eventually retired to Live Oak, Florida.

Carlson

Probably Roy Carlson, the anchor winch operator on the D-Day crew, had the easiest transition back into civilian life. When the war ended, he was part of a construction battalion unit in the Aleutians (for the rest of his life, a cold wind still gave his inner ear a dreadful pain), and so he was happy to make as early a departure from the navy as he could. He went straight back to the Oregon logging camps and picked up right where he'd left off. After he built up his reputation among the loggers in the area, he bought his own logging truck and went into business for himself. After his retirement, he worked for a time with the Astoria Public Works Department.

One Last Combat

The man to have probably the worst transition was Luke Carter, the gunner on the Atlantic crew. He reported to the receiving station at the Norfolk navy base on

January 27, 1945, but for some reason orders to another ship never materialized. More than four months later, just before the first anniversary of the Normandy invasion, Carter suffered a fainting spell while on liberty. During examinations shortly after the incident, Carter told the doctors he'd had two other episodes—one while on watch aboard the 614 that was the cause of his shooting himself in the foot, and once again while on liberty in London. He was diagnosed with "combat fatigue" and hospitalized for observation for more than a month, but the doctors could find nothing wrong with him and soon pronounced him fit for duty. However, he did not go to sea again until after the war.

In late September, he got on the pre-commissioning crew of the USS *Joseph P. Kennedy Jr.* (DD 850), a new Gearing-class destroyer going through its qualification trials. On that crew, he served as mount captain on a 40mm gun mounted on the bridge wing. He was discharged within three days of the *Kennedy*'s commissioning. Once released in Nashville, he telegraphed his mother with typical literary flair: "Home is the sailor, home from the sea."

But Carter would not feel at home, even in Etowah, for some time yet. Navy life had actually been something of an adventure for the free-spirited Carter, and he found himself having a little trouble settling in to life with his Baptist family. He decided that life as a college boy might suit him a touch better than railroading with his dad, but he really couldn't see himself returning to high school. So he took the GED test as quickly as he could, getting the certificate in May 1946, and with the promise of the GI Bill he began shopping for colleges. During this time, he also got back in touch with Frank Pequigney, and the two of them finally got accepted to Tennessee Wesleyan College in Athens, just a few miles north of Etowah. At that time Wesleyan was a two-year school, but it would perhaps be a safe introduction back into academics for Carter and perhaps a southern lark for Pequigney. It turned out to be more of an adventure than Pequigney had thought.

Before the reunion of the two LCT 614 crewmen could take place, Carter had, like Homer's Odysseus, come home from sea to find that he had one last battle to fight. True, he had no Penelope to reclaim, but he and other returning veterans discovered that the suitors to political office in McMinn County were totally unsuitable and needed to be shooed away, if not outright shot.

The story of the celebrated "Battle of Athens" has been told in more detail elsewhere (famed journalist T. H. White covered it for *Harper's* magazine in April 1947, and Lones Seiber described it with a bit more historical perspective for

American Heritage in its February/March 1985 issue). Basically, throughout the 1930s and early 1940s, a political machine run by Memphis politician E. H. Crump gained control of most of Tennessee's political offices. A local toady, Etowah car dealer Paul Cantrell, worked with McMinn County sheriff Pat Mansfield to gain control of the local offices. With local law enforcement providing muscle, the machine quickly tightened its grip to the point that by the mid-1940s the corruption was fairly blatant. Gambling houses operated under the armed protection of the "deputies," and travelers through town—either in their own cars or on the bus line—found themselves in the courthouse being fined for some infraction or another. On election days, the sheriff and his boys would guard the polling places, then gather up the ballot boxes so they could be counted in the safety of the county jail in Athens (just a couple of blocks from the Tennessee Wesleyan campus). After a few hours the sheriff would emerge to announce that—surprise!—the machine's ticket had won again.

As McMinn County geared up for the Democratic primary in August 1946, the returning veterans didn't like the sham of democracy that they found. A group of them formed a competing ticket, running on the promise that "each vote will be counted as cast," and launched an intense campaign against the machine. As duly certified competing candidates, the veterans gained permission to place their own poll watchers at the voting stations. In response, Mansfield called in "deputies" from outside the county; some two hundred thugs armed with pistols and badges arrived. Everyone in the county knew a fight was brewing; the only question was how bloody it would become.

On the primary day, August 1, 1946, tensions ran high. Some of the veterans watching the polls got roughed up; a few of the "deputies" who were caught alone were spirited away into the woods, where they were left without their clothes; and one black voter was shot and wounded by a machine thug. But the veterans maintained their discipline until voting ended and the sheriff's armed escorts arrived to cart the ballot boxes to the jail. With no or little military experience among them, the thugs guarded the jail from inside, covering the door and the few windows. As the sheriff and his men began opening the ballot boxes behind the thick brick walls of the jail, the veterans began disappearing into the warm Tennessee summer evening. But they weren't going home to admit defeat.

A main group of veterans gathered at the National Guard armory. Accounts differ about whether they broke in or if someone among them happened to have a key, but soon they had a hefty arsenal of World War I–era Enfield rifles, at least two

Thompson submachine guns, several .45 pistols, and a far from skimpy supply of ammunition. Other veterans went home to fetch their own weapons: hunting rifles, shotguns, anything they had ammunition for.

Carter was among the latter group. He was still nineteen, a year and almost two months away from turning voting age (now fully two years past his experience in Normandy), but he had driven the short way to Athens to lend what support he could. He knew his time had come when his fellow veterans went home to get their guns. Between him and his dad, he had plenty of rifles, shotguns, and pistols to choose from, but he could do better than that. He grabbed his best souvenir from off the beaches, the MP-40 Schmeisser submachine gun.

Back in Athens, Carter joined the other veterans who had surrounded the jail. Once they were in position on rooftops and along a hill that overlooked the brick building, a representative walked out onto the street in front of the jail and told Mansfield and his thugs that they were surrounded and should surrender the ballot boxes. A few shots rang out from the jail, and as the veteran scampered for cover, the other veterans opened fire.

At first, the veterans kept up a fierce volume of fire. The noise had to be horrendous, with the booming of the shotguns and the blasts from the hunting rifles and Enfields punctuated by the sharper barking of the pistols and the rattle of the Thompsons and Carter's Schmeisser. Unfortunately (from his perspective), Carter had only one magazine for the MP-40 and probably just a few boxes of 9mm ammunition. He would fire off a few quick bursts, then spend a minute or more thumbing rounds into the magazine, and shoot those off in the next few seconds. The Schmeisser was likely out of action well within the first half hour of the siege.

Although the veterans had plenty of accumulated combat experience to back up their weapons and ammunition, they were hampered by a lack of communications and no real command structure. But they did have discipline enough to understand that their task wasn't the destruction of an "enemy" position but simply to keep up enough fire onto the stronghold to convince its occupants that their position was untenable. But the deputies, probably fearing a bloodbath (particularly, with their own blood) if they left the safety of the jail, stayed inside with their heads down. Toward dawn, the veterans began to worry about the arrival of state police (the governor had apparently alerted the National Guard to respond but then inexplicably called them off) and knew they had to force the issue. Some of the veterans raided nearby farm and construction supplies and found a few boxes of dynamite. After a few blasts, the deputies gave up.

That morning, up in the Bronx, Frank Pequigney opened up the *New York Times* to be stunned by the front-page headline: "Tennessee Sheriff Is Slain in Primary Day Violence." And underneath in smaller type: "Crowd Storms Athens Jail to Rescue War Veterans Held as Hostages—State Guard Is Sent—McKellar Wins." The early reporting got to the newspaper before full details became available, so the second paragraph gave Pequigney erroneous details: "At least two persons were killed and a score or more were wounded. The major disorders were at Athens." The two prominent mentions of Athens definitely caught Pequigney's attention.

"Son of a bitch," he thought to himself. "What the hell kind of a place has Carter got me going to?"

Over the next few days, though, the articles in the *Times* described how the veterans, having created a power vacuum, had restored order to the town, closed down the gambling houses, and, once the election board counted the ballots in the few untainted boxes they could find, handed over their authority to the duly elected officials. As it turned out, despite the thousands of rounds fired at the jail, no one died and probably fewer than fifteen people were wounded. Even more remarkable, although the veterans violated any number of federal and state laws, ranging from removing weapons from a National Guard armory to committing assault with deadly weapons to firing into an occupied building, no charges were ever filed. The fact that Tennessee allowed the veterans a free hand in reestablishing democracy in the county was its way of admitting to the corruption of the Crump machine without having a messy trial on its hands. So as the situation settled down and the *New York Times*'s subsequent reporting described a town returning to its normal self, Pequigney decided he could safely travel to Athens to begin his college studies.

Sunday Dinner with the Carters

As it turned out, the reunion of LCT 614's former crewmates was stronger—and stranger—than either had anticipated. Tennessee Wesleyan College, swamped by the influx of some 220 returning veterans (which raised the college's total enrollment to 531), scrambled to find housing and hire sufficient faculty. Although the school had required residency, it asked the veterans to find temporary housing off campus until the dormitories could be expanded. Since his family lived just ten miles away, Carter arranged for Pequigney to stay with them in Etowah.

The experiment in higher education ultimately failed for both men. Carter was certainly smart enough to succeed in college (he later earned his certified public accountant's certificate through self study and without a college degree), but he just simply couldn't settle down to the studies. Whether owing to what we would now recognize as post-traumatic stress (the "combat fatigue" of his last year in the navy gave him trouble for the rest of his life) or girl trouble or some combination of issues, Carter dropped out after just a few weeks of school.

Carter ended up back at sea for a short period. He hitchhiked to New Orleans to try to get onto the crew of a merchant ship. With the glut of unemployed sailors after the war, the only company hiring was a new company called Offshore Navigation, which had been formed to support a survey of the Bahamas funded by a consortium of oil companies. During the spring and summer of 1947, Carter served as navigator aboard the MV *Charlie Bamsu* during the Bahamas Aerial Magnetometer Survey. The little group of war surplus air-sea rescue launches and the surveying aircraft had their share of supply and maintenance problems and at least one brush with a hurricane, but for the young Carter it was a tropical lark.

Pequigney finished that first semester, but because of his father's failing health, he had to return to New York. When his father died the following Thanksgiving, Pequigney had to give up schooling and help support his family. He became a New York City cop and went back to sea, working on the city's police boats. But an event early in that semester doomed the men's friendship.

It happened while Pequigney was still staying with Carter in Etowah, waiting for dorm space to open. Carter's parents were happy to have one of their son's navy buddies staying with them, especially one from such an exotic place as New York. But being unpretentious people, they made no changes to the lifestyle that had brought them through the Depression and the war years. So it turned out that just a few weeks into the semester, the autumnal Sunday dinner was to feature the Carter family staple of squirrel and dumplings. Pequigney knew what was being cooked and was willing to try new and peculiarly southern foods, but Carter, relishing a good joke in the making, made no effort to warn his northern buddy about what to expect. The family gathered at the table, said grace, and then offered Pequigney as household guest the first dip into the pot. Wanting not to seem timid or discourteous, Pequigney scooped deeply into the bowl. Sure enough, squarely on the ladle, perched a squirrel's head.

How Pequigney got through the rest of that Sunday dinner remains a mystery, but that squirrel's head scuttled the last link of friendship formed on the USS LCT(6) 614.

BIBLIOGRAPHY

Private Correspondence
Nick Andin, seaman, LCT 614, letters 1998.
Jack Banks, officer in charge, LCT 614 (Pacific), letters 1997, phone interview 1997.
Roy Carlson, motor machinist mate, LCT 614, heavy correspondence, telephone conversations from 1994 to 2004, personal interview 1994.
Luther E. Carter, gunner's mate, LCT 614.
Fran Coffas, electrician, LCT 614 (Pacific), letters 1996 through 1997.
William Cromer, coxswain, LCT 614, letters 1994 through 1999, personal interview 1999.
Paul DiMarzio, cook, LCT 614 (Pacific), letters, phone interview 1996.
Glenn Dunnegan, gunner, LCT 614 (Pacific), letters 1996.
Richard Gudger, coxswain, LCT 614, letters 1994, personal interview 1996.
Don Irwin, officer in charge, LCT 614, letters, telephone conversations from 1993 until shortly before his death in 2009.
Frederick B. G. Kleen, signalman, LCT 614, telephone interview 2007.
Frank Pequigney, quartermaster, LCT 614, letters, e-mails, and conversations from 1993 through 2011.
George Pillmore, second officer, LCT 614, letters, e-mails, and conversations from 1994 through 2011, personal interview 2004.
Dean Rockwell, commander, LCT Group 35, letters, 1994–1995.
Buster Shaeff, LST 291, personal interview 1994.

Archive Material
Action Report. Commander, Transport Division 59. Occupation of Taku, T'Angku, and Tiensen, China. October 11, 1945.

Action Report. Commander, USS *Arkansas* (BB 33). Operation Neptune. July 3, 1944.
Action Report. Commander, USS *Texas* (BB35). Operation Neptune. June 28, 1944.
Action Report. Deputy Commander, Assault Force O-2. Operation Neptune. July 4, 1944.
Action Reports. LCTs and LCT(A)s in first wave, O-2 sector of Omaha Beach.
Bureau of Ships. File, LCT (6) 614.
———. Schematics, LCT Mark 6.
Conard, B. A. "Summary of Statements by Survivors of the MV Colin." Memorandum, Office of the Chief of Naval Operations. May 23, 1944.
"Force O-2 Roster." Not dated. (Lists LCTs, officers in charge, and second officers.)
Leide, Lt. Cmdr. William. "Action Report, LCT O-2." Commander, LCT-6, Flotillas 12 and 26, June 29, 1944.
———. "Task Unit Orders." Commander, U.S. LCTs Gold Area, July 5, 1944.
Medical and Personnel Records, Luther E. Carter, Gunner's Mate Third Class.
Naval Register's Card, LCT(6) 614.
Navickas, Simon R. "Report of Voyage, MV Colin." Report, July 26, 1944.
Operation Order BB-44. Task Force 124. Northern Europe Area: Neptune. May 20, 1944.
Operation Plan A1703-45. Task Force 78. Operation Campus-Beleaguer. September 19, 1945.
Operation Plan EE-44. CTF 123. Task Force Organization on Far Shore. July 10, 1944, revised November 10, 1944.
Operation Report Neptune. Provisional Engineer Special Brigade Group. September 30, 1944.
Rockwell, Lt. D. L. "Launching DD Tanks on D-Day." Commander, LCT Group 35. July 14, 1944.
Tenth Fleet. Convoy and Routing file, Convoy SC 157, March to April 1944.
USS LST 291. Deck Log, February to May 1944.
USS LST 540. Deck Log, December 18, 1944, to January 18, 1945.
USS LST 1008. Deck Log, March to October 1945.

Secondary Sources

Ambrose, Stephen E. *D-Day June 6, 1944: The Climactic Battle of World War II.* New York: Simon & Schuster, 1994.
Attwoll, Maureen, and Denise Harrison. *Weymouth and Portland at War.* Stanbridge, Dorset, UK: Dovecote Press, 1993.

Balkoski, Joseph. *Beyond the Beachhead.* New York: Dell Books, 1989.
———. *Omaha Beach.* Mechanicsburg, PA: Stackpole Books, 2004.
———. *Utah Beach.* Mechanicsburg, PA: Stackpole Books, 2006.
Ballard, Larry. "Healing Old Wounds." *Waterloo Courier,* December 29, 1993.
Beck, Alfred M., Abe Bortz, Charles W. Lynch, Lida Mayo, and Ralph F. Weld. *The Corps of Engineers: The War Against Germany.* United States Army in World War II Series. Washington, DC: Center of Military History, 1985.
Bemrose, John, J. C. Heggbloom, T. C. Holt, T. C. Richards, and R. J. Watson. "Bahamas Airborne Magnetometer Survey." *Geophysics* 15, no. 1 (1950): 102–9.
Buffetaut, Yves. *D-Day Ships: The Allied Invasion Fleet, June 1944.* Annapolis: Naval Institute Press, 1994.
Chicken, Stephen. *Overlord Coastline: The Major D-Day Locations.* New York: Hippocrene Books, 1993.
Cole, Merle T. *Cradle of Invasion: A History of the U.S. Naval Amphibious Training Base, Solomons, Maryland, 1942–1945.* Solomons, MD: Calvert Marine Museum, 1984.
Cressman, Robert J. *The Official Chronology of the U.S. Navy in World War II.* Annapolis: Naval Institute Press, 2000.
Dyer, George C. *The Amphibians Came to Conquer: The Story of Admiral Richmond Kelly Turner.* Washington, DC: Government Printing Office, 1972.
Ellsberg, Edward. *The Far Shore.* New York: Popular Library, 1961.
Ewing, Joseph H. *29, Let's Go!: A History of the 29th Infantry Division in World War II.* Washington, DC: Infantry Journal Press, 1948.
Gawne, Jonathan. *Spearheading D-Day: American Special Units of the Normandy Invasion.* Paris: Histoire and Collections, 1998.
Grosvenor, Melville Bell. "Landing Craft for Invasion." *National Geographic,* July 1944.
Hart, B. H. Liddell, ed. *The Rommel Papers.* Translated by Paul Pindlay. New York: Harcourt, Brace, 1953.
Hearde, Basil. "The Tin Armada: The Saga of the LCT." *Challenge WWII Special* 1, no. 2 (1994): 25–31, 90–91.
Hughes, Terry, and John Costello. *The Battle of the Atlantic.* New York: Dial Press, 1977.
Kershaw, Alex. *The Bedford Boys: One American Town's Ultimate D-Day Sacrifice.* Cambridge, MA: Da Capo Press, 2003.

Man, John. *The D-Day Atlas: The Definitive Account of the Allied Invasion of Normandy.* New York: Facts on File, 1994.

Memphis Press-Scimitar. "These Memphis War Boats Soon Ready for Battle." October 27, 1944.

Morgan, Sir Frederick. *Overture to Overlord.* New York: Doubleday, 1950.

Morison, Samuel Eliot. *The History of U.S. Naval Operations in World War II.* Vol. 11. New York: Little, Brown, 1957.

Omaha Beachhead. Washington, DC: Historical Division, War Department, 1945.

Pyle, Ernie. *Brave Men.* New York: Henry Holt, 1944.

Roskill, S.W. *The War at Sea: 1939–45.* Vol. 3. London: Her Majesty's Stationery Office, 1961.

Ryan, Cornelius. *The Longest Day.* New York: Simon & Schuster, 1959.

Slaughter, John Robert. *Omaha Beach and Beyond: The Long March of Sergeant Bob Slaughter.* St. Paul, MN: Zenith Press, 2007.

Stillwell, Paul, ed. *Assault on Normandy: First-Person Accounts from the Sea Services.* Annapolis: Naval Institute Press, 1994.

Taylor, David. "Company History." Offshore Navigation Inc. Offshore Crosstalk. www.deltatango.net/ONI/history.htm. Accessed April 26, 2012.

Tent, James Foster. *E-Boat Alert: Defending the Normandy Invasion Fleet.* Annapolis: Naval Institute Press, 1996.

Thomas, Charles S. *The German Navy in the Nazi Era.* Annapolis: Naval Institute Press, 1990.

Tyson, Carolyn A. *A Chronology of the United States Marine Corps, 1935–1946.* Vol. 2. Washington, DC: History and Museums Division, U.S. Marine Corps Headquarters, 1965.

Wolfert, Ira. "LCT, I Love You." *Saturday Evening Post*, January 8, 1944.

INDEX

Accrington, SS (British freighter/rescue ship), 48
Affleck, HMS (frigate), 54
Alaska, USS (battlecruiser), 175
Amphibious Training Base, Camp Bradford, Virginia, 32, 177, 189
Amphibious Training Base, Solomons Island, Maryland, 9, 26–32, 35, 58, 60, 100, 147, 156, 177
Ancon, USS (command ship), 60, 68, 69, 94
Andin, Nicholas, 8, 32, 58, 61, 81, 88, 100, 115, 122–23, 141
Antietam, USS (aircraft carrier), 175, 178
Argonaut, HMS (cruiser), 133
Arizona, USS (battleship), 162
Arromanches, France, 113–14, 119, 121
Arkansas, USS (battleship), 62, 80, 91, 94–95
Arthur Middleton, SS (US freighter), 21
Ashland, USS (landing ship, dock) 178, 184
Astoria, Oregon, 7, 9, 190
Augusta, USS (heavy cruiser), 62, 68, 79–80

Bahamas Aerial Magnetometer Survey, 195
Bailey, Capt. W. O. (Assault Group O-2 commander), 67, 92
Bainbridge Naval Training Station, Maryland, 5, 8, 147
Banks, Lt. j.g. Andrew J. "Jack," 154–55, 158, 163, 173, 176, 182, 185
Barbey, Vice Adm. D. E. (Operation Campus Beleager), 174
"Battle of Athens," 191–94
Bayonne, New Jersey, 41–42, 44
Beagle, HMS (destroyer), 109
Belfast, HMS (cruiser), 133
Bentley, HMS (frigate), 54
Boston, Massachusetts, 8, 40, 42–44, 46, 48, 56, 160
Brantford, HMCS (corvette), 47
Bremerton, USS (heavy cruiser), 185–86
Brockville, HMCS (sloop), 47
Bronx, New York, 6, 194
Buchsbaum, Melvin, 156, 158
Bulolo, HMS (command ship), 100
Butler, Lloyd E., 157–58
Butte, USS (transport), 176

Cabot, USS (light aircraft carrier), 175, 178
Camp Bradford. *See* Amphibious Training Base, Camp Bradford, Virginia
Cape Hatteras, North Carolina, 41
Canham, Col. Charles (116 Infantry Regiment commander), 85–86

INDEX

Carlson, Ens. R. E., 163, 173
Carlson, Roy A., 6–7, 9, 32–33, 35, 37, 43–44, 50, 55, 58, 61, 75, 79–84, 86, 88–91, 95, 101–2, 115, 117, 125, 130, 144, 147–48, 190
Carter, Danny and Winfrey, 1
Carter, Jerry, 1, 3
Carter, Luther E., 1–6, 8, 11, 35, 44, 52, 56–58, 70–71, 73, 95, 100, 103–4, 108, 114–15, 122–23, 131, 134, 136–38, 142, 146, 151–52, 156, 176; combat fatigue, 190–91; cumshaw mission, 132; liberty in England, 146–47; on Omaha Beach, 79–88; return to U.S., 148–49, 164; shoots self, 141–42; at Solomons Island, 26, 29–31; Tennessee Wesleyan College, 191, 194–95 *See also* Battle of Athens
Carter, Noah and Dove, 1–3, 5, 194–95
Carter, Ruby Lee, 1, 3
Catapult Armed Merchant (CAM) ships, 47
Catoctin, USS (command ship), 174
Charles Carroll, USS (transport), 67, 88, 92
Charlie Bamsu, MV (survey vessel), 195
Chattanooga, Tennessee, 5, 11
Chefoo (Yantai), China, 174–75, 180
Cherbourg, France, 94, 109, 126, 134, 142
China, 172–73, 174, 177, 184. *See also* Chefoo (Yantai); Hei Ho River; Peiping (Beijing); Taku; Tientsin; Tsintao (Qingdao)
Clark, Robert N., 8, 29, 31, 58, 61, 84, 115, 142
Cockington, England, 146
Coffas, Francis G. "Sparky," 155–58, 163, 167–68, 176, 183, 185–86
Colbert, USS (transport), 175–76
Colin, MV (Panamanian freighter), 48, 55; sunk by U-boat, 53–54
Conn, Lucian E., 156, 158
Construction Battalion ("Fighting SeaBees"), 9, 158, 163, 165, 171, 180, 182, 190, 208

Convoy BX 100, 44, 48
Convoy SC 157, 46, 49–50, 54–55; composition, 46–48; dodges icebergs, 51–52; scattered by storm, 52
cook (anonymous LCT 614 crewman), 29, 55, 70, 72, 99–100, 108, 129–30, 133, 138, 142
Cota, Brig. Gen. Norman (29th Infantry Division deputy commander), 85–86
Cressy, HMS (World War I armored cruiser), 49
Cromer, William E., 5–6, 9–10, 26, 29, 31, 35–36, 58, 61, 81, 83–84, 88, 93, 99, 102, 115, 122–23, 142, 152, 190; cumshaw mission, 131–32

Dartmouth, England, 144, 188
DD (Duplex Drive) tanks, 64, 68, 74, 76–77, 83, 98
DeHaven, USS (destroyer), 21
DeWitt, Iowa, 156
Diadem, HMS (cruiser), 133
DiMarzio, Paul F., 156, 159, 176–77, 183, 185
Dowling, John J., 8, 29, 31, 58, 61, 90, 112–13, 115, 128, 142; injured in collision, 106
Dragon, HMS (Polish-manned cruiser), 121
DUKW ("duck" amphibious truck), 41, 63, 91, 101, 116
Dundas, HMCS (corvette), 47
Dunkirk, New York, 32
Dunnegan, Glenn, 156, 159, 176

E-boats, 59, 103, 109–10, 121, 125, 161
Elisabeth Dal, SS (British freighter), 51
Empire MacAlpine, SS (British merchant aircraft carrier), 47
Empire Pibroch, SS (British freighter), 49
Eniwetok, 25, 163–65
Etowah, Tennessee, 3, 11, 87, 146–47, 152, 191–92, 194–95

Farragut, Idaho, 9, 32
Fury, HMS (destroyer), 120

INDEX

Gadila, SS (Dutch merchant aircraft carrier), 47
Geckler, Ens. B. T. (LCT(A) 2307 skipper), 78. *See also* LCT(A) 2307
George, Gerald E., 156, 158, 177
George W. Woodward, SS (US Army transport/hospital ship), 139, 141
Gooseberries. *See* Operation Mulberry
Guadalcanal, 4, 21, 169. *See also* Solomon Islands
Guam, 25, 163, 165
Guam, USS (battlecruiser), 175
Gudger, Richard R., 8, 29, 31, 58, 61, 81, 86, 88, 99, 113, 115, 122–23, 131, 146, 148

Halifax, Nova Scotia, 40, 42–43, 44–46, 48, 56
Hall, Rear Adm. J. L. (Assault Force "O" commander), 62, 67, 69, 78, 89, 94, 97
Hei Ho River, China, 179–84, 186

Inglis, HMS (frigate), 51
Intrepid, USS (aircraft carrier), 175, 178
Irwin, Ens. Donald E., 7, 9–10, 33–36, 38, 41–43, 50–51, 56, 58–61, 64, 68–69, 72, 75, 93–95, 99, 107–9, 112–13, 115, 117–18, 120, 125, 128–29, 131, 135–37, 142, 148–51, 154, 187–88; encounter with merchant skipper, 122–23; learning seamanship, 100–105; at Omaha Beach, 80–91; stay in hospital ship, 138–39; training as skipper, 31–32; visit to Paris, 139–40
Isis, HMS (destroyer), 121

Jack Singer, SS (US freighter), 169, 172
Jarvis, John G., 8–9, 32–33, 43, 57–58, 61, 86, 103, 115, 149, 151–52, 155, 157–58, 176; longer quarantine, 45–46; tracer through life jacket, 82; wounded, 87, 91, 94
Jinsen (Inchon), Korea, 172–73, 177, 184–86

Johnson, Ens. Jack "Cooky," 24
Johnson, Woodrow A., 8, 29, 57–58, 61, 70–71, 82, 86–87, 103, 125, 132, 141–42
Joseph P. Kennedy Jr., USS (destroyer), 191

kamikaze attacks, 157, 167, 170
Kelly, Francis J., 60, 71, 115, 122, 130, 149, 155, 157–58, 176, 183
Kirk, Rear Adm. Alan G. (U.S. sector commander), 68, 105
Kleen, Frederick B. G., 8, 56, 57–60, 71, 80, 86–88, 91, 100–102, 106, 109, 113, 115, 122, 125, 141, 148
Korea. *See* Jinsen
Korean War, 190

Laden, Lt. R. M. (LST 1008 commander), 158, 161–63, 167–68, 170–71, 173
LaGrange, USS (transport), 170
Landing Craft, Assault (LCA), 62–63
Landing Craft, Infantry (Large) (LCI(L)), 60, 63, 72, 84, 88, 92, 116, 120, 142, 144, 151, 152, 168, 174, 176, 190
Landing Craft, Mechanized (LCM), 13, 24, 63–64, 77–78, 84, 112, 120, 150, 178, 180
Landing Craft, Tank (LCT): British designs, 13–14; Mark 5 design, 14–15; Mark 6 design, 16–20; operational use, 21–25; re-designated LCU, 16–17; re-designated LSU, 16; value in amphibious operations, 22, 96–97, 180–81
Landing Craft, Tank, conversions: LCF, 66; LCG, 24, 66; LCT(A), 64–73; LCT(R), 66–68
Landing Craft, Vehicle and Personnel (LCVP), 23, 59, 67–68, 88, 90, 92, 94, 97, 124, 130, 163, 169, 198
Landing Ship, Tank (LST), 12–16, 19, 40, 67–68, 127, 139–40, 176–77
LCH 86, 67, 91

INDEX

LCI(L) 91, 84, 92
LCI(L) 92, 84, 92
LCI(L) 507. *See* "Mary"
LCT 21, 21
LCT 33, 23
LCT 63, 21
LCT 146, 24
LCT 181, 21
LCT 182, 24
LCT 322, 21, 24
LCT 404, 153
LCT 413, 67
LCT 501, 16
LCT 535, 64, 76
LCT 536, 65, 79–80, 83
LCT 569, 64, 81
LCT 571, 65, 95, 97
LCT 573, 17, 65
LCT 586, 64, 76
LCT 587, 64, 76
LCT 588, 64, 76
LCT 589, 64, 76
LCT 590, 64, 77, 83
LCT 591, 64, 76
LCT 601, 64, 142, 188–89
LCT 612, 64, 79, 83, 87, 131
LCT 613, 64, 79, 83
LCT 614, 19, 21, 25, 26, 33, 41, 56 74; aboard LST 291, 37–56; aboard LST 540, 150–51; aboard LST 1008, 158–73; at Omaha Beach, 74–75, 79–91, 93–94; at Gold Beach, 100–48, 111–15, –119–21, 122–25, 129–33, 134–43; Channel Storm, 115–18; collision damage, 152–54; crew (original) forms, 28–29, 32–33; crew (Pacific) forms, 155–57; D-Day assignment, 63–64, 68–69; in China, 181–84; in Korea, 184–86; in Plymouth, England, 57–59, 148–51; in Portland, England, 59–61, 69–73; launch and trials, 21, 28; launched from LST 291, 55–56; launched from LST 1008, 173; learning seamanship, 104–16; loading for D-Day, 71–73; repair in England, 144–46; salutes King George VI, 69. *See also* Operation Campus Beleager; LST 291; LST 540; LST 1008
LCT 622, 64, 80, 87
LCT 625, 155–56
LCT 703, 64, 80, 87, 92
LCT 704, 64, 81
LCT 713, 64, 76
LCT 1186, 166
LCT(A) 2050, 64, 77
LCT(A) 2075, 64, 77
LCT(A) 2124, 64, 77
LCT(A) 2227, 64, 77
LCT(A) 2229, 64, 77
LCT(A) 2273, 64, 78
LCT(A) 2275, 64, 78
LCT(A) 2307, 64, 77–78
LCT Flotilla 1, 29, 32. *See also* Amphibious Training Base, Solomons Island
LCT Flotilla 5 (Lt. Edgar M. Jaeger: LCTs 58, 60, 62, 63, 156, 158, 159, 181, 322, 323, 367, and 369), 21
LCT Flotilla 12 (Lt. Cmdr. William Leide), 59–60, 65, 67, 97–99, 130, 144, 148–50, 151–52, 155, 189; Group 34 (Lt. M. E. Wierenga), 97–98; Group 35 (Lt. Dean Rockwell), 59, 64, 98; Group 36 (Lt. D. A. de la Houssaye), 97–98. *See also* Dean Rockwell; "Mary"; William Leide
LCT Flotilla 18, 67
LCT Flotilla 19 (Lt. Cmdr. L. B. Pruitt), 98
LCT Flotilla 23 Group 67, 24
LCT Flotilla 26 (Lt. A. Macaulay), 65, 67, 97–98; Group 76 (Lt. F. C. Wilson), 98; Group 77 (Lt. J. Hintermister), 98; Group 78 (Lt. B. J. Burch), 98
LCT Flotilla 31 (Pacific voyage, Lt. Cmdr. C. V. Dilley), 25
LCT Flotilla 43 (Lt. Arthur M. Rose), 159, 163
LCT Group 115, 172

LCTs, Assault Group O-1 (Lt. j.g. J. E. Barry: LCTs 537, 549, 598, 599, 600, 601, 602, and 603), 64
LCTs H+70 wave (Omaha Beach, LCTs 705 and 775), 64
LCTs H+90 wave (Omaha Beach, LCTs 29, 197, 207, 332, and 364), 64–65
LCTs H+120 wave (Omaha Beach, LCTs 27, 30, 80, 147, 149, 153, 214, 244, 294, 615, 616, and 776), 65
LCTs H+180 wave (Omaha Beach, LCTs 570, 617, 714, 767, and LCT(A) 2297), 65
LCTs H+225 wave (Omaha Beach, LCTs 571, 572, 573, 665, 666, and 813), 65
Le Havre, France, 109–10, 121, 125, 142; air raids on, 110
LeJeune, USS (transport), 148–49, 151
Leide, Lt. Cmdr. William (LCT Flotilla 12 commander), 59, 61, 65, 67, 69, 74–75, 80, 83, 87, 96, 97–99, 102, 113, 120–21 123, 130, 139, 146; at Omaha Beach, 89, 91–92, 94–95, 97; orders to LCTs on Gold, 126–28; Rhine River crossing, 150
Leon, USS (transport), 176
Linsen (German radio-controlled explosive boats), 125
Little Creek, Virginia, 30–32, 151, 154, 189
Lobnitz pier head. *See* Operation Mulberry
London, England, 106, 146–47, 149, 191
Long Island, New York, 6, 42, 149
Long, Robert C., 8, 29–30, 44
Louis, HMS (frigate), 51
LST 174, 155
LST 226, 111
LST 291, 33–35, 40–42, 44, 55–56, 57, 151, 158, 163, 176; hits rock, 42–43; in Convoy SC-157, 46, 50–52, 54–55; loads LCT 614, 37; in New Orleans, 36–38; quarantined, 45–46; shakedown, 35–36

LST 294, 34
LST 307, 111
LST 314, 109–10
LST 331, 111
LST 332, 111
LST 350, 111
LST 376, 109–10
LST 540, 150–51
LST 603, 189
LST 637, 154, 187–88
LST 758, 190
LST 1008, 158–73, 176, 187; air raids at Okinawa, 168–69; begins wartime routine, 163–65; engineering problems, 159–60, 162, 168 171; launches LCT 614, 173; submarine scare, 167
LST Flotilla 17 (Capt. J. D. Shaw), 49
Lyme Bay E-boat attack, 59

Manitowoc Shipbuilding Company, Manitowoc, Wisconsin, 16
"Mary" (LCT Flotilla 12 headquarters), 97–98, 115, 127–28, 141. *See also* LCT Flotilla 12
Maryland, USS (battleship), 167
McNair, Lt. A. G. (LST 291 commander), 34–36, 41–43, 51–52, 56
Meanticut, SS (US freighter), 52
Mediterranean theater, 8, 15, 22–23, 96, 142, 155
Memphis, Tennessee, 11, 16–17, 21, 189, 192
merchant aircraft carrier (MAC), 47, 49
Minneapolis, USS (heavy cruiser), 175, 178
Minnesota, 8–9
Mississinewa, USS (oiler), 167
Mistel (German guided bomb), 109
ML 153, HMS (launch), 74–75, 89, 92, 95
ML 189, HMS (launch), 74
Moorsom, HMS (frigate), 51
Mounsey, HMS (frigate), 51
Murphy, William, 153–54

Navickas, Lt. j.g. Simon R., 48, 53–54. *See also* Colin
Navy Armed Guard, 48, 53–54, 148
Neger (German human torpedoes), 121
Nelson, HMS (battleship), 110–11
New Jersey, 8, 41, 56
New Orleans, Louisiana, 21, 32–34, 36–37, 39–40, 44, 189
New Orleans, USS (heavy cruiser), 175, 178
New York (state), 7–8, 16, 151
New York City, 6, 38, 40–41, 46, 48, 60, 131, 149, 151, 195
New York, USS (battleship), 156
Nicholson, B. W. L. (convoy commodore), 49, 51–52, 55
Nordstrom, Ens. W. H., 87, 189. *See also* LCT 622
North Carolina, 8, 40, 113

Oak Hill, USS (landing ship, dock), 184
Okinawa, 25, 157, 166–68, 171, 173, 174–76; last attacks on, 170; LST 1008/LCT 614 at, 168–70
Operation Campus Beleager (Northern China occupation), 174–76, 177–80; LCTs' value in, 180–81
Operation Epsom (attack on Caen, France), 119, 133
Operation Husky (Sicily invasion), 16, 22
Operation Mulberry (Normandy artificial harbors), 104–5, 115–16, 118, 120–21, 124, 126–27, 137–38, 142–43
Operation Neptune (seaborne phase of Normandy Invasion), 62–63, 96, 104
Operation Olympic (planned invasion of Japan), 157, 166–67, 169–70, 187
Orion, HMS (World War I battleship), 49

Panama Canal, 159–61, 164
Panama City, Florida, 33–34, 44
Paris, France, 134, 137, 139–40, 142

Pearl Harbor, 4, 7, 25, 155, 161–63, 164–65, 167, 170, 188
Peiping (Beijing), China, 180, 184
Pennsylvania, USS (battleship), 170
Pequigney, Frank, 6–7, 9, 26, 29–31, 35, 40, 44–45, 50, 57–58, 60, 71, 74, 79–80, 100, 102, 115, 122, 133, 141, 144, 146, 149–50, 155–57, 158–60, 169, 176, 181–86; at Omaha Beach, 82, 88–89, 94–95; courts-martial, 137–38, 151–52; in Portland air raid, 70–71; learning to drive, 131; Sunday dinner with Carters, 195; Tennessee Wesleyan College, 191–95
Phoenix caissons. *See* Operation Mulberry
Pidgeon, Frank, 189
Pidgeon-Thomas Iron Company, Memphis, Tennessee, 11, 16–17, 26, 41, 112, 189
Pillmore, Ens. George A., 60–61, 68–69, 75, 99–101, 109, 113, 116, 120, 122, 125, 128, 131–32, 135, 138, 142, 188–90; and Carter's wounding, 141; and Dowling's injury, 106; at Omaha Beach, 80–82, 85, 87, 90–91; in temporary command of LCT 614, 140–41
Plymouth, England, 55–56, 57, 59, 70, 74, 148–51, 176
Portland, England, 59–60, 71–72, 74, 79, 93, 106, 162, 172; air raid on, 70–71

Qu'Appelle, HMCS (destroyer), 54
Quorn, HMS (destroyer escort), 125

Red Ball Express, 139
Red Deer, HMCS (sloop), 47
Rhoades, Ens. J. S., 78. *See also* LCT(A) 2275
Rockey, Maj. Gen. K. E. (Operation Campus Beleager), 174
Rockwell, Lt. Dean (LCT Group 35 commander), 59, 64–65, 74, 76, 83,

INDEX

98, 119, 123, 132, 136–37, 138–39, 149, 152. *See also* LCT Flotilla 12, Group 35
Rodney, HMS (battleship), 110–11, 133

Sabin, Capt. L. S. (Gunfire Support Group commander), 65, 67, 78
Saipan, 166–68, 170–71
Saltash, England, 59–60, 64, 148–49
San Francisco, USS (heavy cruiser), 175, 178
Schenectady, New York, 133, 189–90
Scylla, HMS (cruiser), 125
Seth, West Virginia, 154
Singsheim, LeRoy, 133, 141–42, 149, 151–52
Skeena, HMCS (destroyer), 54
Solomon Islands, 4, 21, 24
Solomons Island, Maryland. *See* Amphibious Training Base, Solomons Island, Maryland
St. Boniface, HMCS (sloop), 47
Stefanowicz, Walter "Sparky," 8, 29–30, 33, 57–58, 61, 70–71, 79–80, 82, 86, 88–89, 100, 103, 108, 124, 132
Strule, HMS (frigate), 51
Submarines: German, 4, 6, 40, 47–50, 52, 53–54, 55, 105, 125, 151, 159, 161; Japanese, 6–7, 24, 161–62, 164, 167, 169
Susan B. Anthony, USS (transport), 156

Taku, China, 174–83
Taylor, Lemuel, 60–61
Texas, USS (battleship), 62, 91–92, 156
Thomaston, Georgia, 5, 152
Tientsin, China, 174–75, 179–84
Timmins, HMCS (corvette), 47
Torquay, England, 146
Townsend, Edward G., 156, 158
Tsingtao (Qingdao), China, 173, 174–75, 180, 184, 186
Tuscaloosa, USS (heavy cruiser), 175, 178

Ulithi, 25, 164, 167

US Army units
  1st Infantry Division, 61
  3rd Army, 150
  6th Engineer Special Brigade, 64, 72
  13th Engineer Battalion, 172
  21st Radio Security Section, 163, 165
  29th Infantry Division, 61, 85–86, 92
  51st Military Police Battalion, 172–73
  58th Armored Field Artillery Battalion, 65, 67
  66th Portable Surgical Hospital, 172
  81st Chemical Battalion, 65
  86th Field Hospital, 172
  116th Infantry Regiment, 64, 68, 72, 82, 85, 87
  149th Combat Engineer Battalion, 68, 72
  448th Engineer Depot Company, 172
  467th Antiaircraft Artillery Battalion, 65
  741st Tank Battalion, 64
  743rd Tank Battalion, 64–65
  967th Quartermaster Service Company, 65
  3063rd Quartermaster Company, 172
  3565th Ordnance Company, 72
US Coast Guard, 7, 62, 91, 95
US Marine units
  1st Marine Air Wing, 174
  1st Marine Division, 166, 174
  6th Marine Division, 174, 180
  7th Marine Regiment, 179
Utah, USS (target ship), 162

V-1 (German "buzz bomb" rocket), 106, 147
V-2 (German rocket), 147
Ver-sur-Mer, France, 134

Vian, Rear Adm. Sir Philip (British sector commander), 105, 110, 116, 118, 125

Wajda, Chester J., 60–61, 86, 149, 151, 155, 158, 176
Warspite, HMS (battleship), 110–11
West Nilus, SS (US freighter), 52
Whale floating jetties. *See* Operation Mulberry
Wolverine, SS (US freighter), 52
Wright, Capt. W.D. (Assault Group O-2 deputy commander), 67–68, 81, 89, 91–92, 97

Yellow Sea, 181, 184; threat of mines in, 172, 175, 177
York, Sgt. Alvin, 3, 8

ABOUT THE AUTHOR

Tom Carter grew up in a U.S. Navy family. His father served aboard a landing craft in Normandy, an uncle served on the USS *West Virginia* (BB 48), and a brother served on the USS *America* (CV 66). Carter served three years as a gunner's mate aboard the USS *Semmes* (DDG 18), making deployments to the Persian Gulf in 1976 and to the Mediterranean in 1977. After college, Carter worked for newspapers as a reporter, news editor, night editor, and copy editor. He earned a PhD in communications from the University of Tennessee and now teaches journalism and British literature at Roanoke College in Salem, Virginia.